ORDNANCE SURVEY MEMOIRS OF IRELAND

Volume Thirty-one

PARISHES OF COUNTY LONDONDERRY XI
1821, 1833, 1836–7

Published 1995.
The Institute of Irish Studies,
The Queen's University of Belfast,
Belfast.
In association with
The Royal Irish Academy,
Dawson Street,
Dublin.

Reprint 2014 by Ulster Historical Foundation

Grateful acknowledgement is made to the Economic and Social Research Council and the Department of Education for Northern Ireland for their financial assistance at different stages of this publication programme.

Copyright 1995.

All rights reserved. No part of this publication may be reproduced, stored in a retrieval system or transmitted, in any form or by any means, electronic, mechanical, photocopying, recording or otherwise, without the prior permission of the publisher.

British Library Cataloguing-in-Publication Data.
A catalogue record for this book is available from the British Library.

ISBN: 978-0-85389-550-3

Printed in Ireland by SPRINT-print Ltd.

Ordnance Survey Memoirs of Ireland

VOLUME THIRTY-ONE

Parishes of County Londonderry XI
1821, 1833, 1836–7

South Londonderry

Edited by Angélique Day and Patrick McWilliams

The Institute of Irish Studies
in association with
The Royal Irish Academy

EDITORIAL BOARD

Angélique Day (General Editor)
Patrick S. McWilliams (Executive Editor)
Lisa English (Assistant Editor)
Dr B.M. Walker (Publishing Director)
Professor R.H. Buchanan

CONTENTS

	Page
Introduction	ix
Brief history of the Irish Ordnance Survey and Memoirs	ix
Definition of terms used	x
Note on Memoirs of County Londonderry	xi

Parishes in County Londonderry

Ballynascreen	1
Desertlyn	35
Desertmartin	52
Kilcronaghan	64
Lissan	89
Miscellaneous Papers	111

List of selected maps and drawings

County Londonderry, with parish boundaries	vi
County Londonderry, 1837, by Samuel Lewis	viii
Draperstown, OS map, 1830s	2
Market House at Draperstown	4
Ancient circle in Strawmore townland	10
East window and interior of old church in Ballynascreen	28
Elevated stone and giant's grave in Ballymully townland	43
Tobermore, OS map, 1830s	65
Ancient boat from Calmore townland	70
Lissan Glebe House	97

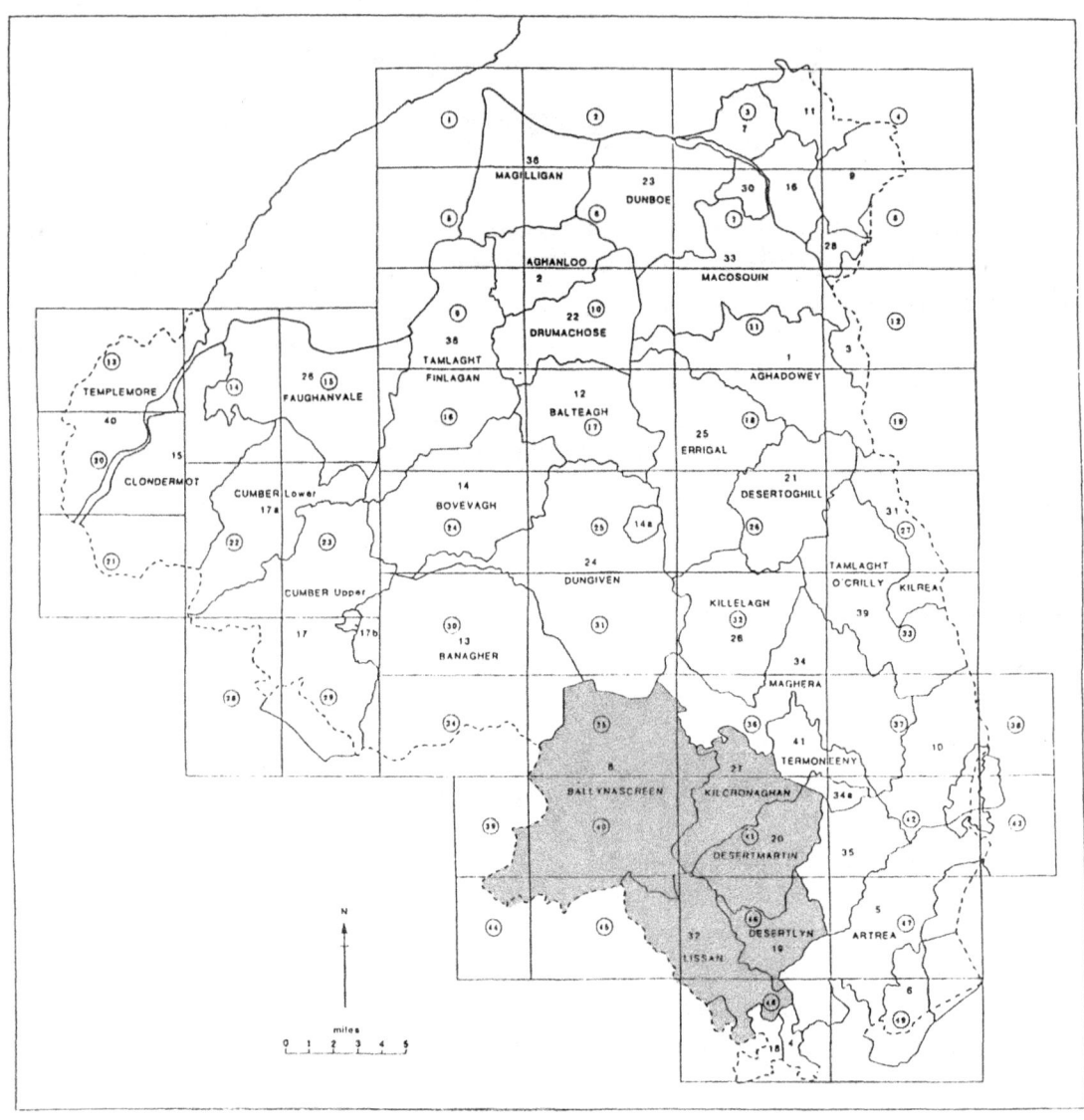

ACKNOWLEDGEMENTS

During the course of the transcription and publication project many have advised and encouraged us in this gigantic task. Thanks must first be given to the Royal Irish Academy, particularly former librarian Mrs Brigid Dolan and her staff, for making the original manuscripts available to us. We are also indebted to Siobhán O'Rafferty for her continuing help in deciphering indistinct passages of manuscript.

We should like to acknowledge the following individuals for their special contributions. Dr Brian Trainor led the way with his edition of the Antrim Memoir and provided vital help on the steering committee. Dr Ann Hamlin also provided valuable support, especially during the most trying stages of the project. Professor R.H. Buchanan's unfailing encouragment has been instrumental in the development of the project to the present. Without Dr Kieran Devine the initial stages of the transcription and the computerising work would never have been completed successfully: the project owes a great deal to his constant help and advice. Dr Kay Muhr's continuing contribution to the work of the transcription project is deeply appreciated, as is that of former editor Nçir°n Dobson. Mr W.C. Kerr's interest and expertise have been invaluable. Professor Anne Crookshank and Dr Edward McParland were most generous with practical help and advice concerning the drawings amongst the Memoir manuscripts. We would like to thank the Director of the Ordnance Survey, Dublin and the keepers of the fire-proof store, among them Leonard Hines. Finally, all students of the nineteenth-century Ordnance Survey of Ireland owe a great deal to the pioneering work of Professor J.H. Andrews, and his kind help in the first days of the project is gratefully recorded.

The essential task of inputting the texts from audio tapes was done by Miss Eileen Kingan, Mrs Christine Robertson, Miss Eilis Smyth, Miss Lynn Murray and, most importantly, Miss Maureen Carr.

We are grateful to the Linen Hall Library for lending us their copies of the first edition 6" Ordnance Survey Maps: also to Ms Maura Pringle of QUB Cartography Department for the index maps showing the parish boundaries. For providing financial assistance at crucial times for the maintenance of the project, we would like to take this opportunity of thanking the trustees of the Esme Mitchell trust and The Public Record Office of Northern Ireland.

Left:
Map of parishes of County Londonderry. The area described in this volume, the parishes of South Londonderry, has been shaded to highlight its location. The square grids represent the 1830s 6" Ordnance Survey maps. The encircled numbers relate to the map numbers as presented in the bound volumes of maps for the county. The parishes have been numbered in all cases and named in full where possible, except those in the following list: Agivey 3, Arboe 4, Ballinderry 6, Ballyaghran 7, Ballyrashane 9, Ballyscullion 10, Ballywillin 11, Bovevagh 14a, Coleraine 16, Derryloran (no Memoir) 18, Kildollagh 28, Killowen 30, Maghera 34a, Magherafelt 35

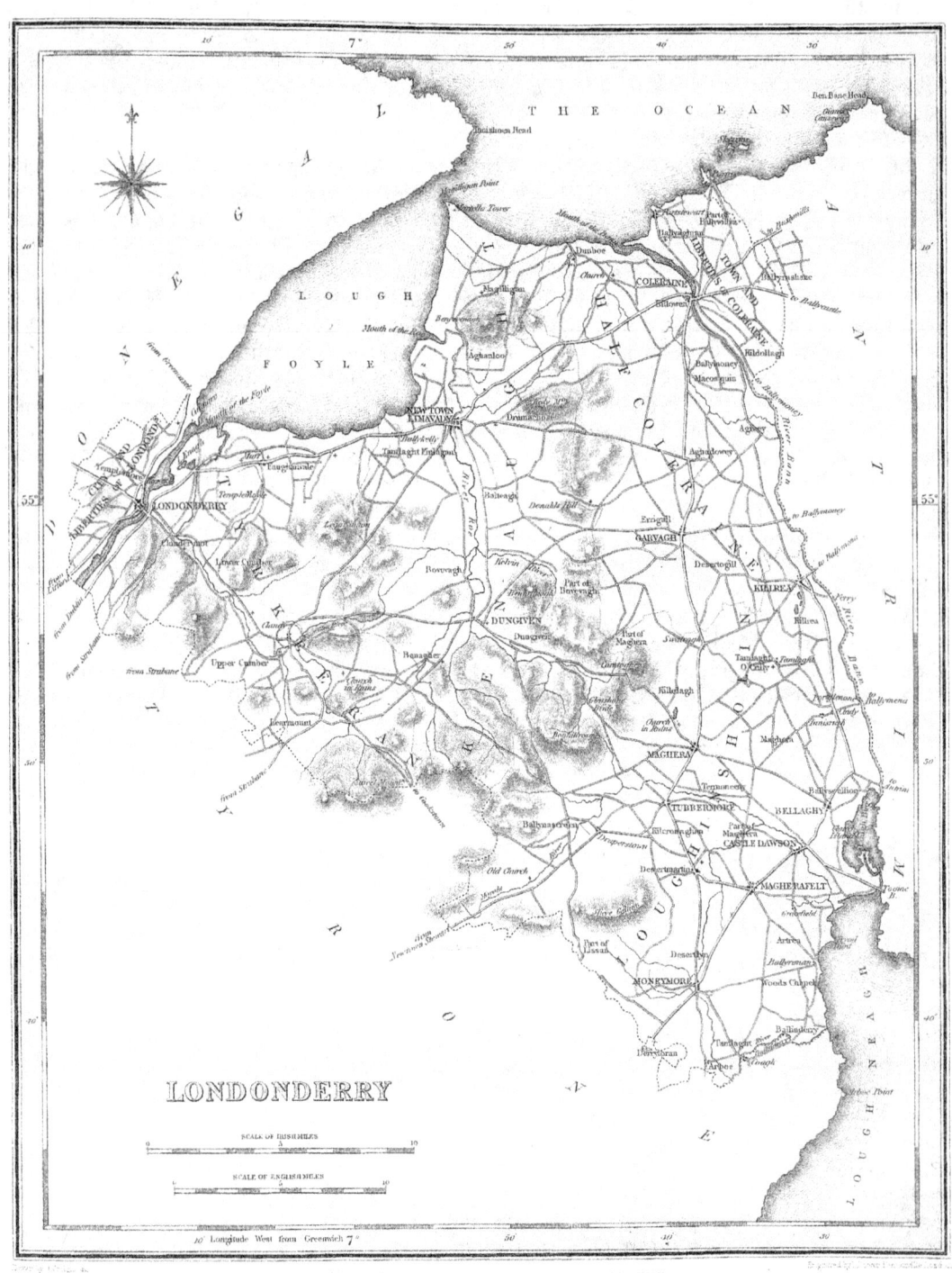

Map of County Londonderry, from Samuel Lewis' *Atlas of the counties of Ireland* (London, 1837)

INTRODUCTION AND GUIDE TO THE PUBLICATION OF THE ORDNANCE SURVEY MEMOIRS

The following text of the Ordnance Survey Memoirs was first transcribed by a team working in the Institute of Irish Studies at The Queen's University of Belfast, on a computerised index of the material. For this publication programme the text has been further edited: spellings have been modernised in most cases, although where the original spelling was thought to be of any interest it has been retained and is indicated by angle brackets in the text. Variant spellings for townland and lesser place-names have been preserved, although parish and major place-names have been standardised and the original spelling given in angle brackets. Names of prominent people, for instance landlords, have been standardised where possible, but original spellings of names in lists of informants, emigration tables and on tombstones have been retained. We have not altered the Memoir writers' anglicisation of names and words in Irish.

Punctuation has been modernised and is the responsibility of the editors. Editorial additions are indicated by square brackets: a question mark before and after a word indicates a queried reading and tentatively inserted information respectively. Original drawings are referred to in the text, and some have been reproduced. Manuscript page references have been omitted from this series. Because of the huge variation in size of Memoirs for different counties, the following editorial policy has been adopted: where there are numerous duplicating and overlapping accounts, the most complete and finished account, normally the Memoir proper, has been presented, with additional unique information from other accounts like the Fair Sheets entered into a separate section, clearly titled and identified; where the Memoir material is less, nothing has been omitted. To achieve standard volume size, parishes have been associated on the basis of propinquity.

There are considerable differences in the volume of information recorded for different areas: counties Antrim and Londonderry are exceptionally well covered, while the other counties do not have quite the same detail. This series is the first systematic publication of the parish Memoirs, although individual parishes have been published by pioneering local history societies. The entire transcriptions of the Memoirs made in the course of the indexing project can be consulted in the Public Record Office of Northern Ireland and the library at the Queen's University of Belfast. The manuscripts of the Ordnance Survey Memoirs are in the Royal Irish Academy, Dublin.

Brief history of the Irish Ordnance Survey in the nineteenth century and the writing of the Ordnance Survey Memoirs

In 1824 a House of Commons committee recommended a townland survey of Ireland with maps at the scale of 6", to facilitate a uniform valuation for local taxation. The Duke of Wellington, then prime minister, authorised this, the first Ordnance Survey of Ireland. The survey was directed by Colonel Thomas Colby, who had under his command officers of the Royal Engineers and three companies of sappers and miners. In addition to this, civil assistants were recruited to help with sketching, drawing and engraving of maps, and eventually, in the 1830s, the writing of the Memoirs.

The Memoirs were written descriptions intended to accompany the maps, containing information which could not be fitted on to them. Colonel Colby always considered additional information to be necessary to clarify place-names and other distinctive features of each parish; this was to be written up in reports by the officers. Much information about parishes resulted from research into place-names and was used in the writing of the Memoirs. The term "Memoir" comes from the abbreviation of the word "Aide-Memoire." It was also used in the 18th century to describe topographical descriptions accompanying maps.

In 1833 Colby's assistant, Lieutenant Thomas Larcom, developed the scope of the officers' reports by stipulating the headings or "Heads of Inquiry" under which information was to be reported, and including topics of social as well as economic interest. By this time civil assistants were writing some of the Memoirs under the supervision of the officers, as well as collecting information in the Fair Sheets.

The first "Memoirs" are officers' reports covering Antrim in 1830, and work continued on the Antrim parishes right through the decade, with special activity in 1838 and 1839. Counties Down and Tyrone were written up from 1833 to 1837, with both officers and civil assistants working on Memoirs. In Londonderry and Fermanagh research and writing started in 1834. Armagh was worked on in 1835, 1837 and 1838. Much labour was expended in the Londonderry parishes. The plans to publish the Memoirs commenced with the parish of Templemore, containing the city and liberties of Derry, which came out in 1837 after a great deal of expense and effort.

Between 1839 and 1840 the Memoir scheme collapsed. Sir Robert Peel's government could not countenance the expenditure of money and time on such an exercise; despite a parliamentary commission favouring the continuation of the writing of the Memoirs, the scheme was halted before the southern half of the country was covered. The manuscripts remained unpublished and most were removed to the Royal Irish Academy, Dublin from the Ordnance Survey, Phoenix Park. Other records of the Ordnance Survey, including some material from the Memoir scheme, have recently been transferred to the National Archives, Bishop Street, Dublin.

The Memoirs are a uniquely detailed source for the history of the northern half of Ireland immediately before the Great Famine. They document the landscape and situation, buildings and antiquities, land-holdings and population, employment and livelihood of the parishes. They act as a nineteenth-century Domesday book and are essential to the understanding of the cultural heritage of our communities. It is planned to produce a volume of evaluative essays to put the material in its full context, with information on other sources and on the writers of the Memoirs.

Definition of descriptive terms

Memoir (sometimes Statistical Memoir): an account of a parish written according to the prescribed form outlined in the instructions known as "Heads of Inquiry", and normally divided into three sections: Natural Features and History; Modern and Ancient Topography; Social and Productive Economy.

Fair Sheets: "information gathered for the Memoirs", an original title describing paragraphs of information following no particular order, often with marginal headings, signed and dated by the civil assistant responsible.

Statistical Remarks/Accounts: both titles are employed by the Engineer officers in their descriptions of the parish with marginal headings, often similar in layout to the Memoir.

Office Copies: these are copies of early drafts, generally officers' accounts and must have been made for office purposes.

Ordnance Survey Memoirs for County Londonderry

This volume, the eleventh for the county and the thirty-first in the series, contains the Memoirs for five parishes in south Derry, on the east side of the Sperrins near the rise of the Moyola river beneath Slieve Gallion, an area containing the towns and villages of Desertmartin, Draperstown, Moneyneany, part of Moneymore and Tobermore. For spelling of parish names, the editors have adhered to the form printed in the 1961 Census of Population.

The earliest account is by the schoolmaster John McCloskey, who wrote an accomplished account of 3 parishes in 1821 for the North West Society, thus providing a broader viewpoint and an interesting comparison to the main Memoir writers whose parish descriptions were produced between 1836 and 1837. We know that John O'Donovan, whose place-name notes for Ballynascreen survive in the Memoir material, met McCloskey in Maghera while he was doing fieldwork for the Topographical Department in 1834. O'Donovan described him as "a sensible, clever and worthy man, universally liked and respected by all classes" (*John O'Donovan's Letters from County Londonderry*, Ballinascreen Historical Society, 1992).

There is one officer's report for Desertlyn, written in 1833, as well as finished Memoir accounts by James Boyle, Charles Ligar and John Stokes, with Fair Sheets by Thomas Fagan and John Bleakly. Altogether, the information provides a well-rounded portrait of these parishes, with fascinating additional detail on beliefs and traditional stories, comparable to volume 30 (Banagher).

The Drapers' Company, one of the London Livery Companies, had significant landholdings in this area and, through their agents, promoted improving works, provided employment, built bridges and buildings, and set standards in housing and schooling. We are told that in Lissan cottiers were forbidden to beg, but the company exerted pressure on the larger farmers to keep their cottier tenants' cottages in good repair. In Desertlyn, the Drapers' Company school pupils wore "smock frocks." Despite influences for modernisation through education and market forces, the strength of traditional beliefs and customs remained undiminished, particularly in rural areas.

In Ballynascreen the Irish language was still widely understood and used, and there are references to the last living bard, Dominic Kelly. McCloskey, a decade earlier, talks of a traditional story teller, one O'Donnell and quotes the satirical verse of Christopher Conway, giving some idea of the lively tradition of racy wit expressed not only in Irish but also in Latin! Stations to Lough Patrick on the Tyrone border were performed regularly and belief in the powers of fairies and "the gentry" to affect people's livelihood was as commonplace among Presbyterians as their Catholic neighbours.

There are interesting allusions to the use of the Ballynascreen bell throughout these parishes in determining the truth of assertions or swearings, thus illustrating the persistence of a very ancient practice in the religious judicial domain. References are made to the "churn" or celebration for the harvesters held by farmers once the crops were safely gathered in, so a great range of cultural practices are touched on.

There are accounts of the fairs held in the area, with goods and prices; particular mention is made of the horse fair at Moneymore, and the fairs at Ballynascreen where ballads and books were on sale along with linen yarn and webs, livestock and hardware. Bleakly is interesting about individual townlands and explains the variation in appearance of houses by season and the occupation of the inhabitant. In Lissan, he notes that besom-making that had been taken up as a result of the decline in the local domestic economy and that this affected the tidiness of homesteads. Through his focus on individual townlands, it is clear that local prosperity depended on the extent of economic diversity. School and emigration statistics for Ballynascreen and Lissan give valuable indications of the aspirations and movement of the population in the area.

The career of the former Presbyterian minister, Alexander Carson, is described in the material for Kilcronaghan and a full list of his theological works appended. There are also references to his Baptist meeting house and school in Desertlyn. Otherwise, accounts of individuals like Kallan More, chief of the Irish Phoenicians, and Big Teag from Slieve Gallion who killed the black bull hindering St Patrick from building Armagh Cathedral, mix legend with history in a fascinating blend.

The editors would like to acknowledge the pioneering role of the Ballinascreen Historical Society, who transcribed and published the Memoirs for Ballynascreen (1981), Desertmartin and Kilcronaghan (1986), as well as the Statistical Reports for the parishes of Ballynascreen, Kilcronaghan and Desertmartin (1983).

Drawings in the Memoir papers are listed below and are cross-referenced in the text; some are illustrated. The manuscript material is to be found in Boxes 30, 37, 42, 43 and 48 of the Royal Irish Academy's collection of Ordnance Survey Memoirs, and section references are given beside each parish below in their printed order.

Ballynascreen	Box 30 III 1, 2, 3, 5, 4
Desertlyn	Box 37 I 1, 3
Desertmartin	Box 37 II 3, 1 and 2
Kilcronaghan	Box 42 I 2, 1, 3, 4, 5
Lissan	Box 43 I 1, 3
Miscellaneous Papers	Box 48 I 2

Drawings

Ballynascreen (sections 1 and 3):

New market house at Draperstown, front elevation with dimensions [illustrated].

Plan of Draperstown, showing buildings intended by the company, with scale.

Ornamented recess at side of east window of old church in Ballynascreen, with dimensions.

View of the east window from the interior, showing recess [illustrated].

Door of old church.

Cross in Ballynascreen churchyard, with annotations and dimensions.

Stones at doorway of old church, with dimensions.

Old windows in parish church, with dimensions.

Grave in Tullybrick, with dimensions.

2 standing stones, with dimensions, ground plan and annotations.

Parishes of County Londonderry xiii

Part of ancient circle in Strawmore, with outline of a person's figure, and dimensions of largest stone [illustrated].

Plan of standing stone circle, with dimensions and scale; view from point A, with dimensions of largest stone.

View of interior of old church in Ballynascreen [illustrated].

Front, side and enlarged end view of stone mould, with dimensions.

Remains of giant's grave in Cloane.

Mether from Labby, with dimensions.

2 views of ornamented quern in Glenavney, with dimensions.

2 views of ornamented quern in bed of the Moyola, with dimensions.

2 views of unfinished quern in Corick, with dimensions.

2 views and section of oak dish from Brackagh.

Carved stone in Moneyneany, with dimensions [by J. Stokes].

Stone quern found in Moyard, with devices cut on surface.

Shaped stone found in Moneyneany, full size.

2 views of iron axe found in Strawmore.

Oak lossett [dish] found in Brackagh, with dimensions.

Brass battleaxe found in Derrynoyd.

Flint stone or arrowhead found in Tonaght, full size.

Section drawing of Giant's Chair in Corick mountain [by T. Fagan].

Desertlyn (section 3):

Desertlyn old church, plan with dimensions and scale.

Giant's grave in Ballymully, plan with dimensions and scale [illustrated].

Elevated stone in Ballymully, south view with dimensions; ground plan with dimensions [illustrated].

Stone hatchet found in Moymucklemurry, front and side views, full size.

2 stone hatchets found in Moymucklemurry, full size.

Stone hatchet found in Mucklemurry, full size and section.

4 flint arrowheads, full size.

Brass rings found in Dunronan, full size, with annotations [by C.W. Ligar].

Desertmartin (section 3):

Stake of oak piles in Shillin lough, with dimensions [by J. Stokes].

Gold gorget found in Rosegarland, full size.

Copper article found in Carncose, full size, side and overviews.

Silver coin in Rosegarland, both faces.

Copper hatchet found in Moneysterling, full size, side view and section.

Brass hatchet found in Brackagh Slieve Gallion, full size, side view and section.

Flint spear or arrowhead found in Annagh, full size.

Brass spear or arrowhead found in Durnascallon, full size [by C.W. Ligar].

Kilcronaghan (sections 2-4):

Pointed stick found in Coolsarragh.

3 crosses in churchyard of Kilcronaghan old church.

Oar found in Calmore.

Door of Kilcronaghan church; view from the interior of window in west gable, with dimensions.

Brooch, side view and overhead view showing decorative detail.

2 stone rings, one side view, one overhead view with dimensions.

Felt hat found in a bog.

Part of stone bowl with an ornamented handle, side and overhead views.

Spearhead found in Coolsarragh, with dimensions; arrowhead, side view and section.

Ancient boat found in Calmore, side and overhead views with dimensions [illustrated]. [Last 6 by J. Stokes, from collection of Revd J.S. Knox].

Brass ring found in Calmore, full size.

Brass halbert found in Slieve Gallion [by T. Fagan].

Date stone over door of Tobermore Presbyterian meeting house [by J. Bleakly].

Lissan (sections 1 and 3):

Lissan Glebe House, east view [illustrated] [by J. Stokes].

Giant's grave near Lough-na-Muck with key and dimensions [by J. Bleakly].

Parish of Ballynascreen <Ballinascreen>, County Londonderry

Memoir by J. Stokes, 1836

NATURAL FEATURES

Hills

The principal summits of this parish are Moneyconey, Crockmore, summit of Spellhoagh, Moydamlaght. The first is 1,602 feet above the sea, the second 1,571, the third 1,869, the fourth 1,805. The fourth is connected at right angles with a lower mountain called Coolnasillagh, which is 1,371 feet above the sea.

These mountains, with the western flank of Sliabh Gallion, form 2 large valleys. The most southern of these separates Sliabh Gallion from Moneyconey and Crockmore, and is watered by the River Moyola. It bears south west and north east, and at the north eastern end, where it becomes broad and irregular and is ornamented by the village of Draperstown, it is met by the second valley bearing west and east, and watered by the Douglas river, a tributary to the Moyola. It separates the shoulder of Crockmore and the descending ridges of Spellhoagh from the Moydamlaght and Coolnasillagh mountain.

From the manner in which those 2 former mountains are disposed, this second valley partakes of the character of an amphitheatre rising on 3 sides from Derrynoyd Lodge.

The most northern part of the parish is filled with low hills belonging to Coolnasillagh and Sliabh Gallion, the most southern with a table land standing at the head of the Moyola. The head of the first valley here spoken of is narrow and confined, and is called the Sixtowns glen. All the summits mentioned, from Sliabh Gallion to Coolnasillagh, are connected with one another by high ground, so that neither of the 2 great valleys formed by them extend beyond the limits of the parish.

Lakes and Rivers

For the dimensions of Lough Patrick, Lough Ouske and Lough, see the maps. They are shallow, being not more than 15 feet in depth.

Of the course of the River Moyola, there are 9 and three-quarters statute miles within the parish, from its source to its exit into the parish of Maghera. It has a swift rippling current and is very inconstant as to its breadth, having the appearance in dry weather of but an insignificant rivulet. At other times it is a broad rushing flood. Its banks are low and of soft materials, and in those times of flood it does them great mischief. No sufficient care is taken by any of the proprietors to fortify them, except the Drapers' Company, who have done so to some degree, by putting down bushes along the banks. There is much sand and gravel washed down.

50 feet is its average fall per mile throughout the parish. Between Moneyguiggy and Mulnavoo it is 16 feet per mile. Between Moykeeran, Tonagh and Straw on the one hand and Strawmore with Derrynoyd on the other it is 25 feet. The latter tract is the best place for mills or machinery. The general direction of this river is from south west to north east. It rises on the western side of Moneyconey mountain.

Of the course of the Douglas river, there [are] 4 and a half miles. It has the same mischievous character as the Moyola and its average fall per mile throughout its course is 183 feet. Between the townlands of Derrynoyd and Cloane, which is the best place for erecting mills or machinery, it is 32 feet per mile. It rises in the precipitous sides of Spellhoagh. From the extent of mountain bog, and the steepness of the ground on every side, each small rivulet becomes, in rainy weather, a dangerous flood, difficult and often impossible for a passenger to cross. Of these, the White water, a tributary of the Moyola, which in dry weather dwindles to 10 feet in width, has been known 3 times to break down a bridge over it, whose curtain wall was upwards of 7 times that length. It was rebuilt again and again at the same place. For the failure of the last attempt see Modern Topography.

There are abundance of springs.

At the village of Draperstown there is a spa well, which has been analysed by Dr Anderson, of that place, as follows. 1,000 grains yielded: alumina, 0.495 grains; peroxide of iron, 3.345 grains; sulphuric acid, 6.191 grains; [total] 10.031 grains.

Bogs

The bogs are few and uninteresting. In the bog of Cloane no other timber has been ever found than sally, oak and fir. The oak was always next the clay but very decayed. Sticks of fir 30 feet long have been dug up. All lie indiscriminately, frequently crossing each other. This flow bog has been only passable for the last 20 years. It is about 20 feet deep.

The bogs of Glenviggan are wet flow bogs or rather quagmires entirely impassable and are believed to be from 8 to 30 feet deep. They are, for the most part, useless for turf and contain no timber.

There are no interesting particulars relative to the thin mountain bogs.

Woods

50 years ago the parish was all well wooded. The hills of Disert and Shanmullagh contained ash trees 50 feet high and there were valuable oak woods at Drumard and Moyheyland. Now it is rare, except where a few stumps and suckers of the ancient wood appear. These are to be found most abundantly on the eastern side of Coolnasillagh mountain, along the hills of Disert and Shanmullagh, and also in the townland of Dunlogan, where the Drapers' Company are fostering the growth of the oak by properly pruning the suckers of the old stumps and protecting them from cattle.

Climate

The air is bracing and healthy from the manner in which the district is enclosed by mountains and the height of the ground itself above the sea. An invalid would be recruited both by the keenness of the air and the variety of the scenery derived from the abundance of uninhabited and heathy country with which he is everywhere surrounded, not only in Ballynascreen but also in the adjacent parishes of Dungiven, Banagher and Bodoney <Badowney>. For further particulars on this head, see Productive Economy.

No meteorological register has been kept.

MODERN TOPOGRAPHY

Draperstown

The village of Draperstown is 3 and a half miles statute from Tobermore, to which it lies in a direction nearly south east. It is on the direct road from Feeny to Magherafelt and is 2 and three-quarters from the road between Cookstown and Dungiven. From Magherafelt it is distant 7 and three-quarters.

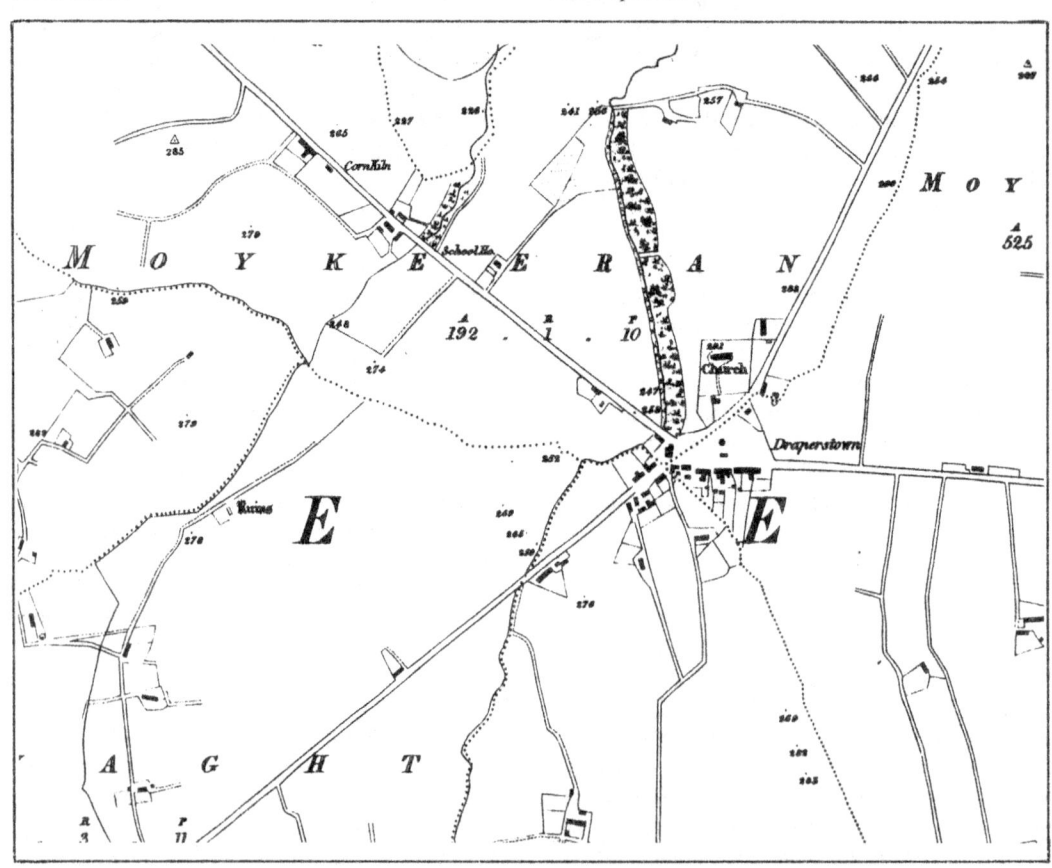

Map of Draperstown from the first 6" O.S. maps, 1830s

Parish of Ballynascreen

It is situated partly on the side and partly at the foot of a sloping hill, and is at present chiefly composed of Patrick Street and of the fairground, a large irregular space. It is surrounded on 2 sides by houses and from the south west angle Patrick Street branches off in a south west direction.

The village will be soon much larger as the company have already laid out new lanes and ranges of buildings, one of which, consisting of an inn, market house, dispensary and shops, is at present (September 1836) in a state of forwardness on the western side of the fairground. This range is in a straight line on the summit of the hill and it will add greatly to [the] picturesque appearance of the village, or town as it will shortly be.

It was founded in 1798 by Laughlin McNamee, a publican, in the following manner.

Before 1797 the cattle fair had been always held in the townland of Moneyneany. In that year, at one of the fairs, the company in McNamee's tent became quarrelsome over their liquor. Their ideas suddenly received a new turn by one of the drunkards exclaiming that if he had a house at the crossroads he would "have a comfortable place to take his glass in," upon which, after some further altercation, another rushed out and, leaping on a cart, proclaimed to the multitudes that the next fair would be held at the crossroads of Moyheyland. They accordingly resorted thither at the time appointed and immediately Laughlin McNamee removed to it and built the first houses. He also soon established a weekly market by giving free cranage and entertainment, and to this day it, as well as the principal part of the fair, is held about his doorway.

With the priest's aid at first, and then the gentry, he kept down quarrelling, and soon had the satisfaction of seeing the fair in a flourishing state and the number of houses increasing. Its name was at first Borbury or the "yellow road," then Moyheyland, then Ballynascreen, then Cross, then Draperstown Cross and finally Draperstown, the name given to it both by the General Post Office and the Company of Drapers.

The church stands at the northern side of the fairground. For a full description of it, see Parish Church. The other public buildings are the market house, inn and dispensary house. The extent of the fronts are marked on the drawings.

The market house is 40 feet by 42 feet. The cost of the inn was about 900 pounds. [Insert footnote: The inn is not yet completely finished as to the offices]. It was begun in 1835, completed and opened in 1836. The cost of the market house will be about 1,000 pounds. It was begun in 1835 and finished in September 1836, as far as the exterior mason work is concerned. The cost of building the dispensary house, which is also a residence for Dr Savage, was about 900 pounds. Many more buildings are contemplated. (For their situation, see drawings which contain a rough plan of the town as it at present stands, with the projected improvements marked in red ink).

Houses

As might be expected, this embryo town is not yet lighted, paved or watched. The following are the descriptions of houses built at different times.

In 1832: 2 houses, side by side, slated, of stone and 1-storey high.

In 1834: 1 house, slated, stone and 3-storey high; 2 houses, slated, stone and 1-storey high.

In 1835: 1 house, slated, stone and 1-storey high.

In 1836: 4 houses, slated, stone and 3-storey high, including the garret.

SOCIAL AND PRODUCTIVE ECONOMY

Local Government

It is believed that a petty sessions will soon be established here, the court to be held in the large room of the market house. The offences are brought to Maghera.

General Remarks

There are no local laws or customs to prevent persons, not possessing exclusive privileges, from setting up shops or factories, or working at any trade they may deem advantageous to themselves. The most marked habit of the people is that of dram-drinking and tippling. They are, however, peaceable and industrious.

Trades and Occupations

Except the Draperstown branch of the North West Farming Society, there are no societies for the encouragement of useful arts or inventions.

The following are their trades and occupations: spirit sellers 6, blacksmith and spirit seller 1, grocers and spirit sellers 2, labourers 4, grocers 4, dry lodgers 3, shoemakers 3, tailors 3, small farmers 3, nailer 1, tavern keeper 1, grocer and haberdasher 1, grocer, ironmonger and deal merchant 1, national schoolmaster 1, grocer and clothier 1, carpenter 1, wheelwright 1, woollen draper 1, washerwoman 1.

There is a house for the constabulary police and a tenement in which a revenue policeman lodges, also one house waste and unoccupied, and a company dispensary.

Goods at Fair

The following are the particulars of the fair of Draperstown held on 7th October 1836, showing the number of head of cattle brought.

Horses: total 387, prices from 4 pounds to 12 pounds; black cattle: total 1,225, prices from 3 pounds to 7 pounds; sheep and lambs: total 1,035, prices from 5s to 1 pound 5s; asses: total 3, prices from 10s to 1 pound; pigs: total 217, various costs; stands of sucking pigs: total 7, prices from 4s to 6s.

Fine linen yarn per spangle, 1s 8d to 1s 10d; coarse linen yarn per spangle, 1s 6d to 1s 8d; fine linen per yard, 1s 4d; coarse linen per yard, 8d; coarse flax per lb., 4d ha'penny, per stone, 5s 8d; fine flax per lb., 10d to 1s.

Woollen stockings per pair, 1s 3d; woollen socks per pair, 7d; flannel per yard, 1s 2d; sacken per yard, 8d.

Men's shoes per pair, 4s to 6s; women's shoes per pair, 3s to 4s.

Woollen hats each 2s; wool per lb., 1s 2d.

Beef per lb., 3d ha'penny; mutton per lb., 4d ha'penny; cheese per lb., 8d; bacon per lb., 7d.

Eels per lb., 2d ha'penny; salt herrings per score, 1s.

Eggs per dozen, 5d.

Slide cars each 2s 6d.

Potato baskets 7d; noggins 4d; crocks 2s; stable brooms 2d; apples per bushel, 2s; plums per bushel, 2s.

Old clothes, bed clothes, books, cottons, tinware, etc.

Houses

There are 24 houses thatched and 19 slated. Most of the new houses have been built at the foot of the hill up to 1836.

Fairs and Markets

A fair is held on the first Friday of every month, with a market on every Wednesday. [Insert footnote: The fair was first established by Lucius Carey Esquire, the former proprietor of Moneyneany]. That of September 1836 was considered "slack;" a smaller quantity of sales were effected than usual. There was a show of cattle

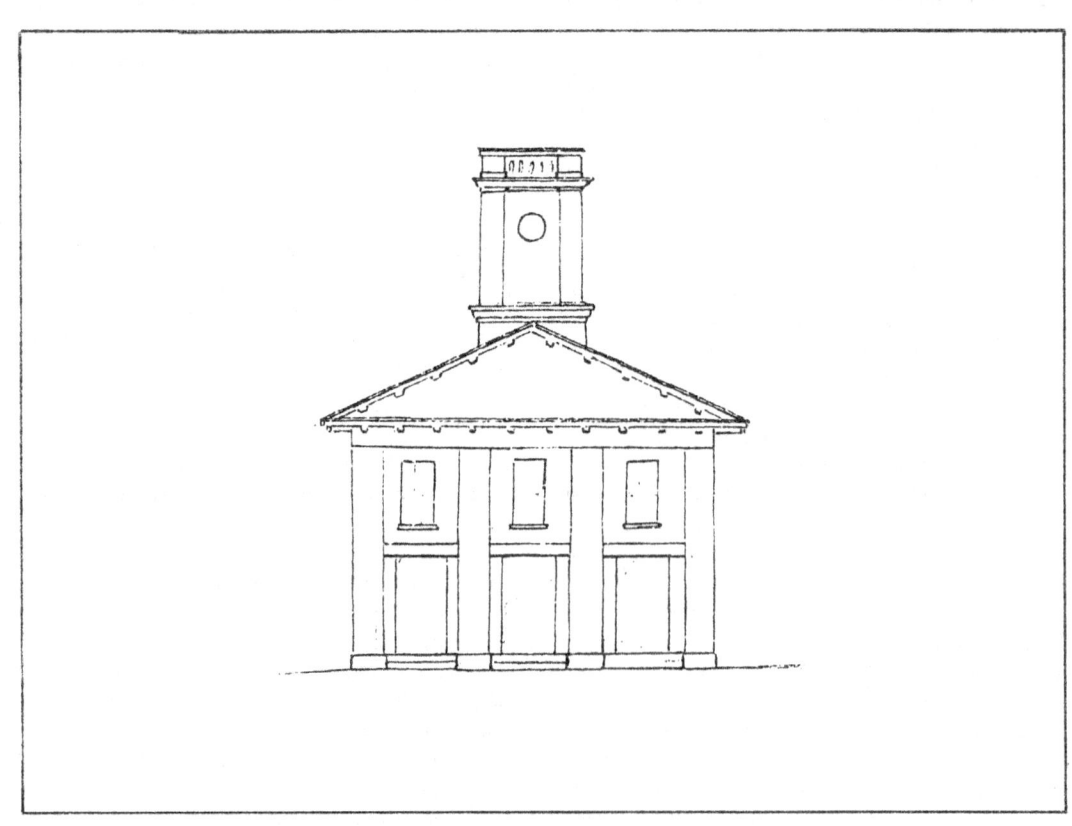

Market house at Draperstown

Parish of Ballynascreen 5

and some inferior horses but they fetched low prices. Milch cows sold from 6 guineas downwards, horses were from 6 to 12 guineas, sheep from 10s to 30s, young pigs 10s, old pigs 4 pounds, heifers from 3 to 4 pounds. Goats are sometimes brought to this fair. If they are with young, they often bring a high price, varying from 15s to 20s. Yarn was from 2s to 1s 6d the spangle. (For further particulars see Productive Economy).

The town is supplied with beef and mutton, the first 3d ha'penny per lb. at an average, the second 4d ha'penny. It is not supplied with poultry, fruit, vegetables or milk. The markets are supplied with beef, mutton, meal and potatoes; the one that succeeds the fair day is always small.

Building Materials

Lime is supplied at Draperstown from Desertmartin, distant 4 miles, at 1s 6d per barrel. Sand is obtained in the parish and laid down at the building ground in Draperstown at 6d per ton. Stone for building is brought from Maghera, distant 5 miles, at 1s 9d and from some quarries in the parish at 1s 6d per ton. Countess slates are procured at Ballyronan, 9 miles off, at 6 pounds 15s per 1,000, lady slates 3 pounds 7s per 1,000, mill slates 3 pounds 15s per ton. The carriage per ton from Ballyronan to Draperstown is 6d.

There are no regular carriers. A branch post from Tobermore to Draperstown was established through the influence of Judge Torrens on 5th January 1831. It goes to Tobermore by a carrier at 10 a.m. and returns at 3 p.m.

Farming Society

There is now a Draperstown farming society. It is identical with the Tobermore and Maghera branch of the original North West Society.

MODERN TOPOGRAPHY

Parish Church

The parish church is a rectangular building 65 feet 10 inches by 24 feet 10 inches from out to out. The side walls are 16 feet high and it is lighted at the sides by 3 lancet-shaped windows. There is also a steeple and spire attached. The interior is in good repair and is warmed by 2 stoves. It contains accommodation for 202 adults, in single and double pews and a flagged alley. The roof and the exterior of the walls are in bad repair and parts of the pinnacles of the steeple have fallen down. The steeple was built in 1793, the church in 1700 or thereabouts. The cost is not known within the parish.

Over the pew of Judge Torrens there is the following inscription, on a handsome tablet: "Sacred to the memory of Anne, the beloved and lamented wife of Judge Torrens. She departed this life at Derrynoyd on 31st May 1832, in the 43rd year of her age. During a long and protracted illness she evinced the characteristic energies of her cultivated mind and her Christian resignation to the will of the Almighty, Deus lumen meum."

There are very few graves in the churchyard, the Protestant parishioners being in the habit of burying in the surrounding parishes. This church will soon be put into a state of complete repair by the Ecclesiastical Board.

Presbyterian Meeting House

The Presbyterian congregation at present (July 1836) meet in the Drapers' Inn. They will, however, soon be more conveniently accommodated with the large room of the new market house and then, when finished, with a separate and regular meeting house of their own, to be built for them by the company. They belong to the Synod of Ulster.

Chapels

The Roman Catholic chapel in the townland of Straw is a plain rectangular building 94 feet by 25 feet from out to out. It [is] situated close to the side of the high road from Draperstown to the old church. It is plain in the inside with an earthen floor. There are broad galleries all around, fitted up with narrow wooden forms. The body of the building is fitted up in the same manner also, and the whole contains accommodation for 1,184 adults. The altar stands at the eastern wall. The interior is lighted by 8 rectangular windows and a few skylights in the roof for the galleries. The side walls are 12 feet high. The roof is slated; all is in good repair. There is a yard with a considerable number of graves.

This building was erected in 1809 on the site of a former chapel and stands 1 and a quarter miles statute from Draperstown. The former chapel was built in 1753.

The Roman Catholic chapel in the townland of Moneyneany is a rectangular building lighted by 5 handsome square windows. It [is] 84 feet by 24 feet 6 inches in the clear. There are no seats but there is accommodation for at least 1,200. There is a gallery running all round which can contain as much as the body of the building. The floor is earthen. The exterior is in good repair, with a slated roof. It was finished in 1832 and begun in the year 1813 but the cost cannot be exactly known, having been partly contributed in horse and manual labour, with materials of all kinds. The altar stands at the east wall. The side walls are about 15 feet high.

This building stands 2 and three-quarter miles statute from Draperstown, on the road to Londonderry.

Gentlemen's Seats

Derrynoyd Lodge, the seat of the Honourable Justice Torrens, is situated in the townland of Derrynoyd, and at the distance of 1 and five-eighth miles statute from Draperstown. It is on the Dungiven road and stands on some low ground that had formerly been an almost impassable bog but which now, by the indefatigable exertions of its proprietor, is converted into a rich demesne covered and ornamented with extensive plantations.

The house was first built in 1809 on a very small scale. It remained thatched until the year 1816, when the roof was slated and a series of additions and enlargements commenced. These were carried on occasionally until the original cottage has become a large 2-storey house with ample accommodation, [crossed out: both within and without], but with the architecture, as might be expected, rather irregular.

The extent of demesne and ornamental ground attached is about [blank], with a handsome avenue half a mile long, and rendered very picturesque by the surrounding mountains.

Ballynascreen Glebe, at present the residence of the Revd [blank] Brownlow, is a handsome 2-storey house on the road from Draperstown to Tobermore and at the distance of 1 and three-eighth miles statute from the former village. A small lawn separates it from the road and it is surrounded by good full-grown trees. [Crossed out: It was built in the year [blank]; not known within the parish].

Robert Ogilby Esquire of Pellipar near Dungiven has repaired an old house in the townland of Strawmore as a lodge for receiving rents. It is on the road from Cookstown to Dungiven and 2 miles statute from Draperstown. It is a small 2-storey house with a good stable and back yard. It was repaired in the year 1834.

Drapers' Lodge, a small house with lawn, now occupied by Dr Savage, was re-edified in 1823. It is 1 mile from Draperstown on the Desertmartin road.

Bridges

The bridge over the Moyola between the townlands of Derrynoyd and Moykeeran, and on the road from Draperstown to Dungiven, has 2 arches. The southern is 31 feet in span, the northern 30 and a half. The roadway is 19 feet 3 inches wide with parapets 3 feet 9 inches high. All is in excellent repair.

The bridge on the same road between Derrynoyd and Drumderg has 1 arch, span 9 feet 2 inches. The parapets are 2 feet 8 inches, roadway 25 feet 8 inches. All is in good repair. The stream turns sharply at right angles immediately on leaving the arch. There will be soon 100 feet of an embankment, executed by order of the grand jury, to keep off the water in times of flood from the road and curtain walls of the bridge. It will be along the foot of the northern curtain wall, paved and 6 feet wide.

The bridge on the same road and between Moneyneany and Drumderg has 2 arches, the northern 15 feet and the southern 18 feet wide. The parapets are 2 feet 8 inches high and the roadway 20 feet wide. It is over a branch of the Moyola called the Douglas water.

The bridge on the same road and between Moneyneany and Moydamlaght has 1 arch 20 feet in span. The parapets are 3 and a half feet high and the roadway 19 feet 8 inches. It is over a branch of the Douglas water. It was built about 40 years ago, the former one having been carried away by a flood. This branch is the Altayesky <Altayiacky> water. Numerous and impetuous streams pour off the sides of Moydamlaght mountain and are carried off under this road through strong well-built pipes and gullets. The number of these is 20.

The bridge over the Moyola between the townlands of Carnamoney and Moykeeran has 2 arches. The diameter of the western is 28 feet, that of the eastern the same. The parapets are 2 feet 8 inches high and the roadway 17 feet 6 inches broad, all in good repair. It was finished in the year 1831 and commenced in 1828. It was the first bridge ever erected on the spot. The inhabitants of the extreme western end of the Drapers' [estate] were much inconvenienced for want of it, that river having cut them off from all communication with the neighbouring market towns, unless they went round by Moneyneany bridges or those of the parish of Maghera and Kilcronaghan. Being on a by-road the circumstance was never paid attention to by the grand jury. At length the Drapers' Company with their accustomed liberality remedied it by building a bridge at their own expense.

They also built at their own expense the bridge between Cloane and Derrynoyd. It has 4 arches, the diameter of each 13 feet 9 inches. The roadway is 17 feet 7 inches wide and the parapets 3 feet 6 inches. All is in good repair. It is over the Douglas water, on a by-road, and was built in 1834. All is in good repair.

Other Bridges

The bridge between the townlands of Moneyneany and Moydamlaght is 25 feet in span, with parapets 2 feet 3 inches high. The roadway is 18 feet 8 inches wide. All is in good repair. It was built in 1831 at the expense of the county. It was on the road from Moneyneany to Maghera.

The bridge between the townlands of Dunmurry and Clough, and on the same road, has 1 arch 20 feet in span with parapets 3 feet 10 inches and roadway 19 feet wide. All is in good repair.

The bridge on the same road, and between the townlands of Carnamoney and Cloane, has 1 arch 9 feet in diameter. The parapets are in a decayed state. The roadway is 16 feet 4 inches wide.

The bridge on the same road, and between the townlands of Ballinure and Carnamoney, has 1 arch 10 feet in diameter; parapets none, roadway 17 feet wide.

The bridge over the Moyola between the townlands of Doon and Disert, and on the road from Cookstown to Dungiven, has 3 arches each 21 feet in span. The parapets are 4 feet 8 inches high with a roadway 21 feet wide. It was built about 60 years ago, 3 years after the road was opened through the parish. On being first built it was broken down by a remarkably sudden flood which took place so unexpectedly that many of the workmen's cars and implements were swept away. All is in good repair.

The bridge over the Moyola between the townlands of Tullybrick and Moneyconey, and close to the old church, has 2 arches. The span of each is 14 and a half feet. The roadway is 18 feet wide with parapets 2 feet high. All is in good repair. This bridge was built in 1834 at the expense of the county. [Insert marginal note: This bridge was first built in 1773, secondly in 1795. It is on the road from Draperstown to the old church].

The bridge in Tullybrick, on the high road from Draperstown to Omagh, in the county Tyrone and over a small tributary to the Moyola, has 1 arch 14 feet in diameter. The roadway is 21 feet wide. There are no parapets at present, the roadway has been filled up by the cutting down of a steep hill at the northern end. The arch is in good repair.

Between the townlands of Straw and Disert, over a tributary to the Moyola called the White Water, there is at present a bridge in the course of being built at the expense of the county. The inhabitants of the southern end of the parish were very much inconvenienced for want of it, the river being subject to impetuous floods which have, in some instances, swept passengers away. It will have 3 arches, each 21 feet in diameter. It was broken down and much damaged by a heavy flood on 3rd September 1836. It is on the road from Draperstown to Omagh, which is the principal line of communication between Draperstown and the southern part of the parish.

The bridge on the road from Draperstown to Tobermore, and between the townlands of Moyheeland and Glebe, has 1 arch 15 feet in diameter. The roadway is 18 feet wide with parapets 2 and a half feet high. All is in good repair.

The bridge on the same road between Glebe and Moneyguiggy has 1 arch 16 feet in diameter. There is a roadway 20 feet wide, with parapets 2 feet 10 inches high. All is in good repair.

The bridge in the townland of Gortnaskey has 1 arch 16 feet in diameter. The roadway is 20 feet with parapets 2 and a half high. All is in good repair. It is on the road from Draperstown to Desertmartin.

A footbridge or plank of fir, elevated on supports and protected by an iron railing, was put over the Moyola between Straw and Doon in 1830, at the private expense of the adjoining townlands, for their accommodation in going to the chapel at Straw. It was torn away by the river before it was finally built.

The bridge between Corick and Brackagh, and on the road from Dungiven to Cookstown, has 1 arch 17 feet in span. The parapets are in bad repair and are 4 and half feet high. The roadway is 17 feet 8 inches.

All the bridges of the parish are either over the Moyola or over tributaries to it.

Mills

The machinery of the flax mill in Straw tenanted by Peter Kelly is contained in an excellent 2-storey house, slated and worked by a breast wheel 12 feet 6 inches in diameter and 2 feet across the paddles. The fall of water is 2 feet. There is a tuck mill in an adjoining room with a wheel of the same dimensions worked by the same stream and fall.

The machinery of the corn mill in Straw tenanted by John Smith is contained in a bad thatched house with the gable end cracked throughout. It is worked by an undershot wheel 13 feet 2 inches in diameter, and 1 foot 11 inches across the paddles. The supply of water is good but the mill lead <lade> very leaky and dilapidated.

The machinery of the corn mill in Cavanreagh tenanted by Neill McKelvy is contained in a good slated house and worked by a breast wheel 13 feet 6 inches in diameter and 2 feet across the paddles. The supply of water is not constant, being but a small mountain stream. There are 2 kilns adjacent, the one slated and the other thatched.

The machinery of the flax mill in Moneyguiggy tenanted by John Dixon is contained in a good slated house and worked by a breast wheel 12 feet 2 inches in diameter and 2 feet 4 inches across the paddles. The cog wheel is 6 feet 6 inches in diameter. The supply of water is good.

Roads

The principal lines of road here are 21 feet wide, clear of banks, drains and fences. The most interesting of them is the high road from Draperstown to Feeny. In the year 1798 the Revd Gardiner Young, then the rector of Ballynascreen, and [blank] Hunter Esquire of Feeny made the first attempt to lay out and finish a line of road across the mountains between the 2 places, by county presentments. It was begun but not completed. In 1828 Judge Torrens took it up and had it finished, but it is not so well laid out as it might have been. That part of it within this parish cannot, however, be altered for the better.

There are about 300 perches of a road between Moneyguiggy and Duntybrian, on the high road from Dungiven to Moneymore, contracted for, for 7 years beginning from 1835, at 2d per perch.

There is a 7 years' contract for 1,755 perches of road from Draperstown to Tobermore at 1d ha'penny a perch, beginning at 1834.

2,163 perches of road from the chapel at Straw along the road to Omagh, and as far as the parish mearing, have been contracted for, for 7 years at 2d per perch from [crossed out: spring] 1835. It is remarkable that 34 years ago this road did not extend further than the old church. Beyond it, that is in the most southern parts of the parish, there were then no roads at all of any kind. Since that time the high road has been carried on towards Omagh by successive presentments.

As to any improvement that might be suggested in the general direction of the lines of road, it may be stated that, excepting the Feeny road on the Ballynascreen side of the mountains, they are all so badly laid out that the most profitable change would be to cancel them altogether; but as this cannot be done, attention should be paid to their improvement by simply cutting down, where practicable, whatever hills rise across them.

Of these, the most important is the Black hill, a ridge rising across the road to Tobermore and forming an awkward acclivity and declivity of nearly 78 feet high. It is the more important as it would be a great obstruction to the Belfast and Londonderry coach, in case that vehicle should be brought by Draperstown and Feeny, as is contemplated by the company. On the top of it this Tobermore road is intersected at right angles by a by-road between Duntybrian and Moneyguiggy, coming on the eastern side from the parish of Kilcronaghan and going on the western to the Forge bridge over the Moyola.

It would be advisable to lay this out anew, making it cross the first-mentioned road at the foot of the hill and on the Tobermore side of it, from thence to proceed in a straight line to that bridge. It could be sloped gently down the hill by making it branch off from the present line at the neighbourhood of the Danish fort that stands in the eastern part of Duntybrian.

The principal lines all radiate from Draperstown. They are: from Draperstown to Dungiven, 5 and a half statute miles; from Draperstown to Feeny, 5 and a quarter statute miles; from Draperstown to Tobermore, 2 and a half statute miles; from Draperstown to Magherafelt, 1 and one-eighth statute miles; from Draperstown to Omagh, 8 statute miles. They are all in excellent order.

The cross and by-roads are not unnecessarily numerous when the small size of most of the farms is considered. There is nothing to prevent any further improvement in communications.

ANCIENT TOPOGRAPHY

Ecclesiastical: Old Church

The stones of the old church of Ballynascreen are large and carefully fitted. The mortar has an ancient appearance and is very hard and coarse. It is a rectangle 72 feet by 25 feet from out to out. The walls are 3 feet thick. The side walls are 16 feet high from the floor. The door seems to have been originally 3 feet wide; it is at present 6 feet 9 inches high and 5 feet wide and, from the decay of the building, is such a shapeless aperture that its form cannot be ascertained. Neither can the original form of the windows, of which there seems to have been 2 on the western wall and 1 on the eastern, be made out.

On the southern side of the eastern window there is a small recess in a dilapidated state, but with some Gothic ornaments still adhering to it. It is represented in drawings. There is a tradition

Parish of Ballynascreen

that human bones were found in it. A drawing represents the eastern window.

In the yard the following names appear: McWilliams, Mulloy, O'Kelly, Gallagher, McNeill, O'Keelt, Clerkan, Dougherty, O'Haran, McNamee. The tombstone of Father Terence Rogers is so ill spelled and cut as to be illegible, except in one part which says: "I do not wonder if sun and moon should change at the expiration of his age."

It is remarkable that fragments of Gothic pillars appear mixed up with the masonry round the doorway.

This circumstance shows that the present church was erected from the fragments of a former building. This church was roofed with shingles of oak timber up to about the year 1700 and a portion of it [was] on the walls up to about the year 1776. A hole in the west gable called the "Bell Hole" was perfect up to 1794.

This ruin is still well preserved. It stands on the banks of the River Moyola, at the opening of the Sixtowns glen, and is enclosed on every side by cliffs and rising grounds. The situation is still lonely and must have been singularly so when the country was wild and covered with woods.

The tradition is that this church was first erected as a college by St Patrick and afterwards converted into a church by St Columbkille. Before that time it is said that the parish was known by the same Irish name as Glenshane.

While it was building the architects were greatly disturbed by a "pesht" or monster who pulled down their work by night. A bell rung in the air and guided them to a new place, and on their arrival at it their ringing leader fell down from above upon McGillian's garment [crossed out: and then upon McGurk's. These 2 individuals disputed the possession but at length the latter held it]. It continued to be preserved to the present time as an object for swearing upon and is now in the possession of a man in the parish of Listress <Lisdress>, county Tyrone.

It should be added that, according to tradition, this church is the central one of the 9 churches found by St Columbkille viz. Ballynascreen, Desertlyn, Desertcreat, Termonmaguirk <Tarmonmcgurk>, Killelagh <Killylagh>, Bodoney, Magherafelt, Maghera and Dungiven.

Glen: Bolie Columbkille

In Tullybrick mountain, about 1 and a half miles from its site, there is a glen called Bolie Columbkille. It is so called on account of its having been selected by the above saint according to tradition as a place for meditation and prayer. A cross which had formerly belonged to the building is now converted into a tombstone in the graveyard.

Burial Grounds

In a part of the townland of Davagh and county Tyrone, but in a piece of ground that formerly belonged to the county of Londonderry, there is an eminence called Templemoyle. It is an ancient burying ground and had been a site selected for a church which was never erected. On its summit there are a number of stones sunk on their ends in the ground and partly appearing above the surface. These are said to stand at the heads of graves now obliterated by the weather. Many skulls and human bones were once found in it. They were afterwards interred in the same place.

In the townland of Moydamlaght 2 ancient thorns mark the situation of a fort which, according to tradition, was the site upon which the first attempt was made to build the church of Ballynascreen. It was fruitless, all that was built by day being pulled down by night. Many skulls and bones were found in it a number of years ago.

Friars Well

In the townland of Mulnavoo there is a spring called the Friars Well. The townland was the residence of friars for many years and this well took its name from them. No other particulars are remembered by the inhabitants.

Draperstown Church

In the back wall, i.e. the northern wall, of the church of Draperstown there are 2 windows of old-fashioned architecture and a door. They were examined to ascertain, from the want of any better source of information, the era at which the building was erected. The tradition of the people is that it was about the year 1700.

Military Remains

There are no castles.

Pagan: Forts and Carns

For the number of forts, see the Ordnance maps. They are all of the usual form. It is remarkable that in the townland of Moneyneany there were formerly 7 forts within call of each other. The tradition of the people is that this townland was formerly a sort of stronghold to the ancient inhabitants, it being bounded on both sides by rapid streams and steep cliffs which served not only as a fortification against their enemies, but also as a means of communication along the edge of the water with the other parts of the country.

There are very few carns. In the townland of Owenreagh, and in the mountain grazing of Patrick Connor, there is a heap of stones occupying a space 45 feet long and 20 feet wide. Its summit is about 5 feet higher than the level of the hill on which it stands. It is composed of stones of a different kind from any at present on the mountain. The carn has been dug into at some former period but nothing was then exposed to view more than a few large flat stones, similar to [those] that are found to enclose and cover giant's graves in other places. It is believed by the inhabitants to be a monument raised over the graves of giants but it is at present an unintelligible heap.

In the townland of Drumderg there is a carn with the top stripped off, leaving exposed to view in the centre a small pit which formerly contained the urn of ashes. It is said that Davige Dawna Mackadrille, a foreign chief who came to fight some of the Irish Phoenicians, was killed by Coocoolun and buried here, it being the site of the battle. The hill was then called Drimadirig and the monument Killeahouma.

In that subdivision of the townland of Tullybrick locally called Bolie Columbkille, and in a secluded marshy valley, there are the remains of a giant's grave of the usual form. [In the] drawings is a view from the north of the remaining canopy stone. It was not thought worthwhile to make the ground plan as it was entirely in a dilapidated state.

In the same subdivision there is a standing stone 2 and a half feet high, 2 feet broad and 1 foot thick. It is believed that this was the stake to which St Columbkille's cow was tethered when she was out grazing and it is called in Irish "the grey cow's tether stake!"

There are the ruins of a remarkable carn in the townland of Strawmore called Slaughte; see drawing. The curved line on which these stones stand indicate a circle of 40 feet in diameter. They are the great stones that had been laid round at the bottom of the carn to hinder the smaller ones from rolling off.

In the townland of Glengomna there is a re-

Ancient circle in Strawmore

markable edifice, the traces of which are represented in the drawings. It is on a high and sloping side of the mountain Crockmore. The house was earthen with semicircular ends. The row of standing stones marked AA is an ancient fence.

In the townland of Corick there is a stone called the Giant's Chair.

No coves or underground caverns built artificially of stone have yet been found. Many caves there are but they had been made in modern times, especially during the last rebellion. There is one in Corick.

Miscellaneous Discoveries

In a sand-hill in the townland of Disert, and about 7 feet beneath the surface, there was found in 1820 an ancient crock containing a quantity of calcined bones and ashes. The crock was beautifully carved on the surface but mouldered away on being raised up.

An iron foundry formerly stood in Mulnavoo and holding of James Lyle. Some pieces of iron bars were found beneath the surface of its ruins in 1833.

In Derrynoyd, and holding of Denis Henry, there is a stone with 2 circular holes in it. One of the holes is 9 inches in diameter and 6 inches deep; the other an inch smaller. 3 other stones with holes in them were formerly to be seen in the same townland but have been destroyed.

In Glengomna, and holding of John McCormick, there are 2 stones with holes in them also. These appear to have been moulds for the purpose of casting cannon-balls.

A stone mould for casting spearheads in was found about 5 feet under the surface of a bog, and within 700 yards of a Danish fort in the townland of Drumderg, in the year 1831.

In Glebe there was discovered, at the depth of 3 feet, a grave 7 feet long and 3 feet broad enclosed by stones and roofed with long flat ones. In the interior there was a quantity of rich black earth.

In Strawmore there was found in 1822 5 ancient crocks containing calcined bones and ashes. They were carved on the surface and covered on the mouth with flat stones. On being removed they mouldered down and fell to pieces.

In Cavanreagh in the year 1815 a grave 5 feet long, 2 and a half broad and 2 feet deep was found enclosed by a stone wall. It contained a quantity of rich black earth.

There are a considerable number of methers in this parish. For a drawing of an ornamented one, see drawings. They are all of the same form and are made of yew wood.

For 2 ornamented querns, see drawings. [In the] drawings is an unfinished one. The circumstance of the first of these having been found in the bed of the Moyola is singular and seems to indicate that the river in changing its course, as it frequently does, had rooted up some old building.

An ancient oak dish or "lossett," as it is called by the parishioners, was found about the year 1726 in a small lough or pool in the townland of Brackagh. It is at present in the possession of James McBride of that townland and was transmitted to him from his ancestor.

[Insert footnote: Priest Quin of Omagh, who was formerly priest of this parish, has a very interesting collection of bells, antiques, manuscripts, dishes, etc. found not only here but also in Desertmartin and Magherafelt].

The fragment of a carved stone found in Moydamlaght during the summer of 1836 is represented in the drawings. It seems to have been the end of one of the arms of a large cross.

In the townland of Corick, on the sloping side of a hill called the Chair hill, there is a natural rock accidently in the form of a chair. It is 3 feet 2 inches high and 3 feet broad.

Derivation of Names

The parish of Ballynascreen is said to have taken its name from a small screen erected to shelter the priest during the building of the old church. This is the tradition among them.

The name given to the adjacent parish of Bodoney is said to have had its origin in the following circumstance. The daughter of a man of rank in the south of Ireland was mad and fled from her friends, who eagerly pursued her and at length discovered her sleeping in the verge of a wood in the above parish. She was naked when found and they immediately erected a small hut of branches over her to screen her from the inclemency of the weather. This was done on Sunday and the house called "the Sunday hut" or Buogh-a-Donaye.

Tradition says that the townland of Moneyneany derived its name from the following circumstances. Its valleys were a favourite place with the old Irish warriors to learn their exercises and also to perform great exploits and tricks by magic. It was consequently called Meen-na-neenthus or "the plains of wonders."

In the same townland there is an ancient spring well called Toberawathymeel or the "earless dog's well." A Sir Volvett, who lived here once and who had the reputation of being a magician, kept a large earless dog continually chained at the well to prevent the other inhabitants from drinking or using any of the water. It appears to be of a mineral nature (see Natural Features). The people assert that it will curdle new milk after being boiled.

Monuments

Rows of sharp-pointed sticks have often been found sunk in the subsoil beneath the bogs in this parish.

2 monuments, one of them apparently a giant's grave: in the upper end of the townland of Cloane, i.e. the highest part of it, there are 2 ancient monuments in a very dilapidated state. One of them is apparently a giant's grave but the other is evidently the remains of a cairn which once occupied a circular space about 30 feet in diameter. It is lower down the hill and is distant from the first monument 5 chains, on a line bearing south west from it. The first monument is a parallelogram of 4 stones at each side and one at each end. The highest is but 4 feet from the ground. The rest are partly covered with the moss and turf of the mountain. The form of it corresponds with that which is usual in giant's graves. The only indication of a cromlech is a stone lying horizontally and partly buried at the northern end; see drawings for a general view.

The stones that remain of the cairn before mentioned are a few of those that had been originally set round the edge to keep the smaller ones from rolling off.

MODERN TOPOGRAPHY

General Appearance and Scenery

The general appearance and scenery of this parish strikes a stranger on first entering it as being pretty, not grand or majestic. The mountains that enclose it on every side have, when approached closely, a tame character from the regular slope of their sides. They look much better at a distance. Nevertheless there are some parts that possess a character of great wildness, such as the approach to the Eshka in the townland of Altayesky (see Natural Features) and the approach to the great rock of Craignashoke in Moydamlaght, which is nearly a perpendicular wall of basalt 200 feet deep and inhabited by eagles.

The glens are none of them remarkably deep. The broad slopes of these mountains, if well covered with trees, would have a very beautiful and picturesque appearance.

SOCIAL ECONOMY

Early Improvements

Next to the Drapers' Company, the proprietor who has shown most anxiety for the welfare of the district has been the Honourable Justice Torrens. For his efforts in that cause too much praise cannot be awarded. From the great difficulty that has been met with of acquiring information here, no very particular details of the progress of improvement in the parish can be entered into.

50 years ago it was covered in many parts with the ancient forest and 70 years ago there were few, if any, regularly formed communications, either by bridges or otherwise. The people were satisfied with riding along the edges of the Moyola water and ascending to their houses by bridle tracks. This state of things continued in the most southern part until 1800. Yet now the district exhibits a different aspect and appears to be steadily improving.

It may be stated that part of the impetus it has received has been produced by the combined exertions of the company and the Honourable Justice Torrens. Mr Stevenson, too, has been paying great attention to the improvement of his estate in the Sixtowns and has, by rearranging his farms, been effectively destroying the rundale system. He is also laying out his wastelands in lots and settling good tenants on them.

The following excellent notice shows the anxiety of the Drapers' Company to produce cleanliness, a quality not always to be found among the parishioners: "We hereby remind the tenantry of the said estate of their negligence and inattention to the regulations of their landlords respecting the whitewashing of their houses, both inside and outside, once every year. It is painful for us to do anything that may appear harsh or severe towards the tenantry, but we are determined to enforce this regulation by obliging every individual who does not immediately attend to it, to pay up his rent to last May, and where they are not able to do so, to remove them from off the estate. Signed Rowley and John Rowley Miller, Moneymore, 13th June 1836."

Prevailing Names

There is a mixture of Scotch, Irish and English names: Duffy, Loughran, Conway, McCloskey, Kelly, McBride, O'Kane, Higerty, McGlade, McNamee, McKenna, Regan, Russell, Mullen, O'Neill, Murray, Hamilton, Lenon. Many English names are on the tombstones in the Catholic chapel yard at Straw.

Parish of Ballynascreen

Obstructions to Improvement

There is a disputed boundary between Robert Ogilby Esquire of Pellipar and John Stevenson Esquire of Fort William at the townland of Disert.

The rundale system will soon be obliterated.

It is remarkable that there is an obstruction to improvement derived from the inhabitants themselves. The Irish inhabitants view with much suspicion the exertions of the company. Religious bigotry has also been used to induce the people to counteract their efforts and if unsuccessful in that, at least to render them unthankful for those efforts.

Local Government

There are at present (October 1836) 4 constabulary police in Draperstown, with 15 revenue police and 1 revenue lieutenant. There are no resident magistrates nor are there any manor courts or petty sessions. No outrages have been very recently committed of any kind. One murder occurred in this year. Illicit distillation is carried on in the mountains and is usually concealed very ingeniously. There are no insurances.

Murders

The following are the murders that have taken place in the parish since the year 1831: James Trolen, farmer, was killed by Patrick Duffy, farmer, in 1831. They both lived in the townland of Cahore. The cause was a drinking dispute. The murderer absconded.

Edward Murphy, labourer, was killed in the year 1833 by John Haghey, farmer. They both lived in Draperstown. The cause was a drinking dispute. The murderer absconded and fled to America.

John Toner, farmer, was killed in the year 1834 by Philip Kelly, farmer. They both lived in the townland of Straw. The cause was a drinking dispute. The murderer absconded.

Thomas Robinson, farmer, was killed in 1836 by Thomas Lusk, a farmer. They both lived in Drumard. The murderer has absconded.

Emigration

The following is the number of persons that have emigrated from the parish of Ballynascreen during the years 1834 and 1835.

1834: 3 females under 10 years, 8 males and 4 females 10 and below 20 years, 19 males and 12 females 20 and below 30 years, 6 males and 1 female 30 and below 40 years, 1 male and 3 females 40 and below 50 years, total 57, males 34, females 23.

1835: 1 male and 2 females under 10 years, 2 males and 3 females 10 and below 20 years, 20 males and 10 females 20 and below 30 years, 7 males and 3 females 30 and below 40 years, 1 male 50 and below 60 years, total 49, males 31, females 18.

125 persons are in the habit of emigrating annually to England and Scotland for harvest work.

Longevity

It is not uncommon to see among the mountaineers individuals more than 80 years old reaping corn and performing other agricultural operations.

Dispensaries

Report of the Worshipful Drapers' Ballynascreen dispensary from 12th May 1835 till 12th May 1836: total number of cases 4,517; of which there were relieved 79, incurable 39, dead 27, cured 2,039, secondary application 2,075, still on the books 258.

The following is the same report from the 12th May 1834 to 12th May 1835: total number of cases 4,001; of which there were relieved 90, incurable 22, dead 30, cured 1,848, secondary application 1,881, still on the books 130.

Report of the Ballynascreen county dispensary from the 28th June 1835 till 28th June 1836: total number of cases 3,788; of which there were relieved 327, dead 28, cured 3,033, still on the books 400, [signed] John Savage, surgeon.

Dyspepsia is the most prevailing disease. Scrofula and dropsy are of frequent occurrence. Common continued fever occasionally prevails, at times assuming a typhoid type. Inflammatory diseases such as rheumatism and pneumonia abound in spring, autumn and winter. Exanthematous diseases are not generally speaking violent.

Dr Savage having the attendance of the 2 dispensaries finds himself, from the incessant nature of his employment, unable to give more detailed information.

Schools

This parish receives little or no instruction from the Sunday School Society. On the 8th May the parish priest pronounced a curse from the altar against any person of his congregation who should send their children to the Irish schools and also against any Roman Catholic teacher who would teach in one of them. However, tacit permission has been since given.

Sunday School

[Insert addition: There is but 1 Sunday school. It is held in the parish church. It contains 17 males and 39 females, of which 45 are of the Established Church and 11 are Presbyterian; none are exclusively Sunday school scholars. It is superintended by Mr Brownlow, the curate, and is of very little importance. It was established 13 years ago and there are 4 teachers, 1 male and 3 females. The hours of attendance are from 10.30 a.m. until 12. It is not connected with any society and commences with prayer only.

Mr Brownlow's name is the Reverend John Brownlow].

Poor

The following are the number and names of paupers on the church list who receive relief from the poor box collection: Widow McDaid, Margaret Devine, Widow McGuiggan, John McCloskey, Bartholemew McKenna, Michael McAllister, Ann McFillan, Patrick McWilliams, Widow Henry, Margaret McEntire, Ann Diamond, Mary McLaughlin, Bridget Hagan, Jane Mooney, Rose Convery, Charles Stewart, John McGeagh, Patrick Quigly, Widow McBride, Widow Murphy, John Hunter, Mary Berrymore, Jane Mundell.

There are but 2 instances in which applicants have been rejected from want of funds. Nothing is given from the poor box to applicants not enrolled, unless from the curate's private purse. The annual collection for 1834 was 16 pounds 9d, for 1835 15 pounds 1s 9d. Age, infirmity, the death of male parents and bad health have been the general causes of their destitution.

Income of the Clergy

Religion: the income of the priest is stated to be 150 pounds per annum. That of the rector is not known within the parish.

Habits of the People

For the proportion of sects, see public documents.

The general style of the cottages is, on the Drapers' estate, superior to what it is on any other portion of the parish. It is most inferior in the Sixtowns glen, where it is not uncommon to meet with roofs covered with a thick growth of grass, with dirty doors and dungheaps to correspond. In the interior their comfort and cleanliness is of a similar character. Near the old church there are some houses, a shade more comfortable, belonging to the Scottish settlers.

There are no mud houses. The food of the people is similar to that of the surrounding parishes.

The longevity of the people here is not remarkable. Robert White of Moneyneany died 17th March 1827 aged 106. His age and death is inscribed on a stone in the chapel yard of that townland.

The mountaineers are very much addicted to early marriages. Instances are known of such occurring at the early age of 14 and 15.

There are few parishes that have retained its ancient Irish character so long. Up to 20 years ago the old wooden mether or drinking vessel was in common use. The old songs are still sung and the Irish language universally spoken. There have been some ancient manuscripts among the people (see Ancient Topography).

Bard

Dominic Kelly, a schoolmaster who lived in the townland of Doon 80 years ago, seems to have been the last bard among them. He composed several songs of great beauty and at length became deranged. His melodies are known by the name of "The Colonel's Songs," that being a title which he assumed to himself during his madness.

Traditions regarding Lough Patrick

An important haunt of superstition is Lough Patrick, which is a small oval-shaped lake occupying about 1 and a half acres, Cunningham measure, and situated in Owenreagh mountain. Stations have been performed at this place from time immemorial. It is believed that when St Patrick was journeying through this district, that he with others began a station on the site and that while performing it some of his followers became thirsty and demanded from him a drink. The saint, to supply their demand, worked a miracle and ordered for them first a spring, and then in consequence there was produced the lough.

A station was then annually held at it for penances and cures of bodily disease. They were well attended from the 3 kingdoms until denounced by the Catholic clergy in consequence of improper conduct on the part of the visitants. However, they are still kept up by a few strangers. The visitors, in performing the station, go praying on their knees 3 [times] round the lough and 9

Parish of Ballynascreen

times round a small tummock at its southern end. At the conclusion the patient is dipped in the lough and a piece of wearing apparel, a lock of hair or some pins are left on the tummock. It is surrounded by a ring worn in the sod by the pressure of the devotees' knees.

Superstitions

There are the usual superstitions about fairies, gentle bushes, etc. In the autumn of 1836 a man in the townland of Bancran was, it seems, so annoyed by the fairies that he was obliged to desert his house. Though the annoyance may be explained by natural causes, yet the strong belief that exists to the contrary serves to show the prevalence of the superstition.

Copy of a memorandum made of O'Haran's words, when examined on the subject of fairies. The full particulars of this event are as follows. They have been thought worthy of insertion as they serve to illustrate the habits of the people.

Denis O'Haran of Bancran Glebe says that about 1 month ago his wife saw a white woman in the byre. She came in then in a great fright and told him, but when he went out he saw nothing. 7 days afterwards he went out and saw the gentle people in the byre. Memorandum: as to these gentle people. He first said, when asked if there was room in the barn for any more of them, that he could not tell. Afterwards that "it was as full as it could hold," which he said in answer to one of the bystanders, who explained and repeated the question. Yet he contradicted himself again saying that at first he did not understand the question, afterwards that he did.

About 3 weeks after saying this, he saw, in company with another called Jemmy Burns of Derrynoyd, 3 hours after nightfall, the "people" again. They appeared like boys, 4 feet high with green jackets and caps. There were more than 60 of them. He saw them between 5 and 10 yards off, all in a body, in a little lane 6 feet wide; the boy Jemmy Burns (a full-grown man could not see them) in 4 days after this he deserted the house altogether.

As for the wife, she saw the white woman one night in her own bedroom lying across her "weans." She came back into the kitchen and fainted. Her husband went down and saw nothing. (Memo: contradiction again?) One of his neighbours says that he beat the children and then when the wife went to grip the white woman it felt like a roll of wool).

At another time she was in the kitchen when the white woman came up to the room door, looked at her and went away again. She also heard a shout outside with voices and noises on the roof, and at the same time she heard a voice which declared that "for all the trouble he had been at in building the house, he maybe would not be alive that day 12 months." She also heard music like the sound of pipers. 3 days after this O'Haran pulled down the house, though he had solemnly promised another person to set up again in it "to make trial once more." 5 days after was the time appointed. His neighbours were so sunk in superstition that they believe he has been paid the price of his house in good British currency by the fairies! It is remarkable that the versions of this story, circulated by his neighbours of the same townland, contradict the above. He contradicted himself, also, in his own story. Now from these circumstances is not this conclusion justifiable, that even as in the parish of Banagher Finn McCool's fingers were carved on the rock at Feeny on purpose, to produce superstition, also in this parish has Denis O'Haran acted as agent to others for the purpose of strengthening the decaying superstition of the people. See Memoir of Banagher, in which that opinion is also advanced about the print of the man's knee at the door of the old church. It would appear that no other explanation can satisfactorily be given for his own inconsistency in the relation which he gave.

Of the same stamp as the above is a legend current among them about a pesht or monster who, it seems, played the same tricks as the great serpent of Laignapieste. A puppy was once found in the wood of Doon by one of the parishioners, who brought him home. To his astonishment it grew up to be a pesht and forthwith began to devour all the cattle in the country. The alarm produced by this was so great that a reward was offered by the rulers, of all the country that could be seen at one view, to whoever would kill it. He was accordingly killed, letting fall in the chase sundry parts of his bowels in different parts of the country still pointed out. After all the killer was cheated in his bargain. They brought him up to Spellhoagh Gap, a place more than a thousand feet above the sea, but from which nothing can be seen but a barren boggy ravine. This specimen is a sufficient sample of the remaining legends of the parish.

Music

There is a great deal of ancient music here. Some of an inferior description has been composed by the mountaineers only 20 years ago. The songs of Ossian are still recited.

Dress

The costume of the people is similar to that of the parish of Dungiven. No Scotch caps appear anywhere.

Emigration

See tables; the migrants act in the same manner with respect to their families as in the parishes of Dungiven and Banagher. [Insert note: See also Thomas Fagan's Fair Sheets].

Remarkable Events

In August 1829 part of the great rock of Craignashoke in the townland of Moydamlaght fell down with a loud noise. It is said that the report was heard to the distance of 5 miles. It is a decaying basaltic rock and its disruption is attributed to the action of the weather.

Table of Schools

[Table contains the following headings: name, situation and description, when established, income and expenditure, physical, intellectual and moral education, number of pupils subdivided by age, sex and religion, name and religion of master and mistress].

[J. Bleakly] Derrynoyd national school, situated in the townland of Derrynoyd, near to the Honourable Justice Torrens' house, a good house, slated, 33 feet 10 inches by 15 feet 10 inches, established 1827; income: from the National Board per annum 8 pounds, from the Honourable Judge Torrens per annum 5 pounds, from pupils 6 pounds; intellectual education: books published by the National Board; moral education: visited by the clergy of the Established Church and the Honourable Judge Torrens, catechism on Saturday by the master; number of pupils: males, 22 under 10 years of age, 5 from 10 to 15, 27 total males; females, 25 under 10 years of age, 4 from 10 to 15, 29 total females; total number of pupils 56, 4 Protestants, 5 Presbyterians, 47 Roman Catholics; master Bristow Miniss, Presbyterian.

Bancran Glebe, on the road from the Cross to Derry, a good slated house, 22 by 15, built by subscription, established 1831; income: from the Revd William Knox, rector, 10 pounds per annum, from pupils 6 pounds; intellectual education: books published by the Kildare Place Society, with *Thompson's and Gough's Arithmetic*; moral education: visited by the Revd John Brownlow, curate, Authorised Version of Scriptures is taught and catechism on Saturday; number of pupils: males, 24 under 10 years of age, 22 from 10 to 15, 46 total males; females, 20 under 10 years of age, 10 from 10 to 15, 16 over 15, 30 [sic] total females; total number of pupils 76, all Roman Catholics; master William Ferguson, Roman Catholic.

Moykeeran, on the leading road from Draperstown to Dungiven, a good house, slated at the expense of the rector, the Revd William Knox, and supported by him, established 1833; income: from the Revd William Knox, rector, 10 pounds 8s, from the curate, the Revd John Brownlow, 2 pounds 8s, from pupils 8 pounds; intellectual education; books published by the Kildare Place Society, with *Thompson's and Gough's Arithmetic, Lennie and Murray's English grammar*; moral education: visited by the clergy of the Established Church, Authorised Version of Scripture and catechism on Saturday; number of pupils: males, 22 under 10 years of age, 7 from 10 to 15, 3 over 15, 32 total males; females, 23 under 10 years of age, 4 from 10 to 15, 27 total females; total number of pupils 59, 20 Protestants, 11 Presbyterians, 25 Roman Catholics, 3 other denominations; master Robert Noon, Established Church.

Brackagh Disert national school, on the leading road from Draperstown to Cookstown, a good house, thatched, established in 1829 and in 1834 under the National Board; income: from the National Board per annum 8 pounds, from pupils 2 pounds; intellectual education: books published by the National Board only are used; moral education: visited by the Revd Patrick O'Loughlin P.P.; number of pupils: males, 19 under 10 years of age, 9 from 10 to 15, 1 over 15, 29 total males; females: 14 under 10 years of age, 17 from 10 to 15, 2 over 15, 33 total females; total number of pupils 62, all Roman Catholics; master John O'Neil, Roman Catholic.

Straw national school, on the leading road from Draperstown to Cookstown, a good house, slated, established 1833; income: from the National Board per annum 8 pounds, from pupils 16 pounds; intellectual education: books published by the National Board, with *Bonnycastle's Algebra* and book-keeping; moral education: visited by the Revd Patrick O'Loughlin P.P., catechism on Saturday by master; number of pupils: males, 32 under 10 years of age, 19 from 10 to 15, 3 over 15, 54 total males; females, 26 under 10 years of age, 7 from 10 to 15, 33 total females; total number of pupils 87, all Roman Catholics; master Thomas McGowan, Roman Catholic. Report for August 1836.

Draperstown national school, held in a room of the teacher's house fitted up for the purpose,

Parish of Ballynascreen

thatched and 12 by 18 feet, established 1833; income; from the National Board per annum 8 pounds, from pupils 16 pounds; intellectual education: books published by the National Board only, with plain and fancy needlework; moral education: visited by the Revd John Brownlow and the Revd Patrick O'Loughlin P.P.; number of pupils: males, 26 under 10 years of age, 4 from 10 to 15, 30 total males; females, 34 under 10 years of age, 5 from 10 to 15, 1 over 15, 40 total females; total number of pupils 70, 4 Protestants, 8 Presbyterians, 58 Roman Catholics; master John O'Kane, Roman Catholic.

Carnamoney male school, held on Monday, Tuesday and Wednesday, situated in the townland of Carnamoney; the schoolhouse and teacher's dwelling are the same as that of the Black hill school and established at the same time; established 1824 in the new schoolhouse, in 1818 in hired house of Drapers' Company; income: from the Drapers' Company 50 pounds per annum; intellectual education: books published by the Kildare Place Society, with *Thompson's and Gough's Arithmetic*, and English grammar; moral education: visited by clergy of all denominations, who are members of the committee, Authorised Version of Scripture is taught; number of pupils: 33 under 10 years of age, 80 from 10 to 15, 20 over 15, total 133, all males, 1 Protestant, 14 Presbyterians, 118 Roman Catholics; master William Diver, Established Church.

Black hill male school, held on Thursday, Friday and Saturday, situated on the Black hill in the townland of Moneyguiggy, on the leading road from Tobermore to the Cross, in the same house in which the female school is held, established 1824; income: from the Drapers' Company per annum for teaching the 2 schools, i.e. Carnamoney and Black hill, 50 pounds; intellectual education: books by the Kildare Place Society, with *Thompson's and Gough's Arithmetic*, and English grammar; moral education: visited by clergy of all denominations and conducted by the same committee; number of pupils: males, 18 under 10 years of age, 49 from 10 to 15, 6 over 15, total 73, all males, 3 Protestants, 15 Presbyterians, 54 Roman Catholics, 1 other denomination; master William Diver, Established Church.

Labby national school, on the leading road from Draperstown to Omagh, a small thatched house, 23 by 14 feet, established 1823, only in the present house since 1825; income: from the National Board 8 pounds, from pupils 8 pounds; intellectual education: books published by the National Board, with *Bonnycastle's Algebra*;

moral education: not visited by any; number of pupils: males, 26 under 10 years of age, 45 from 10 to 15, 20 over 15, 91 total males; females: 57 under 10 years of age, 11 from 10 to 15, 68 total females; total number of pupils 159, 2 Protestants, 16 Presbyterians, 141 Roman Catholics; master John McCloskey, Roman Catholic.

Moneyneany private school, held in Roman Catholic chapel, established in 1823, only 3 years in Roman Catholic chapel; income from pupils 6 pounds; intellectual education: *Universal spelling book and primer*, with *Gough's Arithmetic* and *Murray's English grammar* if required; moral education: not visited by any; number of pupils: males, 8 under 10 years of age, 19 from 10 to 15, 3 over 15, 30 total males; females, 2 under 10 years of age, 15 from 10 to 15, 17 total females; total number of pupils 47, all Roman Catholics; master Rodger O'Kane, Roman Catholic. Report for August 1836.

Black hill public school for females held on Monday, Tuesday and Wednesday, situated on the Black hill in the townland of Moneyguiggy, on the leading road from Tobermore to the Cross, a good house, slated, 41 by 22 feet inside, established 1824; income: from the Worshipful the Drapers' Company per annum, with a good house and small garden attached, 35 pounds; expenditure: built at the expense of the Drapers' Company; physical education: none; intellectual education: books published by the Kildare Place Society, with plain and fancy needlework; moral education: visited by the clergy of all denominations and open to all visitors, and superintended by a committee of the respectable inhabitants; number of pupils: 30 under 10 years of age, 52 from 10 to 15, 82 total pupils, all females, 11 Protestants, 16 Presbyterians, 54 Roman Catholics, 1 other denomination; mistress Elizabeth Moore, Established Church.

Carnamoney female school, held on Thursday, Friday and Saturday, situated in the townland of Carnamoney, a good house of stone, slated, 41 by 22 feet inside, established 1834; income: from the Drapers' Company for teaching both schools per annum 35 pounds; expenditure: the schoolhouse was built at the expense of the Drapers' Company; intellectual education: books published by the Kildare Place Society, with plain and fancy needlework; moral education: visited and superintended as above; number of pupils: 30 under 10 years of age, 42 from 10 to 15, 50 over 15, total 122, all females, 1 Protestant, 10 Presbyterians, 111 Roman Catholics; mistress Elizabeth Moore, Established Church.

[T. Fagan] Tullybrick national school, 3 miles from Draperstown Cross, on the leading road from the above town to Omagh, house thatched, stands 1 storey, 25 by 12 feet inside, 1 door, 2 windows, school requisites in moderate supply, under the Education Board in 1832; income: from the Education Board 10 pounds, from pupils 8 pounds; intellectual education: books published by the Education Board; moral education: visits from the clergy of the Presbyterian and Catholic Churches, all catechisms taught on Saturdays if required; number of pupils: males, 29 under 10 years of age, 1 from 10 to 15, 30 total males; females: 14 under 10 years of age, 6 from 10 to 15, 20 total females; total number of pupils 50, 3 Presbyterians, 47 Roman Catholics; master Daniel McBride, a Roman Catholic.

Drumard national school, 1 and a half miles from Draperstown, on the new line of road to Cookstown, house slated, stands 1 storey, 23 feet 8 inches by 15 feet from out to out, 1 door, 2 windows, school requisites complete, under the Education Board in 1833; income: from the Education Board 8 pounds, from pupils 4 pounds; intellectual education: books published by the Education Board; moral education: visits from the clergy of the Established and Catholic Churches, all catechisms taught on Saturdays if required; number of pupils: males, 20 under 10 years of age, 32 from 10 to 15, 7 over 15, 59 total males; females, 9 under 10 years of age, 6 from 10 to 15, 1 over 15, 16 total females; total number of pupils 75, 5 Protestants, 5 Presbyterians, 58 Roman Catholics, 7 other denominations; master James Rodgers, a Roman Catholic.

Cahore national school at Draperstown, house thatched, stands 2 storeys, 1 door, 4 windows, schoolroom or house 26 by 18 feet 8 inches inside, school requisites in moderate supply, established under the National Board in 1833; income: from the Education Board 8 pounds per annum, from pupils 7 pounds; intellectual education: books published by the Education Board; moral education: visits from the parochial clergy of all denominations, all catechisms taught on Saturdays; number of pupils: males, 18 under 10 years of age, 12 from 10 to 15, 30 total males; females, 35 under 10 years of age, 10 from 10 to 15, 1 over 15, 46 total females; total number of pupils 76, 4 Protestants, 11 Presbyterians, 61 Roman Catholics; mistress Jane O'Kane, Roman Catholic. Report for August and October 1836.

[J. Stokes] Gorteade public school, situated at O'Kane's public house, on the leading road from Maghera to [blank], established 1831 and in 1834 it became connected with the [London Hibernian Society ?]; income: from the London Hibernian Society 4 pounds per annum, from the Mercers' Company 3 pounds, 5 pounds from pupils; expenditure: house rent paid by Mercers' Company, 3 pounds 10s; intellectual education: books published by the London Hibernian Society, with *Thompson's and Gough's Arithmetic*; moral education: visited by the Protestant and Presbyterian clergy, Authorised Version of Scriptures; number of pupils: males, 21 under 10 years of age, 10 from 10 to 15, 5 over 15, 36 total males; females, 11 under 10 years of age, 2 from 10 to 15, 13 total males; total number of pupils 49, 17 Presbyterians, 20 Roman Catholics, 12 other denominations; master William Thompson, Protestant.

Fallagloon public school, situated on the leading road from Dungiven to Knockloghram, a good house, of stone and lime, slated, built [blank], established in 1827; income: from Revd Spencer Knox per annum 2 pounds, until the year 1832 the master received 7 pounds from [blank], 4 pounds from pupils; expenditure: the house is kept in repair by Mr Knox; physical education: none; intellectual education: books published by the Kildare Place Society, with *Thompson's and Gough's Arithmetic, Murray and Lennie's [English grammar]*; moral education: visited by the clergy of the Established church, Authorised Version of Scriptures is taught; number of pupils: males, 15 under 10 years of age, 5 from 10 to 15, 20 total males; females, 11 under 10 years of age, 11 total females; total number of pupils, 31, 3 Protestants, 18 Presbyterians, 10 Independents; master William Losmer, Independent.

Dispensary Reports

Report of the Worshipful Drapers' Ballynascreen dispensary from 12th May 1825 [1835] till 12th May 1836: 2,442 admitted during the year, 258 on the books, 79 relieved, 39 incurable, 27 dead, 2,039 cured, 2,075 secondary application, total 4,517.

Report of the Ballynascreen dispensary from 28th June 1835 till 28th June 1836: 28 dead, 327 relieved, 400 on the books, 3,033 cured, total during the year 3,788; number of patients visited during the above period 478.

Dyspepsia the most prevailing disease, scrofula and dropsy of frequent occurrence. Common continued fever occasionally prevails, at times assuming a typhoid type. Inflammatory diseases, as rheumatism and pneumonia, abound in spring, autumn and winter. Exanthematory diseases not generally speaking virulent. [Signed] John Savage, surgeon.

Parish of Ballynascreen

Appendix to Memoir by J. Stokes

ANCIENT TOPOGRAPHY

Drawings

New market house at Draperstown, front elevation, width 40 feet.

Plan of the town of Draperstown, shewing in red ink the buildings intended by the company, scale 6 inches to a mile.

Ornamented recess at the side of the east window of the old church, with dimensions.

View of the east window from the interior, showing the recess represented in [previous drawing].

Door of the old church.

Cross in Ballynascreen graveyard, with annotations and dimensions.

Stones at the doorway of the old church, with dimensions.

Old windows in the parish church, 10 feet high.

Grave in Tullybrick, with dimensions.

2 standing stones, 4 feet and 3 feet 6 inches high, with ground plan and annotations.

Part of an ancient circle in Strawmore, with outline of a person's figure, largest stone 4 feet.

Plan of standing stone circle, with dimensions, largest stone 4 and a half feet; view from point A, scale 20 feet to an inch.

View of the interior of the old church.

Front, side and enlarged end view of stone mould, with dimensions.

Remains of a giant's grave in Cloane.

Mether from the townland of Labby, main dimensions 6 and a half by 4 inches.

2 views of ornamented quern, townland Glenavney, with dimensions.

2 views of ornamented quern found in the bed of the Moyola, with dimensions.

2 views of unfinished quern found in Corick townland, with dimensions.

2 views and section of an oak dish from Brackagh.

Carved stone found in Moneyneany, with dimensions.

Office Copy of Draft Memoir

NATURAL FEATURES

Hills

The parish of Ballynascreen may be said to comprise the upper valley of the Moyola. It is surrounded on 3 sides by lofty and wild mountains pushing their broad bases to the banks of that river, whilst their bold outlines add beauty and grandeur to the scenery. The tops of these hills are covered with bog.

Lakes and Rivers

Lakes: Lough Patrick, Owenreagh.

The principal river which waters this district is the Moyola. It has its source in the south western corner of the parish, in the townland of Glenviggan, and, flowing north east, traverses the parish in its whole extent. It is the chief outlet for all the lesser streams from the surrounding hills, the principal of which are the Douglas river from the north, flowing through Evishagore glen, and the Blackwater from the south. The remainder are of minor importance.

Bogs

The tops of the hills which surround this parish are covered with bog, whilst the soil of their underfeatures is generally a heavy clay.

Woods

The little wood in the parish at present is chiefly confined to the glebe of Ballynascreen (see Gentlemen's Seats). The Drapers' Company have planted a great deal within the last few years.

MODERN TOPOGRAPHY

Towns

The only village in this parish is called the Cross, from its situation at the point of meeting of the 4 principal roads which traverse it. Considerable improvements to it have long been projected by the Drapers' Company, and since the completion of the new road by Moneyneaney, Glenedra and Feeny to Derry nothing but the encouragement of the landlords is wanting to make the hamlet rise rapidly. The establishment of a good inn is the first requisite, as it will eventually become the principal thoroughfare between Belfast, Armagh and Londonderry.

It is neither a post or market town, both [of] which establishments it will require. A fair is held in it on the first Friday in every month, when a very extensive sale of cattle for exportation takes place. On the completion of the proposed improvements it is to take the name of Draperstown.

Public Buildings

There are 3 Roman Catholic chapels, 1 in Straw, in Strawmore and a third in Owenreagh townland.

Gentlemen's Seats

The glebe of Ballynascreen, which was originally the private property of the late Revd Doctor Torrens, to whose good taste it owes all its present beauty. The only other residence in this parish is Derrynoyd Lodge, the seat of the Honourable Judge Torrens, whose judicious improvements have greatly contributed to adorn the surrounding country.

Communications

Besides the road before mentioned, several others cross the parish. That from Cookstown to Dungiven by Derrynoyd and those from Moneymore and Magherafelt are in general in very good order, but are little frequented on account of the ascent of Moneyneany mountain, the new road by Carntogher being much preferable.

Fair Sheets by Thomas Fagan, September 1836 to January 1837

NATURAL FEATURES

Bogs

The bogs of Moneyconey and Cavanreagh are mountain bogs and vary in depth from 2 to 6 feet. Oak, fir, yew and alder roots are found embedded in these bogs but no trees or windfalls. Roots are often found resting one on the top of another, and burned in varied instances. There are also a number of sharp-pointed sticks found standing upright beneath the surface of the bogs.

MODERN TOPOGRAPHY

Catholic Chapel

The Roman Catholic chapel of Moneyneany was commenced to be built in 1813, roofed in 1828 and galleries were put in it in 1832. The expense of erecting this chapel cannot be at present ascertained as it was so long on hand. Besides, the major part of horse and manual labour, carriage of building materials was done from time to time by the parishioners. Information obtained from Patrick Cassidy, Patrick Crilly and others. 28th October 1836.

Cottage

Mr Ogilby's cottage at Strawmore was repaired 1834.

Bridges

The bridge between Tullybrick and Moneyconey was first built about 1773 and secondly built or repaired 1795.

The new bridge between Tullybrick and Moneyconey was built in 1834. Informant Hugh Bradley.

The Blackwater bridge, on the leading road from Dungiven to Cookstown, has 1 arch span 17 feet, breadth of the road on the bridge 17 feet 8 inches, parapets dilapidated, and averages in height 4 feet 6 inches.

SOCIAL ECONOMY

Judges

The last Catholic judge that presided in Desertmartin previous to the Penal Code was a Rory Mor O'Harran.

Police

Peace police in Draperstown 4, revenue police in Draperstown 15 and a lieutenant.

Manor Court

Mr Ogilby's manor court was held monthly at Strawmore Lodge at some former period, but it is altogether relinquished for the last year. Information obtained from William McCollum, James McNamee and others, 1st October 1836.

Longevity

The late Robert White of Moneyneany died 17th March 1827 aged 106 years and is interred in Moneyneany chapel yard; taken from his tombstone. 19th October 1836.

Catholic Clergy

The Revd Patrick O'Loughlin is parish priest of Ballynascreen and vicar of the diocese of Derry, and receives average annual income from the above parish 150 pounds. Of this sum, the Revd Menassus O'Kane, Roman Catholic curate, receives annually one-third as his proportion or income. Information obtained from the Revd Patrick O'Loughlin P.P. and vicar, 25th October 1836.

Poor Box Charities

The following is the number and names of paupers on the church list who get relief from the poor box funds occasionally.

Parish of Ballynascreen

Widow McDaid, Widow McGuiggin, Bartholmly McKenna, Ann McFillan, Widow Henery, Ann Dimond, Bridget Hagan, Rose Convery, John McGeoagh, Widow McBride, John Hunter, Margret Devine, John McCloskey, Michael McAlister, Patrick McWilliams, Margret McEntire, Mary McLoughlin, Jane Mooney, Charles Stewart, Patrick Quigly, Widow Murphy, Mary Berryman, Jane Mundle.

There are only 2 instance of applicants being rejected, for want of sufficient funds. The sums given to each applicant on the list vary from 2s 6d to 6s 6d each time, as the funds can afford, but nothing given from the poor box to applicants not enrolled on the church list, unless from the curate's private purse.

Annual collection for 1834, 16 pounds 9d; annual collection for 1835, 15 pounds 1s 9d.

The causes of so many distressed poor applicants on the church list are attributable to different calamities and disappointments, such as death of male parents, age, infirmity and bad health. Information taken from the church poor list and partly obtained from John Moran, sexton, and others, 27th October 1836.

Outrages

The following are of the number of outrages of various shades that have occurred within the above parish in 1831 and subsequent years up to the present period, and also the causes.

James Trolen, farmer, killed by Patrick Duffy, farmer, in 1831; both lived in Cahore; cause: a dispute about a pass or bridle road. Duffy evaded detection and fled the country.

Edward Murphy, labourer, killed in 1833 by John Haghey, farmer; both lived in Draperstown; cause: a drinking dispute. John Haghey evaded detection and fled to America.

John Toner, farmer, killed in 1834 by Phillip Kelly, farmer, in a drinking dispute. They both lived in Straw. Phillip Kelly evaded detection and fled the country.

Thomas Robinson, farmer, killed in 1836 by Thomas Lusk, a farmer; they both lived in Drumard. Lusk evaded detection and fled the country; cause: a gambling dispute.

Daniel Kelly of Strawmore died on the roadside near Draperstown. He was on his way home from Coleraine sessions in 1835. He is supposed to have died of weakness but the cause of his weakness is not known.

Many other outrages have occurred within the parish within the above period, but of such characters as was either settled by the parties or punished at petty sessions. Informants Hugh Hagan, Mathew McRory and others. 1st November 1836.

Emigration in 1834

The following is a list of the number of persons that have emigrated to America from the undermentioned townlands during the years 1834 and 1835. It will show the name, age and religion of each person, townlands from whence gone, and ports for which emigrated, as enumerated from 29th September to 17th October 1836.

James Reid, 30, Roman Catholic, from Glebe to Quebec.

Patt Henery, 24, Roman Catholic, from Desert to New York.

Charles Connery, 24, Roman Catholic, from Desert to New York.

Charles O'Neill, 24, Bridget O'Neill, 26, Roman Catholics, from Desert to New York.

Thomas Morrin, 24, Roman Catholic, from Desert to New York.

Sophia Kelly, 40, Mary Kelly, 43, Roman Catholics, from Corick to New York.

Michael Kane, 18, Roman Catholic, from Drumard to New York.

Robert Robertson, 21, Established Church, from Drumard to New York.

George Gibson, 24, Thomas Gibson, 21, Established Church, from Drumard to New York.

Andrew Leech, 30, Established Church, from Drumard to New York.

Rosey Bradley, 26, Joseph Bradley, 25, Roman Catholics, from Cloughfin to Quebec.

Elenor McNeill, 30, Roman Catholic, from Cloughfin to Quebec.

Domnick Gillon, 32, Roman Catholic, from Moneyconey to Quebec.

Information obtained from Henery Gillespie, Hugh Bradley and others.

Emigration in 1835

Sally Sargent, 20, Established Church, from Mulnavoo to Quebec.

James Bradley, 25, Elenor Bradley, 22, Roman Catholics, from Glebe to Quebec.

John Henery, 19, Roman Catholic, from Desert to New York.

John Connery, 20, Roman Catholic, from Desert to New York.

Patt Donnelly, 30, James Donnelly, 20, Roman Catholics, from Straw to New York.

John McNally, 30, Roman Catholic, from Moyard to Philadelphia.

Patt Connelly, 25, Roman Catholic, from Moneyconey to New York.

James Bradley, 24, Roman Catholic, from Moneyconey to New York.

Martha Kelly, 35, Anne Kelly, 5, James Kelly, 2, Roman Catholics, from Corick to New York.

Information obtained from Henery Gillespie, Hugh Bradley and others, finished 17th October 1836.

Migration

The following is a list of the number of persons that annually migrate to the English and Scotch harvests from the under-mentioned townlands, as enumerated from 29th September to 17th October 1836.

Glebe, 6 to Scotland.
Straw, 5 to England.
Moneyconey, 3 to England.
Cloughfin, 5 to England.
Cahore, 6 to Scotland.
Drumard, 6 to England, 5 to Scotland.
Tullybrick, 2 to Scotland.

Information obtained from John Mallon, John Bradley and others, finished 17th October 1836.

Ancient Topography

Giant's Graves

In Clone, and holding of Bernard McEldowney, there stands a giant's grave enclosed by large stones.

There is a giant's grave on Corick mountain.

Ancient Crock

On a sand-hill in the townland of Desert, and about 7 feet beneath the surface, there was found in 1820 an ancient crock containing a quantity of calcined bones and ashes. The crock was beautifully carved on the surface. On being removed it fell into small pieces.

Friars Well

In Mulnavoo, and holding of James Sergent, there stands an ancient spring locally called the Friars Well. The townland was the seat of friars for a series of years. The above well took its name from them.

Ancient Foundry

There was an old foundry in Mulnavoo and holding of James Lyle. There was some pieces of iron bars found beneath the surface of its ruins in 1833.

Cromlech

In Drumderg, and holding of Patrick Dimond, there stands the ruins of a cromlech <crumlic> or giant's grave.

Model Stones

In Derrynoyd, and holding of Denny Henry, there stands a moderate sized stone with 2 circular holes in it. One of the holes is 9 inches in diameter and 4 inches in depth; the other is something smaller. There was 3 other stones with circular holes in each of them got in the same townland, but are not to be seen at present. Informants James Sergent, Denny Henry and many others, 29th September 1836.

In Glengavney and holding of John McCormick, and in the neighbourhood of a Danish fort, there stands 2 stones of moderate size with circular holes in each of them, approaching in dimensions to those described in Derrynoyd. At some former period there was a piece of old iron, resembling a saddle, got in the above fort.

Gold in Glengavney

Michael Harron of the above townland got 3 pieces of ancient gold coin and an ancient pot of rare construction beneath the surface in 1835. The coin was subsequently purchased by Robert L. Ogilby <Ogleby> of Dungiven, Esquire. He is to procure the pot also.

Ancient Grave and Coin

Andrew McGuigan of Glebe discovered beneath the surface, [at] a depth of 3 feet, a grave 7 feet long and 3 feet broad, enclosed by a stone building and roofed with long flat stones. In the interior was a quantity of black rich earth.

The above Mr McGuigan found beneath the surface in the same farm some old irons and pieces of ancient silver coin, one of which coins he has at present attached to his beads. It seems to be one [of] Queen Elizabeth's coins.

Meddars

Pat McCullagh of Glengavney has an ancient meddar. Informants Andrew McGuigan, John McCormick and many others, 30th September 1836.

Andrew Clearken of Labby has 2 ancient meddars.

Ancient Bell

Patrick Crilly of Derrynoyd got beneath the surface at some former period an ancient bell 4 square and 7 lbs weight.

Battleaxe

James McCloskey of Derrynoyd got a brass battleaxe beneath the surface at some former period.

Standing Stones

There are a number of ancient standing stones on Glengavney mountain.

The ancient name of the standing stones in Strawmore is Slaughte. Informants Denis O'Hagan, James Keilt and others.

Ancient Quern

The annexed draft [drawing] represents an ancient quern found in a river in Moyard, and stands at present in Hugh Bradley's in the above townland. It approaches to circular shape, 16 inches in diameter and 2 and three-quarter inches in thickness. Devices, as above shown, are cut on its surface and are locally believed to be old letters or a substitute for such. Information obtained from Hugh Bradley, Moyard. 3rd October 1836.

Human Bones

On changing a portion of the leading road from Draperstown Cross to Omagh in 1824, there was found at some depth beneath the surface in Altayesk the skeleton or a quantity of human bones, which were subsquently buried in the spot in which they were found.

Temple Moyle

In a subdivision formerly of Altayesk but now of Davagh and county Tyrone, and in the holding of James and Charles Quin, there stands an eminence locally called Thampel Muill or Temple Moyle, and said to be an ancient burial ground and site selected for a church which was never erected. However, on its summit at present stand a number of stones sunk on their ends in the ground and partly appearing above the surface. These stones are said to stand at the heads of graves that are now absorbed by the soil.

In exploring the eminence at some former period, there was skulls and a quantity of other human bones got beneath its surface. These bones were subsquently interred on the site where found.

The aforesaid change in the situation of this burial ground occurred in consequence of a dispute between Lady Trench and the late Captain Stevenson of Fort William about mearings, at some former period. The result of the dispute was that Mr Stevenson gave way, or submitted, to her agent, William Magill Esquire, who, with his assistant, pointed out a wrong mearing between the 2 counties and thereby left the above burial ground to stand in Tyrone, deprived Mr Stevenson of a large tract of ground and the county Derry of a portion of its former boundaries. The distance between the burial ground and new mearing exceeds 80 yards. Informants Hugh Morran, Pat McNamee and others.

Lough Patrick

Lough Patrick is a small lake, oval shaped, and occupies about 1 and a half acres. It is situated in Owenreagh mountain and grazing of Thomas Dean and others. This lake is a station stage, time immemorial, and is locally said to derive its origin under the following circumstances.

That when St Patrick was on his mission through this part of the above county, that he with others commenced a station on the site of the aforesaid lough; and that while performing the station some of his followers got thirsty and demanded from him a drink, and that the saint caused a spring immediately to gush through the surface, which relieved the wants of all then present; that the spring continued to force the surface till it formed the aforesaid sheet of water, which was from that period dedicated to the saint and called St Patrick's lough, but subsquently changed and called Lough Patrick; that he, or Colum Kille, ordered a station to be annually held at the lough on Midsummer Eve, and for some days subsequent, for promoting religion and also for the cure of various bodily diseases.

These stations were well attended to by hundreds of persons, not only belonging to this country but also from England and Scotland, to a very late period, till the Roman Catholic clergy commenced to denounce the practice in consequence of improper conduct on the part of many of the visitants.

However, the stations are partially held up by strangers, even to the present period. The visitors in performing the station go 3 times round the lough, praying during that time, and 9 times around a small terrace that stands at the south end of the lough and is called a "tummock." They are on their knees and at devotion during the 9 journeys round the tummock; and at the conclusion of the station, if, for the relief or cure of bodily diseases, the patient is dipped in the lough and a remnant of their wearing apparel, a lock of their hair or some pins are left on the tummock, purporting the disorder complained of to be left there, and a return of good health sure or probable to the patient. If a back-going or a sickly child, its colour after leaving the water denotes death sudden or restoration to good health.

The aforesaid tummock is very small and is covered at present with rags left by visitants from time to time, and a ring completely sunk round it by the pressure of the people's knees. Informants Lawrence Hasson, Stephen Dean and others.

Standing Stones

In Owenreagh, and mountain farm of Patrick Flannigan, there stands the ruins of some ancient stone building locally called the Standing Stones. It occupies 52 feet by 27 feet and seemed to be partly enclosed by a wall 3 and a half feet thick, and partly by stone columns, one of which stands on the site at present and stands 5 and a half feet high, 2 feet broad and 2 feet thick. The principal part of the building is now destroyed and the site undergoing cultivation. This old monument stood in view of Lough Patrick. 4th October 1836.

Ancient Carn

In Owenreagh, and mountain grazing of Patrick Connory, there stands an ancient carn of stones which occupies 45 by 30 feet and its summit about 5 feet higher than the level of the hill on which it stands. It was composed of stones of different sizes and different quality from any stones in the mountain.

The carn was explored at some former period, but no account of anything being found in it save that there was stripped, or left exposed to view, in the bottom of it a number of large flat stones, similar to these often found to enclose and cover giant's graves in other parts.

It is thought by some of the local inhabitants to be a monument raised over the graves of giants at some former period, but at present it is a complete pile of ruins. It stands in view of Lough Patrick.

Bolie Columkille

In Tullybrick mountain, and about 1 and a half miles from the old church of Ballynascreen, there stands a glen locally called Bolie Columkille, so called in consequence of it being a secluded place selected by the above saint to retire to in the evenings, while superintending the building of the above old church. It is in this glen that St Colum Kille spent his nights and leisure hours, and also performed stations or devotions during the building of the aforesaid ancient church. The glen since that period has been dedicated to the saint and called Bolie Columkille, which means "St Colum Kille's place of abode or retirement."

Churches

Local tradition says that Ballynascreen ancient church is the centre one of 9 churches founded by St Colum Kille in the north and southern parts of the county Derry and a portion of Tyrone, to wit Ballynascreen, Desertlyn, Desertcreat, Termon, Killelagh <Killylagh>, Bodoney <Badowney>, Maghera, Magherafelt and Dungiven. These churches are called "nie thampelle na ought milie Colum Kille" or "the 9 churches, 8 miles one from the other, founded by St Colum Kille." Informants Lawrence Hasson, Hugh Bradley and others. 6th October 1836.

Stone Mould

The stone mould for casting spearheads was found about 5 feet under the surface of a bog and within about 700 yards of a Danish fort in the townland of Drumderg in 1831. Informant Lawrence Goodwin.

Ancient Crocks

In Strawmore and holding of Patrick McGlade, and about 10 feet beneath the surface of a sandy hill, there was found in 1822 5 ancient crocks containing calcined bones and ashes. They were carved on the surface and covered on the mouth with flat stones. On being removed from their original berth they crumbled down into small pieces.

Derivation of Drumderg

Darige Dawna Mackadrille, a foreign chief who came to fight some of the Irish Phoenicians, is the giant buried in Drumderg, where the ancient standing stones are on the verge of a stream and holding of Patrick Dimond. He was killed by Coocolun and immediately buried in the aforesaid place, it being the site of the battle. The eminence was from that period called Drimadirig and gave name to the townland, though the name has been subsequently changed and called Drumderg. The monument or standing stones are called Kille Ahouma or "the tomb burial ground."

Derivation of Ballynascreen

The above parish took its name from a small shed <shead> or screen erected of stones, clothes, etc.

Parish of Ballynascreen

to shelter the altar and officiating clergy at some time previous, and during the erection of the old church of Ballynascreen. The site and shed was then called Ballynascreen and the church and parish subsequently called after them.

Derivation of Bodoney

The derivation of the parish of Bodoney occurred under the following circumstances: a gentleman's daughter in the south of Ireland got deranged and fled from her friends, who eagerly pursued her course and at length discovered her sleeping in the verge of a wood in the above parish and county Tyrone. She was naked when found and, in order to allow her quiet and unmolested rest, they constructed a small hut over her to screen her from the inclemency of the weather. It was constructed on a Sunday and afterwards called Buoyh-a-donaye or "the Sunday hut." The parish was called after the hut Buoyh-a-donaye but subsequently changed to Bodoney. Information obtained from Peter McRory, Cornelious McNally and others. 10th October 1836.

Derivation of Moneyneany

Tradition says that the above townland derived its name under the following circumstances. Its valleys were a favourite place of the old Irish Phoenicians to learn their exercises and also to perform great exploits and tricks by magic art. It was in consequence called Mean-na-neenthus or "the plains of wonders," which term the townland gets in the Irish language to the present period, though it is called in the English language Moneyneany.

Ancient Coin

In 1824 there was an ancient gold coin got in a Danish fort in Moneyneany and holding of Alexander Doyle. On one side was a large head and on the other side a Spanish harp with the words "30 shillings" across it. Samuel McElree of Dungiven has the coin at present. Informants Cornelious McNally, Peter McRory and others.

In Moneyneany there was found at some former period an ancient silver coin with 12 small crosses and 12 dots or small stars on one side of it. It has been subsequently lost.

Ancient Spring

In Moneyneany, and holding of Henery McDevitt, there stands an ancient spring locally called Toberawathyweell or "the earless dog's well," so called in consequence of a Sir Volvett, a magician that lived in the above townland at some former period, having kept a large earless dog continually chained at the well to prevent other inhabitants from drinking or using any of the water. There is a very singular feeling, local, concerning the water of this well, that if a small quantity of it be applied to new milk immediately taken from the cow, that it will turn it into curds, similar to any acid or sour buttermilk, but either the sweet milk or water must be boiled before they are mixed. Information obtained from Francis Downey, Peter McRory and others.

Tremor at Craignashoke

A large portion of Craignashoke fell in August 1829. It alarmed the inhabitants of its neighbourhood and quaked the surface for a considerable distance round it. Informants James Toner, Bernard Downey and many others. 11th October 1836.

Model Stones and Fort

In Moydamlaght, and holding of Michael Toner, there stands a large landstone with an oval hole cut in it. There were 2 other holes commenced to be cut in it, but not completed. The oval hole is 12 by 10 inches and 6 inches in depth.

Within a short distance of the above stone there stands the remains of a fort. It seems to have stood circular, 40 yards in diameter, but no vestige of it remains at present to be seen but 2 ancient thorns that stood in the parapet. There is also a quantity of forge dross to be seen through the site of the fort. In labouring the site of this fort from time to time within the last 20 years, there were graves and some human skulls and other bones of more than ordinary size got beneath its surface, which skulls and bones were subsequently buried in the site.

It is thought by many of the local inhabitants that the above fort or enclosure was an ancient burial ground, as there was a quantity of human bones got beneath its surface. Besides that, tradition also says that the field in which it stands was the site on which the old church of Ballynascreen was first commenced to be erected, but that all built by day was nightly demolished by some invisible agents and that the building of the church on the site was in consequence obliged to be relinquished. Informants Peter McRory, Cornelious McNally and James Toner. 11th October 1836.

Curious Stone

The annexed draft [drawing] is a representation of the shape and size of a stone artificially brought to the above shape, and found with a quantity of well-shaped flints about 8 feet under the surface of a bog in Moneyneany in 1835. Informant Denis McKenna.

Meddar

There is a small ancient meddar in Moydamlaght and dwelling house of Michael Toner.

Stones

The hole in a stone beneath the fort in Glengamna, and holding of John McCormick, is oval shaped, 12 by 10 inches and 6 inches deep.

The hole in a stone that stands in the parapet of the same fort is circular, 10 inches in diameter and 5 inches in depth. 13th October 1836.

Ancient Axe

The above [2 drawings] represents an ancient iron axe found about 7 feet beneath the surface of a bog in Strawmore in 1836. There was also found with the above axe a set of plough irons of a very odd construction and all said to be of Danish construction. The above is the exact size and shape of the axe, on its flat and also on its side. It belongs to Peter Kelly of the above townland. Note: The enclosed blank [space] embraced the handle. Informants Thomas Leaden and others. 14th October 1836.

Oak Lossett

The above draft [drawing] represents an ancient oak lossett 2 feet 7 inches by 1 foot 11 inches from out to out, and 2 feet 3 inches by 1 foot 9 inches in the clear and 1 and a half inches in thickness. It was found about 1726 in a small lough or pool in Brackagh and stands at present in James McBride's dwelling house in the above townland.

Battleaxe

The annexed draft [drawing] represents a brass battleaxe found about 5 feet beneath the surface of a bog in Derrynoyd in 1826. Information obtained from James McCloskey and James McBride.

Ancient Mill

In Moykeeran and holding of James Stewart, and beneath the surface in the remains of an old wood, there was found in 1814 an ancient millstead with all the grinding machinery; and though on a small scale, the entire of the works were approaching in construction to mills of modern date. The iron works must have been subsequently destroyed and converted to other uses. [Insert note by J. Stokes: Not ancient]. Information obtained from Thomas Leaden and others. 15th October 1836.

Arrowhead

The above [drawing] is the size and shape of an elve or flint stone or arrowhead found beneath the surface in the townland of Tonaght in 1833.

Tether Stake

In that subdivision of Tullybrick locally called Bolie Columkille, and in the holding of Patt Cassidy, there stands a stone column called Backan Naglisha. It stands 2 and a half feet high, 2 feet broad and 1 foot thick. It is locally said that St Colum Kille had a cow called the glashgevlin, which was kept constantly tethered <teddered> on this stone, and that the stone was in consequence called Backanglashgevlin or "the grey cow's tether stake." There is some impression round the neck of the stone said to be caused by the tether by which the cow was confined.

Giant's Graves

In the above Bolie, and holding of Michael Mallon, there stands the ruins of a cromlech locally called the Giant's Graves. The entire occupies 24 by 21 feet and enclosed and divided into subdivisions by large stones set on their ends and sides in the ground, which seemed to be covered by large canopy stones. One of the canopy stones still remains in its original berth, supported on columns and other large stones, and stands 2 feet 9 inches above the surface. It measures 8 feet in length, 4 feet 4 inches in breadth and 14 inches in thickness. There are several large and well-shaped stones still on the premises but many of them dislodged.

It is altogether the ruins of an extensive building and stands in a secluded and marshy valley in the mountain. 17th October 1836.

Giant's Chair and Cave

In Corick mountain, and holding of Hugh McKeon, there stands a stone locally called the Giant's Chair. It approaches to the shape of an old-fashioned chair, with the back reclining backwards. The summit of the back stands 3 feet 2 inches above the surface, 3 feet broad and 1 and a half feet thick. The seat is 15 inches deep or broad; the back stands 1 foot 10 inches high above the seat. It approaches near to the annexed draft [drawing].

In the above mountain, and holding of Michael McFaull, there stands a cave 12 feet long, 4 feet broad and 3 and a half feet high in the interior. It is constructed in a hill, of mossy surface. There are no stones employed in its construction but formed by vacating the above-described space in the hill, and at a great depth beneath the surface. The entrance to it is nearly circular and only sufficient to admit a boy in to it, similar to a trap hole.

Near the extremity of the cave, in one of the side walls, there stands, at arranged distances, 3 square holes or cupboards. They stand at about half the height of the side wall and seem to have been designed to contain some parcels. The side walls and roof are dry but the floor damp. There are a few stones inside that seemed to serve as seats. This cave was discovered by burning the heath on the surface of the hill. 20th October 1836.

Ancient Grave

William Phillips of Cavanreagh, in labouring a sandy hill in the above townland in 1815, got about 3 feet beneath the surface a grave 5 feet long, 2 and a half feet broad and 2 feet deep. It was enclosed by a stone building and contained a quantity of black rich earth. Informants William Phillips, Hugh McBride and others. 21st October 1836.

Ancient Bell

The bell that fell from the air in Moneyconey, at the period that Ballynascreen ancient church was about to be built, was a relic of great veneration in the church for a series of years after it was built; but at length the bell was taken into custody by one of the Gillan family, on whose garment the bell first alighted, and to whom St Colum Kille bequeathed it as their just property.

However, it has been a prevalent practice in the above and other parishes for many centuries back, when any of the parishioners were accused of theft etc., to procure this bell by leaving some pledge in lieu till its safe return. However, the bell was brought to the scene of accusation and there the accused made oath on the bell that they were innocent of the crime they were accused with. This oath so far satisfied the losing party and the public that the accused were not only acquitted but also esteemed as upright persons by all who knew them, during the remainder of their lives. But swearing by the bell at length became practical with the guilty accused, as well as with the innocent; but whenever the guilty made oath on the bell it immediately commenced ringing, which occurrence not only denoted perjury on the part of the guilty persons but also rendered them odious in the sight of all who knew them. Nor did this exposure of the bell end their misfortunes, for there were various instances from time to time of persons who made a false oath on the bell being subsequently visited with insanity, bodily injuries and diseases, desolation of family.

However, time and constant carrying about from place to place has not only deprived the above bell of its best and most useful member, the tongue, but has also reduced the frame to a mere skeleton. A description of its shape could not be attempted without first inspecting it. It stands at present in the parish of Tarmon [Termonmaguirk?] and possession of some of the Gillan family. The practice of swearing on it is denounced by Catholic clergy for some time past. Informants Hugh Bradley, William Phillips, Thomas Deane and many others, finished 22nd October 1836.

Traditions regarding Old Church

Local tradition says that the ancient church of Ballynascreen was commenced to be built on different sites within the above parish, and that all built by day on many of the sites were nightly demolished by some invisible agents, in consequence of which unpleasant and unconjectured obstruction the process of building the church had to be relinquished [at] sundry times; that the last site selected by the people for the church to be built on was east of the Moyola river, immediately opposite and within a short distance of the spot on which the ruins of the above ancient church at present stands. On this selected site, which stands in Tullybrick and holding of Henery Gillespie, there was raised at some former period a portion of the foundation of the church originally laid, but subsequently obliged to be relinquished under the aforesaid circumstances.

There was also discovered on the last-mentioned site within the last 50 years a kiln of lime supposed to have been burned for the use of the church, but that in consequence of the obstruction met with on this site, as well as on others previously selected, this kiln of lime lay unnoticed from that period.

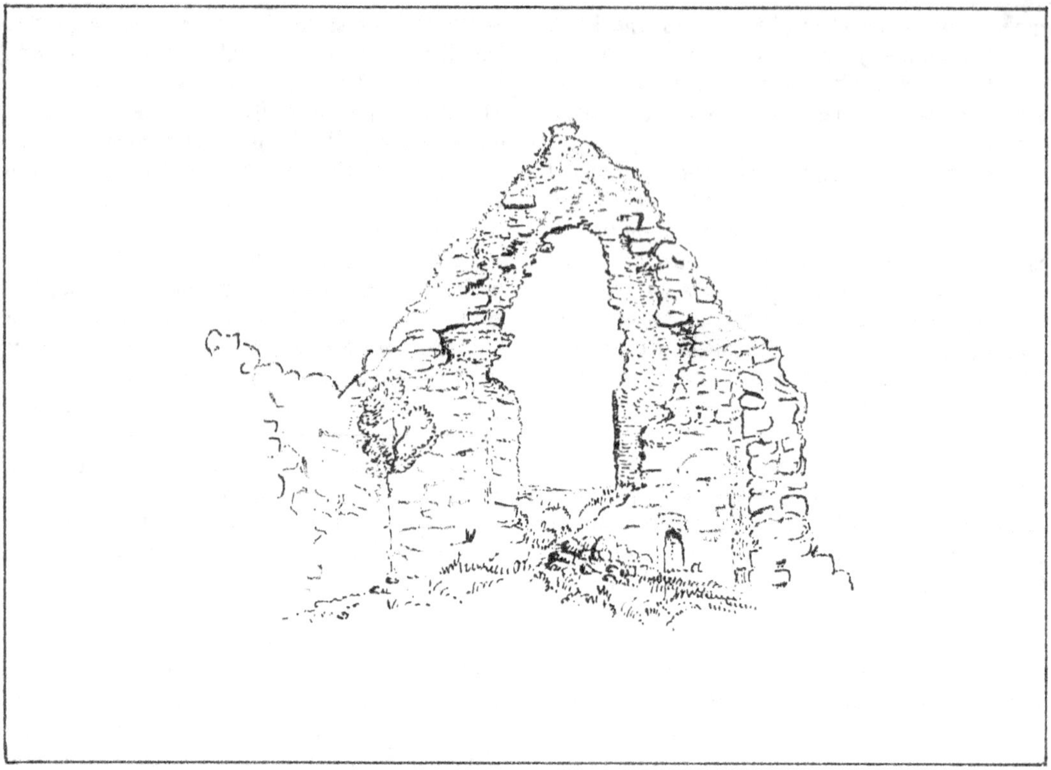

East window of old church

Interior of old church

However, the many disappointments experienced in building the church caused a great sensation and unpleasant feeling among the people, particularly so much regarding the last-mentioned site, that St Colum Kille, who is said to be the founder and superintendent of the church, concluded that the best step that could be taken to appease the minds of the people in such a state of affairs was to call them all together, both lay and ecclesiastic, that they might join together in prayer, invoking the God of Heaven to furnish them with some visible omen whereby they might be enabled to select or choose a fit and proper site to build the church on and be relieved from their long embarrassment. To the above recommendation the people all acceded with one accord and repaired to some befitting place, where they, headed and assisted by the saint, fervently prayed for the aforesaid warning or purposes.

At concluding their devotions the saint announced to all there present the joyous tidings that the Lord accepted their humble but fervent petitions, for that he himself then heard the sweet clangour of a bell, as if descending from the heavens, which he believed was the harbinger of good sent by the Almighty to point out the spot on which the church was to be built and enable them to complete with success their long wished-for and eager pursuit. He also ordered them to spread, each of them, his hood, cloak or other garments, that the bell might be preserved from injury when arriving at the surface.

With this mandate of the saint all present pleasantly complied, each eagerly and attentively watching the nearer approach of the bell, and each person hoping that his garment shall be the happy one to receive the bell; but [blank] hours elapsed before it came to the ground and at length alighted on the garment of a dark man, whom St Colum Kille complimented in the following words and terms: "ais bannaye da vrathe a Duilline no mvrathiv goleirr" or "Gillan your garment is blessed above those of the assembled multitude." The derivation of the Gillans is attributed to these words of the saint.

However, Gillan's garment received the bell on that site where the ruins of the aforesaid ancient church at present stands, and on which site the erection of the church was commenced immediately after the bell and garments having been removed, as the saint concluded that the falling of the bell on that spot was the omen or signal by which they were to abide; and from the moment they commenced the building of the church on this site till they had it completed, there was not the slightest obstruction experienced either by day or by night.

The church was roofed with oak timber and shingled with the same timber. The entire roof remained on the church up to about the year 1700 and a portion of it on the walls up to 1776. There was an oval hole near to the top in the west gable. This hole was called the Bell Hole and was perfect up to 1794.

Patron Day

There was a day annually dedicated to St Colum Kille, which was called the patron day of the parish, or St Colum Kille's Day, and on which day thousands of persons repaired to above ancient church from various parts of the kingdom to perform stations. The place was also well supplied with eatables and drink of different kinds. However, some time about the latter part of the 17th century a great combat or quarrel occurred between the assembled multitude, which put a stop to patrons and stations to a great extent but relinquished altogether for some time past.

Enclosure and Building

In Corick mountain, and grazing of Niece Cleary, there stands the ruins of some ancient enclosure approaching to oblong, 103 by 47 feet. This enclosure is formed by stone columns standing on their ends in the ground and varying in height above the surface from 2 to 5 feet. One of the columns is 5 feet high, 5 feet broad and 3 feet thick. The columns stand several feet, one from the other.

Within a short distance of the enclosure stands 2 other columns that seem to have been in some degree connected with it. All the above stands in the immediate neighbourhood of a river and most barren part of the mountain.

In the above townland, and along the verge of a river or near the union of 2 rivers, there stands the ruins of some ancient building 18 and a half by 10 feet in the clear, walls 3 feet thick and from 1 to 3 feet high. Round it also stands a tract of ground enclosed by an old stone wall.

Stone Model

In Doon, and holding of Widow O'Kane, there stands a stone 3 and a half feet long, 2 feet 2 inches broad, with a circular hole cut in it 14 inches in diameter and 9 and a half inches in depth. It stands in the remains of an old wood. 24th October 1836.

Ancient Bell

Patrick Crilly of Derrynoyd got, about 6 feet beneath the surface in the above townland in 1786, an ancient bell 12 inches in height, 6 inches long and 3 inches broad at the bottom. On the top of the bell there was a place for the hand to go into but the tongue was gone. The Revd Francis Quin P.P. of Omagh procured the bell at 7s and has it at present. It weighs 7 lbs. Information obtained from Patrick Crilly.

Ancient Coin

In Brackagh mountain, and beneath an ancient carn, there was found by William O'Neill about 1804 several pieces of ancient silver coin. They varied in size from that of a shilling to that of a 6-shilling piece, and though in a tolerable state of preservation when found, the date of coinage or king's name could not be judged. The coin has been subsequently sold by weight in Belfast.

Discoveries in Bogs

In the bogs of the above and almost all other townlands within the parish there have been found from time to time, in cutting turf, several rows and circles of sharp-pointed sticks, varying in length from 2 to 4 feet and in various instances sunk in the subsoil beneath several feet in height of bog.

In many of the aforesaid bogs have been also found from time to time, at various depths beneath the surface of the bog, parcels of old butter, wooden vessels of rare construction, plough irons and various other iron instruments and implements, besides large and small shoes made of half-tanned leather and seeming to be constructed out of a solid piece, with only one seam in the entire shoe and that one seam behind the heel. The butter was contained in barks of trees, crocks and pots of very old fashion. Many of the aforesaid articles have been subsequently either destroyed or converted to other uses. Informants Patrick Cassidy, James McBride and many others. 31st October 1836.

Ancient Cave

In Duntibryan and holding of Alexander Martin, and near to a Danish fort, there was discovered about 1815, in making a floor in a dwelling house, and about 5 feet beneath the surface of a sandy soil, a cave containing several small apartments about 3 feet in length, breadth and height, each with arch roof and all walls and roof quite dry and level on the surface. The door or entrance to the cave was very limited, as was also those opening to the different rooms. There was no stones employed in the entire construction, though the cave and attached apartments are locally believed to extend from the spot where it was discovered to the above fort, a distance exceeding 700 yards, through a sandy eminence. The entrance into this cave was subsequently closed up but no part of it destroyed.

There was a number of small earthen crocks of rare construction found deposited in these caves, besides a quantity of other implements which have been subsequently destroyed.

Skeleton and Urn in Duntibryan

In the above townland, and within a short distance of the cave, there was subsequently found, under the roots of a thorn bush, a human skeleton in a tolerable state of preservation. It was again buried on the site where found.

In a sandy hill in the above townland there was found at some former period an ancient earthen urn containing a quantity of calcined bones and ashes, but in a decayed state when found. Informants John and Charles Campbell, 11th November 1836.

Stone Column and Discoveries

In Strawmore, and holding of James Kelly, there stands an ancient stone column 6 feet 10 inches high, 5 feet 9 inches broad and 2 feet 9 inches thick. It is made fast in the ground by 2 smaller stones that stand one on either side of it. In its immediate neighbourhood lies 2 other large stones that seem from their situation to have been connected with the above at some former period.

In exploring round the above column at some former period, there was found beneath the surface at the base of the column a small pot, a hammer and other ancient articles, all of odd construction but corroded by time and rust to a great extent, and have subsequently fallen away.

There was also found beneath the surface in the neighbourhood of the above column a quantity of human bones contained in small chambers enclosed by stone buildings. These bones have been again put down on the site where found.

Battleaxes

In Doon there was found, about 3 feet beneath the surface, a brass battleaxe 2 lbs weight and in shape similar to a saddler's cutting knife, and ornamented on the sides. There was also found in

Parish of Ballynascreen

the same place an iron or steel battleaxe of odd construction. These were found in 1828 and subsequently destroyed in a forge. Informants Paul Kelly, James Keilt and others. 30th December 1836.

Crock of Bones and Old Butter

Daniel Henery, in digging a terrace of gravelly soil in Coolnasillagh in 1824, got about 2 feet beneath its surface an ancient earthen crock containing a quantity of calcined bones and ashes. The crock was in a state of decay when found and has subsequently fallen down.

There have been also found beneath the surface of a clay soil in the above townland in 1827 a parcel of old butter contained in the bark of a tree.

There was found in the same place, and at the aforesaid period, some plough irons of odd construction. All these articles have been subsequently converted to other uses. Informants Daniel Henery and others. 20th January 1837.

Burial Ground and Cromlech

On an eminence in Coolnasillagh, and holding of Charles McKenna, there stands the ruins of an ancient burial ground supposed to have been occupied by the Danes or druids, as it is thickly studded with stones sunk on their ends in the ground and seeming to be placed at the head and foot of graves. Several of these stones vary in height above the surface from 1 to 5 feet and others partly absorbed by the soil. The largest of them is 5 feet high, 3 and a half feet broad and 2 feet thick. There are also 2 stones lying on the site, one of which measures 9 and a half feet long, 2 and a half feet broad and 2 feet thick. The other is 6 and a half feet long, 1 and a half feet broad and 1 and a half feet thick. These 2 stones seem to have been standing at some former period.

These ruins approaches to circular shape and measures 15 yards in diameter, with a few decayed thorns growing among the stones.

East, and within about 200 yards, of the above burial ground there stands the ruins of what appears to have been an ancient cromlech. There are 6 of the stone columns standing, and vary in height above the surface from 1 and a half to 4 feet and in breadth from 2 to 4 feet and in thickness from 8 to 13 inches. Others are lying which measure 6 feet in length.

About 40 yards east of these ruins there lies another stone which measures 7 feet long, 3 feet broad and 1 and a half feet thick, and is said to be standing at some former period. Many more were carried away.

Burial Grounds

In Ballynure, and on a rising eminence in the holding of William Doogan, there stands the ruins of an ancient burial ground supposed to have been occupied by the Danes or druids. The site stands 40 by 40 yards. It was at some former period occupied by graves of various sizes, which were enclosed by stone columns sunk on their ends and sides in the ground, and in many instances supporting canopy stones that covered the entire of many of the graves. A few of these columns still remain on the premises and vary from 1 to 2 and a half feet in height above the surface. Several cart-loads of the columns have been carried away from time to time to arch bridges and gullets. In raising many of the graves in the above burial ground, there have been parcels of decayed bones got beneath the surface.

About 3 furlongs from the above burial ground, and in the mountain of Carnamoney, there stands the remains of another ancient burial ground, in size and construction similar to the one above described; but the greater part of the stone columns by which the graves were enclosed have been removed and buried in bridle roads. Informants William Doogan, Pat Hassin and others. 23rd January 1837.

In Ballynure, and holding of William Doogan, there stands on a handsome eminence the remains of an ancient burial ground said to have been a consecrated one. It contains above 1 acre of ground, enclosed on either side by ravines through which small rivers run.

It is likewise locally said that it was on this ground that the ancient church of Ballynascreen was first commenced to be built and that the ground walls of the church was raised about 110 years ago by the grandfather of the above William Doogan, all except one of the corner stones which still remains in its original berth and measures 3 and a half feet in length, 2 feet in breadth and 1 and a half feet in height. The extent of the foundation as described by Doogan was 62 by 18 feet.

Burials in this graveyard prevailed to a great extent up to the beginning of the 18th century.

As late as 1740 there was 18 young men, of the name of McWilliams, belonging to Carnamoney, and who died by a fever, buried in the above ground, all within 1 year. [Insert marginal note: The most destructive fever recollected overran the above and neighbouring parishes about 1740].

However, the site is now totally under tillage and in labouring it from time to time within the last 60 years there was hundreds of headstones and graves raised; and out of many of these graves, skulls and other human bones lifted that, for their extraordinary size, excited great astonishment among the local inhabitants. All these skulls and bones have been sunk to the proper depth on the site where found. From William Doogan, Charles Boon and others. 23rd January 1837.

PRODUCTIVE ECONOMY

Fair of Draperstown Cross

The following were the commodities offered for sale in the fair of Draperstown Cross held on the 7th of October 1836, also the number of horse cattle, cow cattle, sheep and pigs, also the prices brought by various commodities, as enumerated on the above day.

Horses, total 389, prices 4 pounds to 12 pounds; black cattle, total 1,225, prices 3 pounds to 7 pounds; sheep and lambs, total 1,035, prices 5s to 25s; asses, total 3, prices 10s to 20s; pigs, total 217, various prices; stands of sucking pigs, total 7, prices each 4s to 6s; fine linen yarn per spangle, 1s 8d to 1s 10d; coarse linen yarn per spangle, 1s 6d to 1s 8d; fine linen per yard, 1s 4d; coarse linen per yard, 8d; coarse flax per lb., 4d ha'penny, per stone, 5s 8d; fine flax per lb., 10d to 1s; woollen stockings 1s 3d per pair; woollen socks 7d per pair; flannel 1s 2d per yard; sacken 8d per yard; men's shoes 4s to 6s per pair; women's shoes 3s to 4s per pair; woollen hats 2s each; wool per lb., 1s 2d; beef per lb., 3d ha'penny; mutton per lb., 4d ha'penny; cheese per lb., 8d; bacon per lb., 7d; eels per lb., 2d ha'penny; salt herrings per score, 1s; eggs per dozen, 5d; slide cars each 2s 6d; potato baskets each 7d; noggins each 4d; piece crocks each 2s; stable brooms each 2d; apples per bushel, 2s; plums per bushel, 2s.

The following commodities were in abundant supply: new and old ready-made clothes for both sexes, bedclothes, new and old books and ballads, silks, cottons and calicoes, hardware, delf, china and crockery, tinware, black and whitesmith work, turner's work of all kinds, bread, gingerbread. Information obtained from John Donnelly, James Quin and many others. 7th October 1836.

Building Materials

Lime supplied at Draperstown from Desertmartin, distance 4 miles, per barrel 1s 3d. Sand got in the parish and supplied on the building ground in Draperstown, per ton 6d. Building stones supplied from Maghera, on the building ground, Draperstown, distance 5 miles, per ton 1s 6d to 1s 9d. Flags supplied from Maghera and laid in the work in Draperstown, per square foot 8d. Countess slates procured in Ballyronan, distance 9 miles, price per 1,000, 6 pounds 15s. Lady slates, price per 1,000, 3 pounds 7s. Mill ton slates, price per ton 3 pounds 15s. Queen ton slates, price per ton 3 pounds 5s.

Carriage per ton from Ballyronan to Draperstown, distance 9 miles, 6s.

Reclaiming of Mountain

The mountainous parts of that subdivision of the above parish locally called the Six Townlands, the property of Mr Stevenson of Fort William, which remained a barren and unproductive waste for centuries back, is at present undergoing irrigation and speedy cultivation by the instrumentality of the proprietor, who, within the last few years, has subdivided the mountains into farms of different sizes and told [sold?] them out free, or at least at a very trifling annual rent, for a willful period, to such of his tenantry as are able or willing to cultivate them.

A number of these mountain farms are already occupied by many of those of his tenants who formerly held limited parcels of ground on the lowlands, and are now building farmhouses, office houses and making gardens, small plantings, etc. on these new tenements. They are receiving some assistance of building materials from the proprietor.

This new colonization will, in a few years, not only become a substantial property to the proprietor, but also enable the cultivators of it to provide their growing family with local settlements, such as their former limited holdings in the lowlands would not afford. It will also give local employ to many of the able-bodied young men who, in the absence of such sources, would be obliged to seek a living or asylum in America or some other foreign nation. Informants William Phillips, Patrick Cassidy and others. 17th November 1836.

Derivation of Townland Names by John O'Donovan

NATURAL STATE

Place-Names

Drumard, Drimard, *Druim Ard* "high ridge:" Drumard is better.

Parish of Ballynascreen

Drumderrig, Drumderig, Drimderg: it is for consideration what should be the general anglicising of *dearg*, "red." It is at present spelled darg, derg, derig, derrig. *Dearg*, though reckoned a monosyllable in Irish, is in reality a dissyllable, as r and g will not coalesce.

Duntybryan: Bryan is not always the anglicising of *Brian*, a man's name. It is written Brian also.

Dysert, Desert: it is for consideration what should be the general anglicising of *disert* (i.e. Loch Fasaigh) "a wilderness, a hermitage." It is at present orthographied disert, desert, desart, dysart.

Glengomna, Glengawna (Sampson), Glengawny (Down Survey): query.

Gortnaskea: Gort na Sgeach "field of the briars." Query, should not gh be added to this, Gortnaskeagh?

Awenreagh, Owenreagh, Oanreagh, Ballyowenreagh: it is for consideration what should be the general anglicising of *amhain*, Latin amnis "a river." It is at present orthographied owen, oan, oen, one, awen. The Irish word is pronounced oun. I found *na hamhan* "of the river," anglicised nahown, nahoun, on Down Survey map.

Letters on Ancient Topography, 1837

MEMOIR WRITING

Letter from C.W. Ligar to T. Larcom

Dungannon, 5th April 1837, My Dear Sir,
I send you a copy of an old plan of the Danes Cast in the counties of Down and Armagh which I borrowed from Mr Bell, artist of this town, thinking it may be useful for the Memoirs of those counties at a future period. I have not seen the Danes Cast, but should you require any information respecting it I think we might procure it now that we are working in the neighbourhood.

I also forward part of an old Irish manuscript which Mr Bell obtained from one of the ushers of the Dungannon school, who brought it out of the parish of Ballynascreen in the county of Derry and was using it as a cover for a dictionary. Mr Bell lent it to me for the purpose of transcribing a part and would not allow me to forward it to you or let it go out of my hands; but as I do not value it quite so high, and finding the interlineations difficult to copy, I have forwarded it privately for your inspection.

I am very sorry to hear that you have not been well but hope you are now quite recovered. Yours most truly, [signed] Charles W. Ligar.

I am afraid that I shall never obtain the bell in this neighbourhood: the priest says it is quite hopeless.

Letter from G. Petrie to T. Larcom

My Dear Larcom,
I do not think it will be necessary for O'Donovan or Curry to visit any but the wild parts of the county of Dublin: they would get nothing in the civilized regions. O'Donovan wishes to have the Name Books of the parishes which he visits. Can you send him Kilternan to begin with? They could get out and in on the Enniskerry mail car. There are some curious remains in Glencullen about which there may be traditions. Glanesmol is another valley they should visit. It is the scene of a famous hunt by Finn MacCool and Ossian, and Finn's sighan or seat and Ossian's well are still to be seen. I shall give them every assistance in my power.

I send you O'Donovan's account of the manuscript leaf which you sent. It is not necessary to copy the whole but I have set DuNoyer to make a facsimile of the capitals and a portion of the writing. He is doing it very well.

I am glad that Ligar has fallen in with Bell. His account of the Danes Cast would be most valuable and important. We could verify it by one in the college written in 1682.

When I see O'Keefe, I will tell him to write to you about Oxford. He has been employed these last 4 days in the Royal Irish Academy, copying the *Repertorium [Viride?]*, an account of the churches in the diocese of Dublin written by Archbishop Allen about 300 years ago. It is a very valuable document.

There can be little doubt that the manuscript leaf is a portion of the book of Ballynascreen; what a pity it should be destroyed. I wish if it were possible the messengers could come about 1 o'clock, as I have to be at the schools from 11 till 1. Ever my dear Larcom, yours faithfully, George Petrie, 7th April 1837.

Notes on the Amhra Choluim Chille by John O'Donovan, 1837

Amhra Choluim Chille

This vellum sheet contains a fragment of the well-known ancient Irish poem called *Amhra Choluim Chille* or the "elegy of Columbkille," composed by his contemporary Dallan Forguill, the patron saint of Kildallan in the county of Cavan, of Glendallan in the county of Sligo and of Clonallan in the county of Down. The language is very ancient and would be now totally unintelligible were it not that it has been very copiously glossed, in a language, however, which is itself now obscure enough.

Colgan gives the life of this saint in *Acta Sanctorum*, where he speaks of the poem as follows: Dallan, or Eochy Dallan, flourished AD 580 and was better acquainted with the antiquities of his native country than any other writer of his time. He wrote in Irish, in the antiquated language [insert marginal note: i.e. in the now antiquated], some works which in these latter ages cannot be easily understood, even by the best informed in the Irish tongue. Hence it is that the antiquaries of later times have illustrated them with copious glosses and have been accustomed to expound them in the antiquarian schools as precious monuments of the ancient idiom and antiquities of Ireland.

Dallan's principal poem is in honour of St Columba and was written before that saint had departed from the Synod of Drum Ceat in Ulster in 596. It is entitled *Amhra Coluim Cille*. I have a copy of it, well written but intelligible to very few.

There are several copies of this poem with its gloss in the library of the Royal Irish Academy and also in the college, but the most ancient copy hitherto discovered is in *Leabhar na hUidhri* (*Levar na Heeria*), now in the possession of Messrs Hodges and Smyth, College Green.

The writing on this sheet is good and seems to be in the style of the 14th century. [Signed] J. O'Donovan, 7th April 1837.

Parish of Desertlyn, County Londonderry

Statistical Report by Lieutenant Bailey, 1833

NATURAL FEATURES

Hills

The north western corner of the parish includes one of the lower features of Slieve Gallion, and, sloping gradually to the eastward, forms at the foot of the mountain very precipitous and strongly marked ravines called the Quilly, Cairndaisy and Carrydarragh glens. The remainder is composed of small hills principally of basaltic and white limestone formation.

Rivers

There is no river of any importance; a considerable mountain stream called the Carrydarragh water rises in Lissan parish and flows through the southern extremity of Desertlyn parish. It is subject to rapid floods and the water, not getting off quickly enough, often overflows the meadows in Ballindrum and Moneyhaw below Moneymore.

Bogs

There is a large piece of bog in the townland of Dunronan which supplies many of the tenants from other townlands in the Magherafelt estate with fuel, [insert addition: and throughout the parish there are but few townlands which do not contain patches of greater or less extent]. The inhabitants in the neighbourhood of Moneymore purchase bog in Coltrim, parish of Lissan. Those in the most northern part of the parish get bog in Tyrgan, parish of Desertmartin.

Woods

The before-mentioned ravines, Quilly and Cairndaisy, belong to the Drapers' Company, who have planted them very judiciously. They have a very pretty and picturesque appearance.

MODERN TOPOGRAPHY

Towns: Moneymore

Moneymore, the principal town on the Drapers' Company, is situated partly in Desertlyn <Desertlynn> and partly in Artrea parish. The public buildings consist of a church, a market house with a town hall over it, a dispensary and an inn.

The church, which is a very handsome edifice, was completed in 1833, towards the erection of which the Drapers' Company subscribed 300 pounds. The inn is a large building and is kept remarkably clean and comfortable. The town contains about 130 houses and is quite proverbial for its cleanliness.

PRODUCTIVE AND SOCIAL ECONOMY

Markets and Fairs

A corn market is held on every Friday and a fair on the twenty-first day of each month. About 1,500 webs is the quantity of linen sold on each fair day, the estimated value of which is about 2,500 pounds. It is also celebrated as a cattle fair. There are sometimes 700 or 800 horses and an equal number of horned cattle, but very few sheep.

Conveyances

The public conveyances are the mail coach from Dungannon to Coleraine and a day coach from Cookstown to Belfast. These pass through the town and return every day.

Dispensary

There is an excellent dispensary for the relief of the sick poor on the Drapers' estate. The surgeon receives 100 guineas a year with a good house and a garden, also an allowance of forage for a horse.

Schools

The company have also established 2 very good schools, one for boys, the other for girls. They are both well attended. The master receives 50 pounds (Irish) per annum and the mistress 35 pounds (in the same currency), with houses and turf free. Their salaries are paid by the company.

MODERN TOPOGRAPHY

Communications

The principal roads are those leading from Moneymore to Magherafelt and Desertmartin. They are repaired with broken stone and are kept in good order.

Memoir by James Boyle, October 1836, with Sections by C.W. Ligar

Natural Features

Hills

Completed 2nd October 1836, received 22nd October 1836.

The north west corner of this parish includes one of the lower features of the lofty mountain of Slieve Gallion <Slievegallion> which, sloping gradually eastward, forms the western side of a valley which traverses the centre of the parish from north to south. The average elevation of this valley above the sea is 175 feet. The sides of the feature before mentioned are strongly marked by the very beautiful and precipitous ravines called the Quilly, Carndaisy and Carrydarragh glens, formed by the streams flowing down the side of the mountain.

The highest point in this feature is 1,300 feet above the level of the sea. The surface of the western portion of the parish consists of a variety of hills of basaltic or limestone formation, the highest of which does not exceed an elevation of 465 feet above the level of the sea. A chain of these extend along the eastern side of the parish and, sloping irregularly towards the west, form the eastern side of the valley before mentioned.

The principal points in this parish are Carndaisy, 758 feet, Drumcormick, 611 feet above the sea (on the east side of the parish), Gortagilly, 465 feet, Forsyth's hill, 417 feet, and Long's hill, 347 feet above the sea, on the western side of the parish.

Lakes and Rivers

There are no lakes in this parish.

There is no river in this parish. A considerable stream called the Carrydarragh takes its rise in the adjoining parish of Lissan, at an elevation of 1,500 feet above the sea. It soon after enters on the western boundary of the parish, along which it pursues a south easterly course for some distance. It continues the same course by the town of Moneymore and, descending to a level of 130 feet above the level of the sea, enters the parish of Artrea and finally discharges itself into the Ballinderry river. It flows for 1 and two-third miles through this parish [insert marginal note by C.W. Ligar: and separates it from the parish of Artrea for five-sixths of a mile], in which its extreme breadth is 61 feet and ordinary depth 3 and a half feet.

Its bed is mostly sandy or consists of fine gravel, except in the mountains where it is rocky. In the mountains, particularly in the glen to which it gives its name, its banks are very high and steep, but in the low grounds they are very low and the country through which it flows in many parts nearly level.

Owing to the height of its source and the number of its tributary streams, it is very subject to rapid floods which, from its trifling fall in the low grounds, soon inundate the adjacent country and require some time to subside. These floods are very injurious as they sour the grass, destroy the crops and throw up some sand on the inundated lands.

Its average fall is 1 foot in about 9 and a half feet and it [is] usefully situated for machinery, drainage and irrigation.

There are numerous minor streams which, flowing down the side of the mountain, find their way into that just described. These and the springs with which the parish abounds afford an ample supply of water for domestic purposes.

There are not any hot or mineral springs in the parish.

Bogs

There are numerous small patches but no extensive tracts of bog in this parish. Many, indeed the greater number, of these seem to have originated in the subsiding or partial drainage of lakes of which their sites seem to have been the beds. Their subsoil is usually a reddish and stony clay and their depth varies from 4 to 18 feet.

The principal tract is in the townland of Dunronan (at the east of the parish) and it extends into the adjoining parish of Artrea. Its elevation near the centre is 348 feet above the sea. From the centre it falls gently towards its sides; the deepest part of this bog (as yet known) 12 feet. Oak blocks or stumps, with a few trunks, are found standing on the subsoil. The trunks lie indiscriminately and are not very large. All bear marks of fire. Fir blocks are found in abundance, occupying the same level and broken off at the same height. Very few trunks are found, and those which are bear marks of combustion.

A narrow paved road formerly extended across this bog. It was made of stones (some of which were larger than a man could lift) with a few logs of oak placed transversely. It was 5 feet from the surface and 3 feet from the bottom of the bog, but little of this road now remains.

This bog differs little in any respect, except extent, from the other bogs in this parish.

Parish of Desertlyn

Climate

The climate of the lower part of this parish is very mild and early, and the air pure. Oats is sown in March and April, and reaped in August and September. Wheat is reaped about the end of August. Potatoes are planted in April and the beginning of May, and raised by the 12th November. In the mountainous districts the crops, though sown as early, are 3 weeks later in coming to maturity.

MODERN TOPOGRAPHY

Towns: Moneymore

The neat little market and post town of Moneymore is partly situated at the southern extremity of this parish and partly in the adjoining parish of Artrea. It is seated [situated] on the mail coach road from Dungannon to Coleraine and also on the main road from Cookstown to Belfast. It is 31 and three-quarter miles west of Belfast, 114 miles north of Dublin, 4 miles north of Cookstown and 5 miles south of Magherafelt. It is in the county of Londonderry, barony of Loughinsholin, primacy of Armagh and north west circuit of assize. Its extreme length is five-twelfths of a mile, breadth one-sixth of a mile and circumference 1 mile.

Its situation, though low, is exceedingly pretty. A lofty bank or hill, beautifully planted and wooded, extends near the eastern side of the town which is situated at its base. The adjacent country is richly cultivated and partially planted, and the general appearance of the town itself, which is proverbial for its neatness, cleanliness and uniformity, is exceedingly pleasing and cannot fail to arrest the attention of the traveller.

History of Moneymore

Moneymore is said to be one of the oldest towns in the province. Pynnar, in his survey in the year 1630, states that the castle which stood at the end of the present street (High Street where the schools now stand) "was very complete, that there were 6 good stone and lime houses on either side of the High Street, and that the castle and these 12 houses were all supplied with fresh water from the spring out of the limestone rock near the present quarry above the town." In sinking the foundations for the present schools, some old foundation walls of immense thickness were found, and the earth in about them was very deep and rich and some human bones were found in it.

The source from which the town and castle was originally supplied with water was Lough Lug, a small lake 1 mile east of Moneymore and on the summit of a hill rising to an elevation of 200 feet above; and this fact is further corroborated by the circumstance of several pieces of pipe having been discovered in the ground between the lake and the site of the castle.

It is probably to the erection of this castle that Moneymore owes its origin and it is said that about the time of the siege of Derry by James II this castle was one of considerable importance. As is elsewhere stated, this estate was granted to the Drapers' Company of London by James I, but they did not look after their property until after the restoration of Charles II. They did not, however, come into actual possession of it until the year 1817, previous to which time Sir William Rowley's family had had a lease of it for 61 years.

On the company's getting possession of it in 1817, Moneymore was a dirty, irregular, straggling village, the streets leading to it consisting of wretched mud cabins and the few 2-storey houses constituting the main street (now High Street), with a few exceptions, thatched. The streets were crooked and dirty, and the fairs at Moneymore were invariably scenes of the most violent party riots. Its large horse fair, the largest monthly one, except Moy, in the province of Ulster, and one of the oldest, has been the great support of Moneymore; and probably to it (previous to its coming into the possession of the Drapers) it owes its existence.

Public Buildings: Church

The public buildings in Moneymore, which have all been built either wholly or partly by the Drapers' Company since 1817, consist of the church erected in 1831 by the Drapers' Company and at an expense of 6,000 pounds. It is situated on a rising ground at the east side of the town and a little retired from the street. It is altogether of the chastest style of Saxon architecture and built exactly after the model of Tewkesbury Cathedral in England. It is entirely built of highly polished white sandstone. Its form is an oblong square 93 feet by 52 feet (not including the tower), at the southern end of which stands a very handsome square tower 40 feet high and castellated at the top.

The interior consists of an aisle and naves, the former separated from the latter by 2 rows of 5 lofty arches supported by massive stone pillars. Over the arches on each side is a row of windows, above which is the roof of the aisle. The naves are much lower than the aisle, their roofs reaching only to the bottom of the windows above its arches. They are each lit by a row of windows.

At the northern end of the church is the chancel table, on either side of which is the vestry and robing room. Over the chancel table is a lofty window with a lesser one on each side. Underneath these, and on the wainscoting behind the chancel table, the Lord's Prayer, Ten Commandments and Creed are printed in large gilded Saxon letters.

At the southern end of the church, in the tower and over the doorway, is the choir consisting of a small gallery set apart for the singers. Above the choir is a large circular plate of richly stained glass upon which the royal arms are beautifully painted, and underneath the arms of [blank]. The seats in the aisle and those also in the naves, except a few, are merely forms with backs.

The entrance to the church is through a very beautiful and richly cut doorway in the tower. The ascent to the summit of the tower, from which there is a very beautiful and extensive prospect, is by a winding stone staircase.

[Insert addition by Ligar: Over the entrance, on the inside of the wall and on a small light marble slab, is the following inscription: "This church was erected by the Drapers' Company of London, and at their sole expense, for the use of the parishioners of the adjoining parishes as are tenants of the Drapers' Company, consecrated 29th August 1832]."

The architecture of this church, both internally and externally, is in the most perfect keeping, and finished in the handsomest and most substantial manner; and it is justly allowed to be the handsomest country church in the kingdom. The space in which it stands is enclosed in front by a handsome cast-iron railing extending along the street for 112 yards.

Meeting Houses

The Presbyterian meeting house, which is situated in Stonard Street on the south west side of the town, is a substantial, stone-finished square building, 76 and a half feet long and 50 feet wide. A spacious gallery extends along 3 sides of the building and it is otherwise neatly and comfortably fitted up. It contains accommodation for about 1,000 persons. This house stands in a pretty enclosure tastefully planted with evergreens, and the side fronting the street secured by a neat cast-iron railing. It was erected by the Drapers' Company in 1823 and cost 4,000 pounds.

The Seceders' meeting house is prettily situated in Hammond Street, on the east side of the town. It is a very neat but plain building, stone finished, 61 feet long and 40 feet wide, neatly fitted up internally and containing accommodation for 300 persons. It was erected in 1831 at an expense of 800 pounds, of which 250 pounds was contributed by the Drapers' Company and the remainder by subscription.

Market House

The market house stands near the centre of the town and at the west side of High Street. It is a neat brick building, stone finished and 2-storey. On the front is elevated a handsome cupola under which is an excellent town clock. The under storey contains the public crane and is used as a grain market. The upper storey consists of one large room used as a town hall for holding petty sessions and manor courts in, and in which on market days the linen merchants pay for their webs. It was erected by the Drapers' Company in 1819. It cost 1,000 pounds.

[Insert addition by Ligar: The company are erecting a very handsome and capacious grain store and another market house, which is expected to cost from 5,000 to 6,000 pounds].

Schools

The schools stand at the southern extremity of the same street. They were built by the Drapers' Company in 1820 and consist of 2 schoolhouses, one for boys and one for girls, each calculated to contain 120 scholars. They are spacious, lofty and well ventilated. These schools are connected by a house containing separate apartments for the master and mistress, and present to the street a handsome front of [blank] feet enclosed by an iron railing.

Hotel

The hotel stands next to the market house and the corner of High Street and Stonard Street. It is a pretty stone-finished building and contains a good deal of accommodation. Its interior arrangement is very comfortable and the charges are moderate. It was built by the Drapers' Company in 1819.

Gentlemen's Seats

The official residences are those of: Rowley Miller Esquire, J.P. (chief agent for the Drapers' Company), who resides in the Mansion House situated in High Street. It is a handsome and spacious mansion, 3-storey, with a lesser wing at each end. It is built of cut sandstone and has a portico supported by massive stone columns. It was rebuilt by the company in 1835.

Parish of Desertlyn

Next to the Mansion House is the official residence of John Rowley Miller Esquire, J.P. As joint manager of the Provincial Bank, he is also joint agent with his father for the Drapers' Company. It is a plain, old 2-storey house.

The official residence of the dispensary surgeon, Zachariah Maxwell Esquire, is situated in High Street and next to the market house. It is a neat, 2-storey stone-finished residence with 2 rooms used as a dispensary at one end. It was built by the company in 1819.

The private residences are those of the Revd Matthew Enraght, the Protestant curate, and the Revd John Barnet, Presbyterian clergyman. These are exceedingly nice and modern stone houses, built by the company and situated in Hammond Street. There are 2 similar houses in the same street which are at present unset.

Streets and Houses

Moneymore consists of 6 streets, containing 101 1-storey and 50 2-storey houses. From High Street, which is the principal one and at the centre of the town, extend Lawford Street in a northerly direction, consisting mostly of houses occupied by petty dealers and tradespeople, [and] Smith Street extending north east. The houses in this street have almost all been built by the company and, except a few, are all 1-storey, slated and roughcast, and very neat and uniform; they are occupied by tradesmen and a few shopkeepers.

From High Street extends Stonard Street westward, and consists of a few neat 2-storey houses built by the company and occupied by shopkeepers.

From Stonard Street, Bridge Street extends southward along the road to Stewartstown. It is a very neat little street. The houses were built by the company and are roughcast and uniform in size and appearance. They are occupied either by labourers or tradesmen.

Conyngham Street extends south east from the southern extremity of High Street along the road to Coagh. This street is irregular and straggling, and the houses old and of an indifferent description. They are almost all 1-storey and thatched and, except a few, occupied by the poorer class of labourers or tradesmen.

Hammond Street extends from the middle of Smith Street across Conyngham Street to Bridge Street. Its eastern end consists of very nice 1-storey cottages built of sandstone, in the neatest and most substantial and uniform manner. They are chiefly occupied by tradesmen or labourers.

The streets in Moneymore are of a sufficient width and, with the houses, present an appearance of cleanliness, uniformity and regularity rarely met with. The houses which have been built are of a description combining comfort, neatness and durability, possessing every convenience and in every respect suited to the persons by whom they are occupied. The old houses which are now standing will, whenever their leases expire, be thrown down and new and neater ones be built by the company. Every inducement is held out by them to respectable families to come and settle there, and they will expend any sum that may be desired in building a house, for which they will charge only 5% on the sum expended as rent.

SOCIAL ECONOMY

Local Government

A manor court for the manor of Drapers is held in Moneymore monthly, for the recovery by civil bill of sums not exceeding 5 pounds late Irish currency; Rowley Miller Esquire, seneschal. The average number of trials each sitting is 8, about one-half of which are decreed. The seneschal does not encourage the people to resort to his court, as he considers it would encourage the spirit of litigation.

Petty sessions are held on every alternate Wednesday in Moneymore. There are usually at least 3 magistrates in attendance.

4 constabulary are stationed in Moneymore.

General Character of the Inhabitants

The inhabitants of Moneymore consist of a few shopkeepers and spirit dealers, tradesmen and labourers, and amount to about 700. From the constant employment given to labourers and mechanics, and the habits of regularity and good conduct enforced by the company through their excellent and active agent, the inhabitants of this town are among the most orderly, peaceable and well regulated in the kingdom. Industry and good conduct are encouraged, while the reverse is discountenanced and no immoral or improper person allowed to remain in the town.

Library

There is a small library, consisting of a few useful and religious works, kept by the rector of the parish for the use of the poorer class.

PRODUCTIVE ECONOMY

Bank

A branch of the Provincial Bank of Ireland was

established here in 1835; Rowley and John Rowley Miller Esquires, managers. [Crossed out: The office of the bank is in the agent's house in High Street]. This bank is thriving and its effects on the country will be found equally beneficial here as with other places.

Fairs and Markets

The great monthly fair in Moneymore (said to be one of the oldest established in the province) is held on the 21st of every month. It is a general mart, but horses and cattle of all kinds, linen and yarn constitute the principal sales. [Insert footnote: NB owing to the tolls and customs having been abolished, the quantities of the articles can only be given by estimation]. From 300 to 500 horses, varying in prices from 6 pounds to 40 pounds, 600 to 700 cows and black cattle, a number of pigs and a few sheep are exposed for sale; see appendix for a more detailed account.

About 3,000 pounds worth of linen and 250 pounds worth of yarn are sold in each fair. Some flax, the quantity of which, though small, has increased greatly of late, is also sold, besides which the quantities of beef, mutton, pork, pedlar's goods, hardware, shoes, fruit and vegetables is very considerable and exceeds that of the neighbouring fairs.

As a cattle and horse fair, Moneymore is one of considerable importance and is resorted to by buyers and sellers from this and the neighbouring counties. Some horses and a considerable quantity of cows and pigs are bought up by dealers for exportation to England. The greater number of the horses are those suited for farmers.

A second linen market, to be held on the first Monday in each month, was established in the latter end of 1835. For so far it has continued to prosper, though it as yet is but small and fluctuating. Some yarn and flax and the other commodities offered for sale in the monthly fair (with the exception of cattle) are brought to this market.

A corn market was established about 20 years ago. It is held on Wednesdays and about 40 tons of oats are sold in each market. All these markets are thriving, and as an encouragement to dealers and others to bring their commodities to this market, the Drapers in 1835 abolished all tolls or customs; and though they were set at a considerable yearly rent, they not only gave them up but allowed their tenant 100 pounds per annum compensation.

The commodities offered for sale at the markets and fairs in Moneymore are brought by the farmers in their own carts or cars. The supply of these articles is pretty much the same throughout the year, except during the seasons of seed time and harvest when there is a little decrease.

The supply of butcher's meat, poultry, milk, fruit and eggs is adequate to the consumption of the inhabitants. Except in the fairs, no vegetables are sold. During the summer trout and pullen from Lough Neagh are sometimes brought here.

Table of Grain

Grain and meal sold in Moneymore market. Year ending 1st September 1835: 3,373 sacks of oats, 130 sacks of wheat, 9 sacks of barley, 6 sacks of rye, 62 sacks of meal.

Year ending 1st September 1836: 4,632 sacks of oats, 169 sacks of wheat, 50 sacks of barley, 8 sacks of rye, 116 sacks of meal.

Grazing

There is a little stall feeding and grazing for beef. Grass for cows lets at from 1 pound 10s to 2 pounds 10s per Irish acre.

Building Materials

Timber and slates are procured at Ballyronan, which is 5 and a half miles distant. Their cost there is usually about 10d ha'penny per ton over Belfast prices. Bricks are brought from the kilns along the Bann or in the neighbourhood of Bellaghy, where the usual cost is 10s per 1,000. Stone is abundant, and lime, which may be procured within half a mile of the town, stands when laid down about 8d per barrel.

Insurance and Employment

There are few fire or life insurances.

Labourers, owing to the benevolence of the Drapers' Company, are always in employment at some of their works.

SOCIAL ECONOMY

Conveyances

A mail coach, leaving Dungannon daily at half past 7 a.m. and arriving in Coleraine at 3 p.m., passes through Moneymore at quarter past 10 a.m. The same coach, leaving Coleraine every day at 10 a.m. and arriving in Dungannon at half past 4 p.m., passes through Moneymore at 45 minutes past 2 p.m. The fares by this coach are: inside to Dungannon 4s and inside to Coleraine 8s; outside to Dungannon 2s 6d and outside to Coleraine 5s 6d.

Parish of Desertlyn

A coach, leaving Cookstown every morning (except Sundays) at 5 a.m. and arriving in Belfast at 11 a.m., passes through Moneymore at half past 5 a.m. The same coach, leaving Belfast at 3 p.m. and arriving in Cookstown at 9 p.m., passes through Moneymore at half past 8 p.m. The fares by this coach are: inside to Belfast 7s 6d, inside to Cookstown 9d; outside to Belfast 4s 6d, outside to Cookstown 6d.

[Crossed out: A 2-horse outside car (carrying 8 passengers), with the mail from Dublin, leaves Dungannon daily at 20 minutes before 8 a.m., passes through Moneymore at 10 and arrives in Coleraine at 3 p.m.

A second and similar car, leaving Coleraine daily at 10 p.m., passes thro' Moneymore at 20 minutes past 2 p.m., carries on the Dublin mail from that town, and arrives in Dungannon at 20 minutes before 5 p.m. The fares by this car are: to Coleraine 5s 6d and to Dungannon 2s 6d. Insert marginal note: Taken off the road].

There are 2 regular carriers to Belfast; they require 4 days to make the trip. The usual charge per cwt is from 1s 8d to 2s per cwt, the charge being less for a large quantity than for small packages. During the season for pork and butter there are many more carmen employed.

Dispensary

The Drapers' Company established a dispensary here in 1818 and support it unassisted. In 1833 a sum was granted in addition by the county grand jury, and a similar one raised by subscription. Its effects upon the health and comfort of the poor have been very perceptible. For details, see Table of Benevolence in the appendix.

Schools

2 schools were built here by the Drapers' Company in 1820 and have since been wholly supported by them. The children are educated gratis and clad during their being at school in smock frocks. 10 boys annually from the male school are, upon passing an examination, apprenticed to some tradesmen not residing on the estate, and 10 pounds apprentice fee given with them. [Insert footnote: The object for apprenticing the boys to a tradesman not residing on the estate is to prevent them becoming small farmers and petty tradesmen on it, and to enable the company to enlarge the farms]. There are usually 110 scholars in the male and 120 in the female school.

The parish school is supported by the Honourable and Revd John Pratt Hewitt, who pays the master an annual salary of 15 pounds.

There is a female school supported by the Revd Mr Hewitt, who pays the mistress a salary of 10 pounds per annum.

There is a female school, towards the support of which the Drapers' Company contribute 10 pounds annually, and a male school to which the company contributes 10 pounds annually.

There are besides, 3 Sunday schools supported by the public. For detailed accounts of these schools, see Table of Schools.

Almshouses

There are 2 cottages in Bridge Street belonging to the Drapers' Company which [are] appropriate[d] to the use of 6 aged and infirm persons, 3 in each. The company also grants 10 pounds annually towards their support.

Remarks on Inhabitants

The inhabitants are very orderly, peaceable and industrious, and not prone to or fond of amusement.

2 chaises, 3 post cars, a gig, a hearse and 6 post horses are kept for hire. The charge per mile Irish for chaises is 1s, cars 8d and for the hearse, according to agreement.

The people are civil and obliging, but there are few of the class from which hospitality can be expected.

Progress of Improvement

Moneymore has improved, both as regards its appearance and its inhabitants, more perhaps than any town of its size in the kingdom. In appearance it in reality bears little resemblance to what it was 19 years ago, when it fell into the hands of the company. Its trade also is increasing, and tradesmen and labourers are in constant employment, all owing to the liberality of the Drapers' Company, who intend erecting a large corn store, market place and making several other useful improvements.

Moneymore is, however, near zenith as to trade. It is within 4 miles of the very large and old established weekly market of Cookstown, and within 5 and a quarter miles of Magherafelt, where there are large weekly grain, pork and general markets, besides a large monthly market and monthly fair; and as these towns, which are more than double its size, are equally thriving and increasing in trade, it is not likely to become of more importance than at present.

Modern Topography

Public Buildings in the Parish

Beside those public buildings described under the head of Towns, there is another.

[C.W. Ligar] The Baptist meeting house in the townland of Carndaisy is situated in the glen of that name. It is a low thatched house 22 and a half feet long and 11 and a half feet broad on the inside; erected about the year 1820 for a schoolhouse and soon after its erection was used for divine service by about 20 persons, who had become converts to the Revd Alexander Carson of the parish of Kilcronaghan and who found the distance too great to attend him every Sunday. They have never had a minister, but expound the Scripture to each other. They now amount to 40 persons. A small collection is made on Sundays to defray the expense of bread and wine used in the sacrament which is taken by each every Sunday. The interior of the house is fitted up with loose forms capable of accommodating more than the 40 actual members of the congregation.

Gentlemen's Seats

[J. Boyle] The only gentlemen's residences in the parish are Desertlyn, the residence of Captain Smyth, and Magherascullion, the residence of Dr Patchell, both of which are in the townland of Magherascullion and within 1 mile of Moneymore. They are neat and modern residences, 1-storey, and in the cottage style.

Mills

The machinery of this parish consists of 1 corn mill in the townland of Ballymully; is propelled by a breast water wheel 16 feet in diameter and 2 feet 6 inches broad.

Communications

The main roads in this parish are kept in repair at the expense of the barony of Loughinsholin. Some of the by-roads in its mountainous districts have been made by the Drapers' Company and are kept in repair by them. They are in excellent order, as are also the main roads.

The main roads are: that from Magherafelt to Moneymore, of which there are 3 miles in this parish; the average breadth of this road is 24 feet. It is principally repaired with white limestone. It is kept in excellent order and its direction is good, but it is very hilly and might be rendered less so.

The road from Maghera to Moneymore traverses the centre of the parish from north to south for 2 miles. It is nearly level, in excellent order, and its direction could not be improved. Its average breadth is 22 feet.

There are several pipes which answer all the purposes for which they may be required, but there is nothing in the parish entitled to the name of a bridge.

[Insert addition by Ligar: A bridge is much required on the road from Moneymore to Tulnagee, at the Cross burn. This stream at present rushes across the road and the only means of crossing it is by stepping stones].

General Appearance

This is one parish in which art has lent its hand unsparingly to add to the natural beauty of the country. The diversity of the ground in the eastern and western districts of the parish, the beautiful and richly cultivated valley traversing its centre and the glens and hills on either side, so tastefully planted and situated at the base of a lofty and noble mountain, present a landscape of more than ordinary beauty.

Ancient Topography

Ecclesiastical: Old Church

[C.W. Ligar] Desertlyn old church is situated in the townland of Ballymully, at 1 and one-sixth miles on the north west side of Moneymore. A part of the east gable and south wall is all that remains of it, together with the foundations of the other wall, and which show the building to have been 64 feet long, 24 feet broad and the walls 3 and a quarter feet thick. The graveyard is well enclosed by a strong and still good wall, and there are a great many graves; but few in proportion have been marked by stones. One of the earliest bears the date 1712. A handsome carved stone bearing some family arms is to the Revd Mr Henry Croocks, who died May 24th 1740. Another in its immediate vicinity records the death of his 7 sons and 4 daughters.

The following are all the names which occur on the stones, few of which are of the aborigines of this country, although all classes until lately have buried here; but this may be perhaps occasioned by those persons being unable to erect such frail monuments to their names: McElwain, McGowen, McEldery, McCreight, McGredy, McEleanon, McCorry, McGeown, McGarry, Magil, Broxton, Wilson, Smyth, Reynolds, Adams, Sloan, "Roben Rutherson," Johnstone, Kidd, Downing, "Unity Wright," Martin, Devilin, O'Farrell, O'Grugen, "Pady Henery."

Parish of Desertlyn

There is a Roman Catholic family, the Branans, who still continue to bury here, although most other families of that religion have taken [to the] burying ground in the new chapel yard at Moneymore. In this churchyard there is a fine ash tree which is claimed by the Branans as having grown from a handspoke, used for carrying a coffin, which, after being thrown into the grave as is the custom, sprung up and became a fine tree. It is stated that there was another but which was cut down some time ago.

There is not a church in this county to which some tradition is not recorded of its having been built upon a forewarned site, or that it never could be completed owing to nocturnal interruptions. This church comes under the latter denomination and it is firmly believed by the oldest never to have been roofed or used for divine service. No one recollects that it ever had a roof.

Military Remains

There are no remains of this class of buildings.

Pagan: Giant's Grave

The most remarkable monument of antiquity in the parish is a large heap of stones of an oval form,

Elevated stone in Ballymully

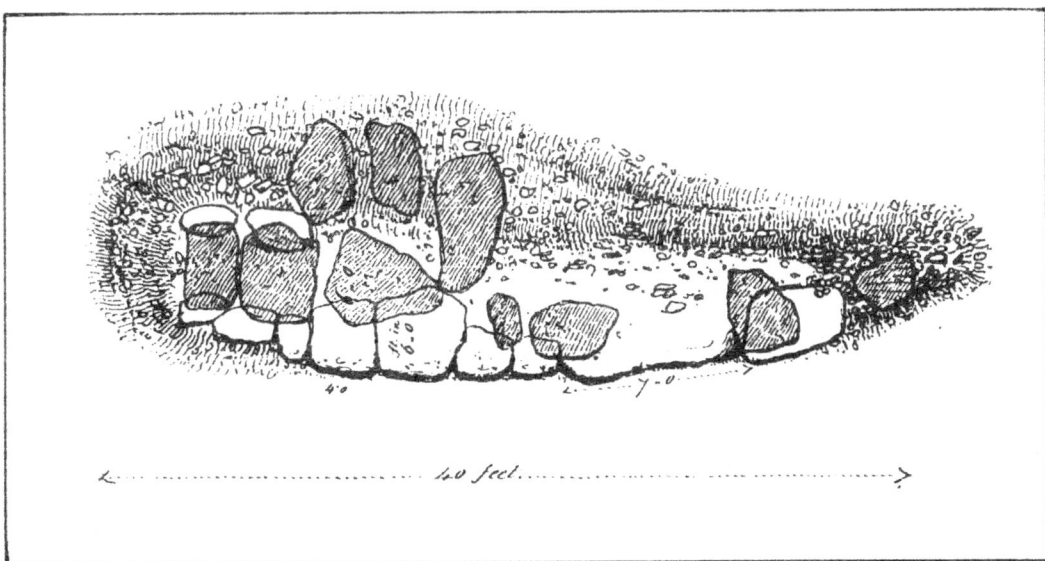

Giant's grave in Ballymully

measuring 40 feet long and 14 feet broad. There appear to have been 3 rows of large stones extending from one end to the other and covered by large flat stones, thus forming 2 distinct and well-formed passages which were of sufficient size to allow a man to crawl through them. These have been much injured and the whole is covered by small stones and thorns. It is not known whether these smaller stones have been thrown on the larger ones by the cultivators of the soil for the purpose of being out of the way, or whether they are coeval with the building.

The whole spot is at present considered very gentle, and not a single twig would be cut from the luxuriant thorns and brambles on any account. It is stated that during a winter, when firing was scarce, the son of a schoolmaster came in the dead hour of night and cut away several branches, and was never known to prosper afterwards.

Some of the largest stones are 6 and 7 feet in length and 6 feet broad. It is locally called the Giant's Grave and is situated in the townland of Ballymully.

At a distance of 40 yards south of the above there is a large stone 4 feet 9 inches long, 3 and a half feet broad and 5 feet deep, supported upon 4 small ones averaging 2 feet high above the ground. Underneath the large stone an urn containing bones and ashes was found. It has been subsequently destroyed.

An urn containing bones and ashes was also found in Tulnagee.

Forts

The largest and best preserved fort is in the townland of Tulnagee. It is of an oval shape, 141 by 113 feet in the interior, with 2 earthen parapets, the highest point of the outer one being 16 feet above the bottom of the ditch. The inside parapet is 5 feet lower than the one beyond it. This uncommon and injudicious arrangement is most perceptible on the north side. Many attempts have been made to dig for treasures in this fort, but the parties have all been frightened away. The last party were driven away, supposing they saw the trees on fire and by the smell of sulphur.

The parapets and interior are covered by a thriving plantation which very much improves that part of the parish and is an effectual protection against the destruction of the fort. Within 20 yards on the north side there is a smaller one, 133 feet in diameter, with only a single parapet. It has been converted into a good garden.

Carrydarragh Fort is of a circular form, 40 yards in diameter and has 2 parapets.

There are 2 forts in Tamnadoey; one is 100 feet in diameter and the other 70 feet. An adze and other iron implements like chisels were found in one of these, on Daniel Wood's farm.

There is a circular-shaped fort in Carndaisy with a single parapet, and is now under cultivation.

In the following townlands there were formerly forts, but have been thrown down for the purpose of cultivation: Tulnagee (this made 3 in the townland), 2 in Quilly, 1 in Dunronan; the one in Ballymuckleheany has been nearly levelled. It was 180 feet in diameter.

Discoveries in Bogs

A brass axe was found in the townland of Tulnagee about 20 years ago, but has since been lost. Another was found in the townland of Larrycormick in a bog in 1826, but has also been lost.

A brass spearhead was found in the townland of Gortagilly about 20 years ago, but is also lost. Another was found in the townland of Ballymuckleheany and since lost.

4 stone hatchets were found in the townland of Moymucklemurry, of different shapes and sizes. One of them is 9 inches long and 3 broad, and is the largest that has been seen in the county. Some of the smaller kind of these have been used as "rubbing bones" by the weavers. They are found to polish the cloth too much and a bone is preferred. From this at first sight it would appear they had been originally intended for this purpose, but the weavers themselves do not think so; and the large size of the one mentioned above would seem to remove the opinion altogether.

4 flint arrowheads were found in this parish. They are used for curing cows of "elfshots," as in other parts of the county. See drawings in the appendix which show their different shapes.

About 60 brass rings, similar to those found in Magherafelt, were found 3 feet under the surface of a bog in the townland of Dunronan, together with a fine set of amber beads forming a rosary. One of the rings, 3 inches in diameter, has 2 smaller ones attached to it; see drawing in the appendix.

SOCIAL ECONOMY

Early Improvements

[J. Boyle] The earliest cause of improvement in this parish is considered to have taken place on its colonisation by the Protestants. The manor of Drapers, in which this parish is included, was granted to that company by James I, but it was not until the restoration of King Charles II that the company looked after their property in this country. The Drapers came into actual possession of the estate in 1817, previous to which time it had been in the possession of Sir William Rowley's family for 61 years.

The colonisation of this parish by Protestants led to improvements in it similar to that of the neighbouring ones. The Roman Catholics were ashamed to keep their children from school, as they did not like to see them inferior to those of their Protestant brethren, and their education may be regarded as one of the most important steps towards civilisation. The causes of improvement subsequent to and consequent upon this were the active exertions of the Protestant clergy and the general introduction of schools supported by charitable institutions, and Sunday schools. The latter have been particularly beneficial.

Progress of Improvement

On the estate falling into the hands of the Drapers' Company in 1817, improvements of every description, both in the estate and its inhabitants, commenced on a very extensive scale. Roads were cut through districts hitherto almost shut out. Schools were built and supported wholly by the company. A dispensary was established and almost wholly supported by them. Advantage was taken of every spot where planting could be advantageously disposed and trees put down. Salutary regulations for promoting order, regularity and good conduct among the tenantry were adopted and enforced, and among these that of rendering any tenant subject to expulsion from the estate for any breach of the revenue laws has not been the least important.

The custom of keeping undertenants, which [is] a sure method of introducing poverty to the country, has been limited to farmers holding a certain extent of farm. The result of these changes has been that the estate is now among the most prosperous, well regulated and improved, both as regards the general aspect of the country, the state of agriculture and the habits, morals and circumstances of its tenantry.

The company have in their estate, both in this and the neighbouring parishes, made and kept in repair upwards of 50 miles of roads and planted 800 acres; they have opened lime and 3 stone quarries in the mountainous districts; they have established a farming society and they keep in constant employment 100 labourers; and altogether they expend nearly their entire income from the estate, amounting to about 10,000 pounds per annum, in their different public works and improvements. The improvements in Moneymore have been noticed elsewhere.

The exertions of the Protestants and Presbyterian clergy of the present day among their flocks has tended much to the improvement in the morals of the people. The linen trade, which is now (1836) in a prosperous state, affords good wages to the manufacturing class and they are now pretty comfortable in their circumstances.

The establishment of grain and other markets for the sale of farm produce, and the affording a facility for its conveyance to market by the opening of new roads, have materially tended to the advantage of the farmer.

Almost all the inhabitants of this parish are of English or Scottish extraction or descent and there are few, if any, of the original inhabitants of the country residing in it.

Obstructions to Improvement

None: on the contrary, there is every encouragement. Some say that the law recently enacted to permit publicans to sell spirituous liquors from the hours of 7 in the morning until 11 at night on weekdays, and from 2 until 11 on Sundays, is quite sufficient to demoralise a whole nation, but especially the Irish.

Local Government

The only magistrate residing in the parish is Rowley Miller of Moneymore, Esquire, who, from his situation as chief agent to the Drapers' Company and his firmness and decision, possesses the respect, esteem and confidence of the people.

There are no police stationed in this parish but there are 5 constabulary in that part of Moneymore situated in the adjoining parish of Artrea. The manor court and petty sessions are also held in Artrea parish.

No outrages have, for a long time, been committed in this parish. Since the Drapers' took possession of the estate in 1817, smuggling and illicit distillation have been put a stop to.

There are a few fire and life insurances. No losses by fire have been recently sustained.

Dispensary

There are no diseases which can be called prevalent in this parish, and the people are now rather more healthy than those in the adjoining parishes. This may be owing to the early establishment of the dispensary, which took place in 1818. No detailed list of diseases, however, is published. For further description of this institution, see Table of Benevolence.

Schools

Schools have done an immensity of good in this parish. There are few parishes in which they have been more generally introduced or where there are the same opportunities afforded of gratuitous instruction. A taste for information and education has thereby been excited among the people, who now avail themselves of the advantages of education. Sunday schools have been particularly beneficial to the rising generation and their effects are very perceptible in the manner in which the sabbath is observed. The Drapers' and other schools in Moneymore, though situated in the parish of Artrea, are those which are principally resorted to by the poorer class in this parish; see Table of Schools.

An infant school is about to be established in the town. The schoolmistress is engaged and the number of pupils are expected to amount to about 70.

Poor

There are no strolling beggars and very few actual paupers residing in this parish. The collections in the different places of worship on Sundays is the only regular provision for them, and this, with the voluntary charity of the people, is quite adequate to their support.

Religion

By the revised census of 1834 there are in this parish 1,100 Episcopalians, 800 Presbyterians of the Synod of Ulster, 300 Seceders and 900 Roman Catholics. The rector of the parish has 500 pounds per annum tithes and pays his curate 75 pounds per annum.

The Presbyterians worship at the meeting house in that part of Moneymore situated in Artrea parish. The officiating minister of this house receives only the stipend, 75 pounds per annum, during the life of the senior clergyman, who is superannuated and receives the regium donum, 100 pounds per annum. The former minister receives 20 pounds annually from the Drapers' Company.

The Seceders of this parish worship at the Seceding meeting houses in the adjoining parishes of Artrea and Desertmartin, to the ministers of which they pay their stipend. These ministers have also each 50 pounds per annum regium donum and 10 pounds per annum from the Drapers' Company.

The Roman Catholics of this parish mostly worship at the chapel near Moneymore and in the parish of Artrea. They support their clergy in the usual manner and the parish priest receives 10 pounds per annum from the Drapers' Company.

Habits of the People: Houses

The cottages on this estate are, with a few exceptions, neat, cleanly and comfortable, built of stone and lime, a few slated but the majority thatched. They consist of from 2 to 3 apartments and are well lit. Their furniture is in general sufficiently good and plentiful. Their cleanliness is perhaps in a great degree attributable to the abundance of lime and the regulations of the Drapers' Company enforcing the use of it in whitewashing.

The farmers' houses are in general comfortable, though many of them are old and display anything but taste in their appearances. They are, however, improving rapidly in their style, and some of those lately built are neat looking and substantial. These houses generally consist of from 3 to 4 apartments, one of which, though seldom used, is called the parlour and well furnished with a clock and glass press. The kitchen is the general resort of the family. The other rooms are used as sleeping apartments.

These houses, though chiefly 1-storey, have a sort of loft which seldom extends over more than the parlour and kitchen. It is used for the servants to sleep in and as a sort of lumber or store-room. The parlour is sometimes floored, the kitchen paved but the rest of the rooms earthen floors.

Food

Bacon, salt beef, eggs, meal, milk and potatoes are the principal food of the farmers. They sometimes use tea, and baker's bread is now more used than formerly, meal less so. They and their servants generally dine together.

The food of the manufacturing class differs little from the farmers except that less animal food is used. Their houses are smaller but in general comfortable.

Cottiers

The habitations of the cottiers or labourers, and also the condition of that class, has been much improved of late years. Formerly many of their cabins were built of mud, but now there are few such. They never consist of more than 2 apart-

Parish of Desertlyn

ments and frequently of only 1. They are now much more cleanly and comfortable than formerly. The cottiers are now, owing to the works carrying on by the company, in better and more constant employment than formerly, and their comforts thereby increased; but potatoes, milk, salt herrings and a little meal constitute their principal food.

Character

The people of this parish are in general an intelligent, moral and industrious race, very honest and peaceable. They are in general sober, but the men are in general more so than the women.

General Economy

The majority of the male population are engaged in the manufacture of linen and the females spin linen yarn, but spinning is now more resorted to as an alternative to idleness rather than from anything that can be earned by it. Most of the manufacturing class possess a cow and from 1 to 3 acres of land.

Turf, which is abundant, is their only fuel.

Dress

The quantities of second-hand and ready-made clothes now sold in the fairs and in shops, together with the low prices of calicoes, afford both sexes opportunities of dressing well at a trifling expense. They not only dress well but very neatly, and their appearance at fairs is very interesting and respectable. An umbrella seems to be an indispensable appendage to the equipment of both sexes, and a watch is an object of ambition to the men.

Marriage and Amusements

They do not marry particularly early; they are in general long lived.

They have not now any regular amusements: going to fairs, dancing, assembling at Easter have been almost totally given up, partly from the increased habits of industry and partly from the exertions of the clergy.

There are no traditions nor is there anything peculiar in their appearance.

Emigration

Emigration has decreased within the last 2 years, [due] chiefly to the improvement in trade and the want of encouragement from those gone out. The entire population of the parish are now in almost regular employment. 17 persons emigrated in 1834 and 30 in 1835 to America.

On average 8 persons migrate annually to the English and Scottish harvests and a few remain behind. The rest return in time for the Irish harvests. They sow and plant for their winter support. See list of the numbers and ages of those who emigrated in 1834 and 1835.

Remarkable Events

None upon record.

Appendix to Memoir by James Boyle

Emigration

[C.W. Ligar] The following is a list of the number of persons who have emigrated to America in the years 1834 and 1835.

1834: 12 males, 5 females, total 17; 1 male under 5 years old, 1 male and 1 female 5 and under 10, 1 male 10 and under 15, 1 male 15 and under 20, 5 males and 1 female 20 and under 25, 1 female 25 and under 30, 3 males and 2 females 30 and under 40, total 17.

1835: 19 males, 11 females, total 30; 1 male and 1 female under 5 years old, 1 male 5 and under 10, 2 females 10 and under 15, 2 males and 2 females 15 and under 20, 8 males and 3 females 20 and under 25, 2 males and 1 female 25 and under 30, 3 males and 1 female 30 and under 40, 2 males and 1 female above 50, total 30.

To New York: 1 in 1834, 3 in 1835.
To Philadelphia: 5 in 1834, 12 in 1835.
To Quebec: 11 in 1834, 15 in 1835.
Total 17 in 1834, 30 in 1835.
Protestants: 11 in 1834, 13 in 1835; Presbyterians: 3 in 1834, 10 in 1835; Roman Catholics: 3 in 1834, 7 in 1835; total: 17 in 1834, 30 in 1835.

Migration

The following persons have migrated from the parish to England and Scotland for harvest work.

From the townland of Ballymully: 1 to England, 1 to Scotland.

From the townland of Larrycormick: 2 to England, 1 to Scotland.

From the townland of Feenanmore: 2 to Scotland.

From the townland of Quilly: 1 to Scotland.
Totals: 3 to England 3, 5 to Scotland.
The ages of these men varies from 18 to 35.

ANCIENT TOPOGRAPHY

Drawings

Desertlyn old church, ground plan with orientation and dimensions, 64 by 24 feet internally, scale 1 inch to 20 feet. 5th September 1836.

Giant's Grave in Ballymully, length 40 feet, ground plan, scale 1 inch to 8 feet. [Insert note: The shaded stones are those supported on the others. 11th October 1836].

South view and ground plan, with dimensions, of an elevated stone under which was found a small urn of ashes and bones; the large stone is 4 feet 9 inches by 3 feet 6 inches by 5 feet; the small ones average 2 feet by 1 foot 6 inches and 1 foot above the ground. 8th September 1836.

Front and side view of stone hatchet found in the townland of Moymucklemurry, full size. 12th October 1836.

2 stone hatchets found in Moymucklemurry, full size.

Stone hatchet found in Moymucklemurry, full size. 13th October 1836.

4 flint arrowheads found in the parish of Desertlyn, full size. 12th October 1836.

Brass rings, full size, found in the townland of Dunronan, 3 feet under the surface of a bog. [Insert note: About 60 other rings of different sizes, but not linked together like those represented above, were found in the same place, together with a set of amber beads forming a rosary]. [Signed] C.W. Ligar, 30th August 1836.

PRODUCTIVE ECONOMY

Moneymore Fair

The following are the numbers of horses, cows etc. exposed for sale on the 2 fair days, 21st July and 22nd August 1836.

Horses: on 21st July 343, on 22nd August 523, varying in price from 3 pounds to 40 pounds.

Cows: on 21st July 675, on 22nd August 697, varying in price from 3 pounds to 11 pounds.

Sheep: on 21st July 283, on 22nd August 374, varying in price from 10s to 3 pounds.

Pigs: on 21st July 117, on 22nd of August 371, varying in price from 10s to 40s.

Goats: on 21st July 17, on 22nd August 11, varying in price from 5s to 10s.

Asses: on 21st July 13, on 22nd August 17, varying in price from 15s to 30s.

Litters of sucking pigs: on 21st July 47, 3s to 10s each.

The following were the average prices of articles: beef per lb., 4d ha'penny; mutton per lb., 5d ha'penny; butter per lb., 8d; cheese per lb., 6d; bacon per lb., 6d ha'penny; linen yarn per spangle, 1s 10d; wool per lb., 1s 2d; flax per stone (14 lbs), 6s 9d; coarse linen per yard, 7d; sacking 7d.

Moneymore: Table of Trades and Occupations

[J. Boyle] Apothecaries 2, bakers 2, builder and joiner 1, butchers 2, blacksmiths 3, agents to bank 2, carpenters 5, clergymen 2, carmen 2, constabulary 4, dressmakers 2, woollen drapers 2, delf and glass shops 2, flax dressers 2, glaziers 1, grocers 13, hotel keepers 1, whitesmiths 1, lodging and entertainment houses 6, publicans' houses 8, hosiers 1, hardware shops 1, haberdashers and milliners 2, leather cutters 1, masons 5, magistrates 2, nailers 1, painters 2, reedmakers 2, shoemakers 5, schoolmasters and mistresses 6, surgeons 2, saddlers 1, sawyers 2, thatchers 1, turners and wheelwrights 2, tailors 2, total 101.

SOCIAL ECONOMY

Moneymore: Drapers' Company's Dispensary

List of the prevailing diseases in this parish.

In 1832: rheumatism, diseases of the eye, affections of the bowels and stomach, catarrhal affections, measles, scrofula, fever, burns, diseases of the skin.

In 1833: worms, fevers, accidents, affections of the stomach and liver, dropsy, ruptures, rheumatism, English cholera morbus, paralysis, sore throats, diseases of kidney, diseases of joints.

In 1834: phthisis pulmonalis, cancers, lunacy, dysentery, affections of the eye, ulcers, influenza, fever, hysteria, scrofula, paralysis, rheumatism, whooping <hooping> cough.

In 1835: smallpox <smallpock>, dropsy, diseases of the ear, fever, retention of urine, wounds, epilepsy, scald head, inflammation of the chest, abscess, measles, jaundice, rheumatism.

Note: The numbers of the different diseases could not be ascertained.

Benevolence: Establishments for the Indigent

[Table contains the following headings: name, object, management, number relieved, funds from public and private sources, annual expense of management, relief afforded, when founded].

2 cottages given by the Drapers' Company; object: to relieve 6 old women; 3 old women live in each of the 2 cottages; number relieved 6; funds: 10 pounds per annum from the Drapers' Company, [crossed out: Mrs Miller] a lady in the town privately supports them and reads to them

Parish of Desertlyn

on Sunday; clothing: the lady makes up what is worn; money 10 pounds; when founded: 1806. The company allows 20 pounds besides, to be distributed by their agent.

Establishments for Mental and Bodily Diseases

Drapers' dispensary; management: a secretary and governors of the neighbouring clergy who vote at the election of the surgeon; number relieved: during the 4 months ending June 1832, 640; for the year ending June 1833, 1,651; for the year ending June 1834, 1,782; for the year ending June 1835, 1,918, total 5,991; annual expense of management: the Drapers' Company give the surgeon a free house, turf and a cow's grass; salaries: the Drapers' Company allow the surgeon 100 pounds salary and 25 for a house; when founded: 1819.

[C.W. Ligar] Moneymore county dispensary: management: by Rowley Miller Esquire, who holds the office of treasurer, secretary; numbers relieved: 1834, 200; 1835, 571; funds from public bodies: 1834, 14 pounds 14s from the county; 1835, 25 pounds from the county; from private individuals: subscriptions amounted to an equal sum with the county grant; annual expense of management: house rent none; salaries: surgeon in 1834 received 14 pounds 14s and 25 pounds in 1835; annual expense of patients: in 1834 14 pounds 14s, in 1835 25 pounds; when founded: 1834.

Moneymore: Schools

[Table contains the following headings: name, situation and description, when established, income and expenditure, physical, intellectual and moral education, number of pupils subdivided by age, sex and religion, name and religion of master and mistress. Insert marginal note by Boyle: These [first 2] schools are situated in that part of the town which is in the parish of Artrea].

Drapers' male school, in a large and well-ventilated schoolroom, well fitted up for the purpose, built at the sole expense of the Drapers' Company in High Street, Moneymore, established in 1820; expenditure in salaries: the master has a free house and turf from the company, besides a salary of 40 pounds; intellectual education: the boys are dressed in smock frocks and learn spelling, reading, writing and arithmetic, books of the Kildare Place Society; moral education: visits from the clergy, Authorised Version of the Scriptures daily, Scripture extracts; number of pupils: 90 under 10 years of age, 20 from 10 to 15, total 110, 48 Protestants, 11 Presbyterians, 51 Roman Catholics; master James McCaul, Protestant.

Drapers' female school, in a similar room to that just mentioned and similarly built and situated, established in 1820; expenditure in salaries: the mistress has the same as above and a salary of 35 pounds; intellectual education: sewing, spelling and reading, books of the Kildare Place Society; moral education: visits from the clergy, Authorised Version of Scriptures daily, Scripture extracts; number of pupils: 94 under 10 years of age, 26 from 10 to 15, total 120, 53 Protestants, 10 Presbyterians, 57 Roman Catholics; mistress Margaret McKeever, Protestant.

Parish school, in a house kept for the purpose in the town of Moneymore; income: from the Honourable and Revd John Hewitt, rector of Desertlyn, annually 15 pounds; intellectual education: spelling, reading, writing, arithmetic, grammar, books of various authors; moral education: visits from the Protestant clergy, Scriptures (Authorised Version) daily; number of pupils: 10 from 10 to 15 years of age, 20 above 15, total 30, all male, 13 Protestants, 3 Presbyterians, 14 Roman Catholics; master John Wade, Protestant.

In a good house the property of the teacher, in the town of Moneymore; income: from the Drapers' Company annually 10 pounds, from pupils 15 pounds; intellectual education: spelling, reading, writing, arithmetic, grammar, also book-keeping, mensuration, books of no particular author; moral education: visits from the Protestant clergy, Scriptures (Authorised Version daily); number of pupils: males, 3 under 10 years of age, 10 from 10 to 15, 7 above 15, total 20; females, 2 under 10 years of age, 3 from 10 to 15, 1 above 15, total 6; total number of pupils 26, 22 Presbyterians, 4 Roman Catholics; master [blank] Kelly, Protestant.

Female school, in a suitable schoolroom the property of the teacher, in the town of Moneymore, established 1835; income: from the Drapers' Company annually 10 pounds, from pupils 10 pounds; intellectual education: spelling, reading, writing, grammar, French, needlework, geography, arithmetic, various authors; moral education: Authorised Version of the Scriptures and catechisms daily; mistress Miss Maguire, Moravian Protestant.

Female school, in a suitable room kept for the purpose in the town of Moneymore; income: from the Honourable Revd Mr Hewitt, rector of Desertlyn, annually 10 pounds; intellectual education: spelling, reading and writing; moral education: visits from the Protestant clergy, Authorised Version of Scripture and catechisms daily; number of pupils: 13 under 10 years of age, 27 from 10 to 15, total 40, 19 Protestants, 4 Presbyterians, 17 Roman Catholics; mistress Mrs Wilson, Protestant.

Church Sunday school, held in the church of Moneymore, established 1831; books from the Sunday School Society; intellectual education: reading, spelling, books of the Sunday School Society; moral education: Authorised Version of Scriptures and church catechisms; number of pupils: males 171, females 162, total 233, all Protestants; gratuitous teachers.

Presbyterian Sunday school, held in the Presbyterian meeting house, Moneymore; books from the Sunday School Society; intellectual education: reading, spelling, books of the Sunday School Society; moral education: Authorised Version of Scripture; number of pupils: males 57, females 43, total 100, all Presbyterians; gratuitous teachers. Memoir completed 12th October 1836.

Schools in the Parish

Carrydarragh London Hibernian school, townland of Carrydarragh, on the by-road from Lissan to Magherafelt; built by subscription, a good room, the forms and desks supplied by the rector; dimensions of room 30 feet by 12 feet, established 1830; income: London Hibernian Society 4 pounds, Revd John Hewitt, rector, 4 pounds, from pupils 3 pounds; physical education none; intellectual education: books published by the London Hibernian Society only, 1 pupil learning arithmetic; moral education: no catechisms, the master examines the children in the Scriptures, no visits from the clergy; number of pupils: males, 17 under 10 years of age, total 17; females, 25 under 10 years of age, 5 from 10 to 15, total 30; total number of pupils 47, 39 Protestants, 8 Presbyterians; master George McLeery, Seceder.

Larrycormick Kildare Street school, townland of Larrycormick, near the leading road from Moneymore to Desertmartin; house is slated and was built by subscriptions and a grant from the Kildare Street Society; room 23 and a half feet by 16 and a half feet and apartments for the master and mistress; there is also a female schoolroom but it has never been used; established 1826; income: Kildare Street Society have not given any money since the alteration in the laws; Miss Jane Maxwell, proprietress of the townland, 6 pounds, and also gave half an acre of land, Honourable and Revd John P. Hewitt, rector, 3 pounds, from pupils 4 pounds; intellectual education: *Dublin Reading and spelling books*, and the Authorised Version of Scriptures; moral education: no catechisms, master examines the children in the Scriptures, visited by the Protestant clergy; number of pupils: males, 22 under 10 years of age, 3 from 10 to 15, total 25; females, 20 under 10 years of age, 2 from 10 to 15, total 22; total number of pupils 47, 27 Protestants, 18 Presbyterians, 2 Roman Catholics; master Andrew Wright, Protestant.

In townland of Quilly, on the leading road from Moneymore to Desertmartin, house repaired by subscriptions, no desks, 28 feet by 16 feet, established 1836, the income not yet known; intellectual education: children procure their own books and bibles; moral education: different kinds of catechisms taught, visited by the Presbyterian clergyman; number of pupils: males, 15 under 10 years of age, 10 from 10 to 15, total 25; females, 24 under 10 years of age, 1 from 10 to 15, total 25; total number of pupils 50, 16 Protestants, 20 Presbyterians, 14 Roman Catholics; master Paul Bradley, Roman Catholic.

Gortagilly school, on the leading road from Moneymore to Magherafelt, house built by local subscription, is slated and well furnished, room 24 feet by 16 feet, established 1832; income: Kildare Street Society gave a grant until the alteration of the law, Sir Robert Bateson Bart, M.P. 5 pounds, the Honourable and Revd John P. Hewitt, rector, 4 pounds, from pupils 20 pounds; intellectual education: books published by the Kildare Street Society, Scriptures; moral education: no catechisms, Authorised Version of the Scriptures, visited by the rector and curate; number of pupils: males, 30 under 10 years of age, 20 from 10 to 15, total 50; females, 20 under 10 years of age, total 20; total number of pupils 70, 7 Protestants, 53 Presbyterians, 10 Roman Catholics; master Adam Beattie, Baptist.

Magherascullion national school, in the townland of Magherascullion, in a room of a dwelling house 14 feet by 14 feet, the interior fitted up by the master assisted by a gift of 3 pounds from the National Board; came under the National Board in 1832, was a private school previously; income: from National Board 8 pounds per annum, from pupils 8 pounds; expenditure: house rent 2 pounds; intellectual education: books published by the National Board; moral education: the Authorised Version of Scripture is read for 1 hour only each day, as appointed by the board, visited by the parish priest; number of pupils: males, 29 under 10 years of age, 10 from 10 to 15, total 39; females, 25 under 10 years of

Parish of Desertlyn

age, 5 from 10 to 15, total 30; total number of pupils 69, 21 Protestants, 4 Presbyterians, 25 Roman Catholics, 19 other denominations; master Thomas McMurray, Protestant.

Sunday Schools

[Table contains the following headings: name, situation, when established, superintendent, number of teachers, number of pupils subdivided by religion and sex, hours of attendance, societies with which connected, observations].

Carrydarragh Sunday school, held in the day schoolhouse, established 1830; superintendent Thomas Kennedy, a Baptist; 6 male teachers, total 6; number of scholars: 28 Protestants, 40 Presbyterians, 2 Roman Catholics, total 70, 30 exclusively Sunday school scholars; hours of attendance: morning class; the London Hibernian Society supply books and the Sunday School Society give bibles.

Carrydarragh Sunday school evening class, held in the day schoolhouse, established 1830; superintendent Thomas Kennedy, a Baptist; number of scholars: 40 Protestants, 60 Presbyterians, total 100, 50 exclusively Sunday school scholars; hours of attendance: evening class.

Gortagilly Sunday school, held in the day schoolhouse, established 1832; superintendent William Macklin, a Presbyterian; teachers: 3 males, 1 female, total 4; number of scholars: 20 Protestants, 38 Presbyterians, 22 Roman Catholics, 12 other denominations, 46 males, 46 females, total 92, 24 exclusively Sunday school scholars; hours of attendance: from 8 to 10 a.m.; the Sunday School Society give books free, but the bibles are sold to the pupils for 1s each; commences with prayer.

Moneymore Sunday school, parish of Desertlyn, held in the Methodist preaching house in Church Street and in the church after divine service, established 1812; superintendent Thomas Harman, who receives 10 guineas per annum from the Drapers' Company for superintending the school; teachers: 6 males, 7 females, total 13; number of scholars: 250 Protestants, 50 Presbyterians, 107 males, 193 females, total 300, 100 exclusively Sunday school scholars; hours of attendance: from 9 till 12 o'clock a.m. in the Methodist preaching house and after divine service in the church; the Sunday School Society for Ireland give books at a reduced price, viz. bibles at 1s each and testaments at 6d each. The money which is paid for the above books is generally collected by the superintendent through the town. This school concludes with prayers only by the superintendent. The Sunday school which is held in the church after divine service is composed of the same children who attend the above Sunday school.

Moneymore Presbyterian Sunday school, in that part of the town in the parish of Artrea, held in the Presbyterian meeting house, Stonard Street, Moneymore, established 1831; superintendent Revd John Barnett, Presbyterian minister; teachers: 3 males, 1 female, total 4; number of scholars: 35 males, 55 females, total 90, all Presbyterians, 75 exclusively Sunday school scholars; hours of attendance: from half past 10 a.m. till 12 o'clock; the Sunday School Society for Ireland give books at a reduced price; commences with singing and prayer.

Quilly Sunday school, parish of Desertlyn, held in the day schoolhouse, established 1835; superintendent Paul Bradley, a Roman Catholic; teachers: 5 males, 1 female, total 6; number of scholars: 20 Protestants, 60 Presbyterians, 50 Roman Catholics, 54 other denominations, 100 males, 84 females, total 184, 20 exclusively Sunday school scholars; hours of attendance: from 8 o'clock till half past 10 a.m.; societies with which connected: none at present; concludes with prayer only.

Parish of Desertmartin, County Londonderry

Memoir by James Boyle, 1836, with additions by J. Stokes and C.W. Ligar

NATURAL FEATURES

Hills

The south western district of this parish includes a portion of the noble and lofty mountain of Slieve Gallion, the summit of which, rising to an elevation of 1,730 feet above the level of the sea, is near its south western boundary. From this it extends north easterly along the west side of the parish, declining at first abruptly and rapidly, but soon after more gently until it finally loses itself in the low, almost level, country near the village of Desertmartin.

The ascent westward from the eastern side of this mountain is rapid and broken by numerous little steps, and these again are intersected by several strongly marked but beautiful little glens or ravines worn by the streams which flow down it.

The most remarkable of these glens are Reuben's, Gortanewry and Quilly glens, which have been beautifully and tastefully planted by the Drapers' Company.

The ground, which is low (not exceeding an average elevation of 270 feet above the sea), falls gradually from the western to the north eastern side of the parish, from which it rises rapidly eastward in the adjoining parish of Magherafelt.

The principal points are Slieve Gallion Carn, 1,625, Brackamore hill, 418, Windy Castle, 1,216 and Tirgan rock, 590 feet above the level of the sea.

Rivers

There is no river in this parish. There are, however, several streams, the principal of which is the Grange or Desertmartin river which is formed by the innumerable small streams which, rising near the summit of Slieve Gallion mountain in this parish, unite in one stream near the base of this mountain. From this it pursues a north east course through the parish, enters that of Maghera, and soon after discharges itself into the River Moyola at an elevation of 140 feet above the sea, and after an entire course of 5 miles. Its average fall is 1 foot in 18 feet, its average breadth 16 feet and depth 18 inches. Its bed is sandy and gravelly, chiefly the latter, and its banks very low.

This stream does serious injury by its inundations which, owing to the height and number of its sources, are frequent and rapid; and owing to its banks being so low, the level country through which it flows is frequently inundated to a great extent. The crops along it are therefore rendered uncertain, the grass soured by constant immersion and quantities of gravel washed over the cultivated land. It is applicable to machinery but is not usefully situated for irrigation.

Another great and chief cause of the mischief done by this stream is a mill-dam which has been formed on it at Curran near the confines of this parish. By this the water is driven back, while were it removed it would have an increased fall of 13 feet; but there is some legal obstruction to the removal of this dam.

The floods in this stream subside naturally but slowly. In the cultivated grounds through which it flows it is confined by embankments.

There is another smaller stream which has its principal source in the parish of Magherafelt at an elevation of about 200 feet above the sea. From this it flows westerly for a short distance and enters the eastern side of this parish, at which point it is 154 feet above the sea. It pursues a north westerly course for 1 and a half miles and discharges itself into the Grange water at an elevation of 140 feet above the sea. Its average fall is 1 foot in 566 feet, its average breadth 11 feet and depth 2 feet. Its bed is soft and sandy, its banks very low and it frequently overflows them, laying the level country through which it flows under water to a considerable extent, rendering the crops uncertain and souring the aftergrass on the meadows. It is slow in subsiding but artificial means are not necessary to drain the flooded country.

It might be applied to machinery but is not usefully situated for irrigation or drainage. Its deposits are trifling and innocent.

Lakes

The small lake called Lough Shillin, from which the barony is said to take its name, is the only one in this parish. It is situated in the townland of Annagh and Stranagard, and at an elevation of 179 feet above the level of the sea. Its form is nearly oval and its extreme dimensions 220 yards long and 176 yards broad. It is 15 feet deep in the deepest part.

Parish of Desertmartin

This parish is amply supplied with spring and river water for domestic uses. There are not any hot or mineral springs.

Bogs

There are several tracts of bog in this parish. None of them, however, are of any extent, except that in the townland of Grange which is very extensive and extends far into the adjoining parishes of Maghera, Kilcronaghan and Termoneeny. Its average elevation above the sea in this parish is 155 feet and above the Grange river, towards which it falls gently, 30 feet. Its depth varies from 5 to 25 feet, its bottom, which is a bed of whitish gravel, being very uneven and traversed by numerous little gravelly ridges which, however, do not rise above the surface of the bog.

Oak trees, some broken and some with the roots attached to the trunks, are found in considerable numbers at the bottom and near the edges of this bog. Several layers of roots, one resting on another, are found in many of the deeper parts of it. The trunks, which are not so numerous, are generally found near them. They do not preserve any particular direction and many of both are scorched or partly burnt; those in the same layer are broken at the same height.

The principal timber is fir and some of it of an enormous size and excellent quality. A good deal of alder is found in this bog. The oak, though large, is not of a good description, nor in a sound state.

There is nothing worthy of notice or description in the other tracts of bog in this parish.

Woods

There is every indication of this parish having been at one time well wooded, both from the quantity of timber found in the bogs and the numerous patches of brushwood to be found scattered over its surface, but which is now rapidly disappearing. The tradition is that within a century the parish had been covered with wood but, except the brushwood, none of it now remains. Hazel is the most prevalent; there is also a little oak and holly.

Climate

In the lower parts of this parish the climate is very mild but rather moist from its very low situation, but the general climate of the parish is healthy and the air pure. Sowing in the low grounds commences in the first week in May and in the more mountainous parts early in April. In the low grounds harvest sets in regularly by the end of August, while in the mountains it does not commence until the beginning of October. Potato setting takes place pretty much about the same time, about the end of April, throughout the parish. In the low grounds they are usually raised by the end of October but are not all raised in the mountains by the end of November.

MODERN TOPOGRAPHY

Towns

There is no town in this parish. Near its centre, and on the road leading from Moneymore to Maghera, is situated the village of Desertmartin, which is dirty, irregular and straggling. It consists of 2 irregular streets, one branching from the other, and containing 56 1-storey and 5 2-storey houses. The former are of an inferior description in point of comfort or cleanliness, many of them being built of mud and almost all thatched. Their inhabitants also are of the poorer class and are mostly engaged as agricultural labourers. The 2-storey houses are of a better description, built of stone and slated.

The situation of Desertmartin is rather cheerful, being seated on the acclivity of a hill, the base of which is watered by a stream called the Desertmartin or Grange river.

The tradition of the inhabitants is that Desertmartin was formerly the assizes town of the county. Some old foundations on the south side of the village are shown as those of the gaol and court house, and the adjacent hill of Knocknagin (the hill of heads), which stands near the eastern side of the town, on the summit of which a platform seems to have been artificially formed, is said to have been the place of execution.

There are not now remaining any other indications of its former greatness. The old church, which stood at the north east side of the village, was thrown down in 1821, up to which time it had been in use. This building was roofed with shingles but bore no marks of antiquity.

There is neither fair nor market now held in Desertmartin. The inhabitants attend those in the neighbouring towns of Magherafelt and Maghera, the former of which is 2 and a half miles and the latter 6 miles distant. There is a patent for holding 5 annual fairs, but no one in or about Desertmartin remembers to have seen more than 2, which were held on 7th November and 27th December; but none have been held since 1821.

Desertmartin seems to be at a stand as to improvements, no houses being or having recently been built.

Public Buildings

There is no public building in the village except a schoolhouse which was built in 1835 at its northern side, at the sole expense of the Honourable and Reverend Arthur William Pomeroy, rector of the parish. It is a plain 2-storey house containing 2 schoolrooms, that on the first floor for the boys and that on the second for the girls. It cost the sum of 200 pounds.

The only gentleman's residence in the village is that of the Revd William Dysart, the Protestant curate.

Public Buildings in the Parish

The public buildings in the parish consist of a church, a Seceders' meeting house, 2 Roman Catholic chapels and 2 schoolhouses.

The church, which is prettily situated on the road from Desertmartin to Maghera, half a mile north of the former village and in the townland of Dromore: it is a pretty and substantial little building, the extreme dimensions of which are 60 feet by 30 feet. It contains accommodations for 280 persons. At its western end is a neat square tower and at its northern side a vestry room. This church was erected in the year 1821 at an expense of 950 pounds, principally defrayed by the Board of First Fruits. It is too small for the congregation.

Meeting House

The Seceders' meeting house stands on the road to Moneymore, about 1 and a half miles from the village of Desertmartin. It was erected by subscription in the year 1795 and is a plain old building 61 feet long and 28 feet wide, with a small aisle attached to its western side. It contains accommodation for 400 persons. It cost when first built 400 pounds, and when repaired in 1825 the Drapers' Company gave 100 pounds.

Catholic Chapels

The Roman Catholic chapel, situated in the townland of Annagh, on the road to Dungiven and a third of a mile north of the village of Desertmartin, is a very old building 70 feet long and 20 feet wide, fitted up with a gallery and containing accommodation for about 700 persons. It is plain and clumsy in its structure.

The second Roman Catholic chapel is situated in the townland of Cullion, near the north west boundary of the parish. It was rebuilt by subscription in 1835. Its dimensions are 58 feet long and 19 feet wide; it accommodates 450 persons.

Schools

The schoolhouse in the townland of Inniscarron was built by the Worshipful the Drapers' Company in the year 1819. It is a plain but suitable building 56 feet long and 34 feet wide, and contains 2 excellent schoolrooms, one for the male and one for the female scholars.

The second school is in the townland of Cranny. It was built by the same company in 1819 and is of similar dimensions with the former schoolhouse.

Gentlemen's Seats

Dromore Glebe, the residence of the Honourable and Reverend Arthur William Pomeroy, rector of this parish, is situated in the townland of Dromore, about half a mile north of the village of Desertmartin. The house is elegant and modern in its construction, and is built of white freestone. It was erected by Mr Pomeroy at an expense of 2,050 pounds in the year 1832. There is a some fine old timber about the house, and the garden and offices are suitable and commodious.

Communications

The main roads in this parish are level, well laid out and kept in repair by the barony. Those in the Drapers' estate are particularly good and many of the by-roads in that district have been made and kept in repair at the expense of the Drapers' Company. The by-roads in their estate are sufficiently numerous and have been of infinite service in opening communications with districts formerly almost shut out. In the eastern district by-roads are much wanting, as in the townlands of Grange and Ballinderry, which are contiguous and contain upwards of 1,000 acres, there is not a yard of public road. Bridges also are much wanting over the Grange river.

The main roads are: the road from Moneymore to Maghera through Desertmartin, which is well laid out, level and in excellent order. There are 4 and a quarter miles of it in this parish and its average breadth is 25 feet.

The road from Magherafelt to Maghera through Tobermore, which traverses the northern part of the parish for 2 and a half miles, is level and kept in good order, its average breadth is 24 feet; and the road from Magherafelt to Desertmartin which is rather hilly but kept in good order; there are 1 and a half miles of this road in this parish and its average breadth is 22 feet.

These roads are easily kept in order as the country through which they pass is mostly sandy

Parish of Desertmartin

or gravelly; they therefore dry rapidly and are smooth. Except the road from Magherafelt to Tobermore, which is made of broken stones, they are repaired with river gravel which is abundant and convenient.

There are several small bridges, or more properly pipes, in this parish. They are in general old but are in sufficient repair.

Mills

The machinery of this parish consists of 3 corn and 2 flax mills. The corn mill in Annagh townland is propelled by a breast water wheel 12 feet diameter and 2 feet broad; the corn mill in Stranagard by a breast water wheel 12 feet in diameter and 1 foot 4 inches broad; the corn mill in Killyboggin by an undershot water wheel 12 feet in diameter and 2 feet broad; the flax mill in Stranagard by a breast water wheel 11 feet in diameter and 1 foot 3 inches broad; and the flax mill in Annagh by a breast water wheel 11 feet in diameter and 1 foot 4 inches broad.

General Appearance and Scenery

Slieve Gallion, which rears its lofty head near the southern boundary of this parish, forms a truly noble and conspicuous feature in the landscape. Its steep side, intersected by several beautifully wooded glens and richly cultivated towards its base, forms a striking contrast to the northern and eastern districts of the parish, which are tame, flat and deficient in planting or anything natural or artificial to interest the eye.

ANCIENT TOPOGRAPHY

Ecclesiastical: Old Church

[J. Stokes] The foundations of the old church of Desertmartin form a rectangle 58 by 24 feet 2 inches, including the thickness of the walls. The only part of the walls that remain is a piece of the north wall, into which a monument to the Boyd family had been inserted. The mortar does not seem old. The stones are unequal in size but well fitted. The graves have accumulated to a level 6 feet higher than the level of the floor. The graveyard is small and crowded, and in a very disadvantageous situation, being close to a stream that floods part of it in the winter, namely the Desertmartin or Grange river.

It is situated at the north eastern side of the village and its bad position was the cause of the church being thrown down in 1821, up to which time it had been in use. This building was roofed with shingles and lighted with lancet-shaped windows which had been latterly made square. There does not appear to be any gravestones older than 1700.

The following families are buried in this yard: Coskchran, McTrainor, McDevitt, Treanor, Trenor, Traner, McConmie, Higgins, McCork, Miller, Leban, Proctor, Bryan, Stokes, Hughes, McCrackin, Mardock. The 12th, 13th and 14th names belong to the rectors of the parish. The name Traner is very abundant in the neighbouring parish of Kilcronaghan. It was introduced by the early English settlers.

It is remarkable that though there are recent burials, there are very few gravestones of recent date, which seems to indicate that those families who lately buried in it were not able to afford one. There are 4 rectors interred, but one, Magee, is without a tombstone.

The following is the inscription on the monument to the Boyd family before mentioned: "Here lyeth the body of Captain James Boyd, who died the 4th day of January 1748 aged 72. He was the youngest son of John Boyd, who died in the year 1687 aged 54, and of Grizle Boyd, otherwise Mongomery, who died in the year 1708 aged 76, who both lye here also interred. This monument was erected in the year 1750 by Olivia Boyd, relick of the said James."

History of Old Church

It is believed among the parishioners that this church was very old and that it was built by St Martin; also that it was originally in connection with a "monastery" which is said to have stood within 300 yards of the shores of Lough Shillin, in the townland of Moneysterlin, and to have been founded by a lady of the name of O'Lynn who was married to Shan More O'Hagan, at the time proprietor of the manor of the Drapers' Company.

The 10 townlands of Ballynascreen were settled upon her at her marriage and which she subsequently gave to endow the monastery. She also prevailed on her husband to erect the artificial island on the lough and build a small cottage or bathing house on it for the accommodation of the nuns, it being a secluded and retired spot and quite apart from the male students and monks. The monastery and lough were named after the maiden name of this lady, the one called *Monaistir O'Linn*, anglicised "O'Linn's monastery;" the other was called Lough O'Linn, since changed to Lough Shillin.

The monastery gave the name to the townland

in which it was situated, but which has since been corrupted into Moneysterlin.

A portion of the cellars of what is said to have been the monastery were dug up in 1835 and the last portion of the bathing house was removed about 5 years ago.

There is a tradition that St Patrick intended to build the old church at Desertmartin in that part of the townland of Longfield now occupied by Patrick Hassan, but that the building materials brought to the site by day were removed at night to the place where the old church at Desertmartin now stands; and that St Patrick attempted to erect the church on the forewarned spot but was prevented by some heathen governor or chief. The building was afterwards completed by St Martin and was, together with the "desert," dedicated to him.

Island in Lough Shillin

An interesting antiquity is the island in Lough Shillin, on which, according to the tradition of some of the parishioners, there formerly stood a small wooden house. The island itself is entirely artificial, having been composed of oak piles with crossbeams joining them, on which was thrown earth etc. A considerable number have been taken out but there are many in it still, and the drawing in the appendix is a representation of one of them standing at the western side. It is 30 feet wide and is partly surrounded on the western side by grass and rushes that have grown through the lowered waters consequent on the drainage of the lake. It has been lately converted into a small vegetable garden. In digging it up a rusty chain and pothook were found, with mutton bones, a horseshoe and a cannon-ball.

In modern times it was inhabited by robbers who kept a curragh of horseskin on the lake and thus rendered themselves inaccessible, it being the only curragh in the whole country round. The inhabitants at length dislodged them by turning in a stream and thus rendering their stronghold dangerous, from the increasing level of the waters. Kilnaclieve is the old name of the district immediately around it.

Military Remains

There is a tradition that the town of Desertmartin was the scene of a battle in the troubles of 1641 between the Presbyterians and the Irish, in which the latter were overcome with the loss of 18,000 men. The commanders were Sir Phelim O'Neill and General Munroe. The only military remains are those of the old jail, part of which probably once belonged to a castle. It is in the course of being pulled down. They at present extend about 40 feet in front. The oldest part of the walls is a gable now forming the end of a cowhouse. It is 17 feet long and averages 2 feet thick, but is thicker by a couple of inches at the bottom than at the top. The mortar appears very ancient. This jail and the attached court house was disused about 100 years ago.

Forts

Knocknagin Fort is on a rising ground commanding the village. The top is nearly flat. It is oval and 100 feet by 82 feet. The circumference of the oval is formed by a ledge 18 feet deep, except at the southern end where it is interrupted by an inclined plane by which to ascend to the top. It is all composed of fine gravel and sand. It was on this spot that criminals were formerly executed. Some executions also took place on the hill over Lough Shillin. This is the most remarkable of the forts. The rest are earthen of the usual form and are marked on the Ordnance map.

[C.W. Ligar] A large stone, 6 feet 10 inches long by 4 feet broad and 3 feet deep, was supported by 6 smaller ones and stood in an old fort in Turgan. It was thrown down a few years since by some persons who supposed a treasure was concealed beneath. The fort was circular, with one parapet and was 140 feet in diameter.

[J. Stokes] Before the cultivation of the country was so far advanced as it is now, 4 Danish forts stood round the village remarkably close to each other. A shout from one could be replied to from the next. They are now destroyed.

Discoveries

Stone hatchets and arrowheads have been frequently found in this parish. None, however, have been obtained of late years; see drawings in the appendix of a gold gorget, brass spearhead etc.

6 years ago, that is in 1830, an old military canteen was found in the townland of Drumanasarragh. It was in a very decayed state. Perhaps it is a remnant of the battle mentioned under the head Military.

Gold Gorgets

[C.W. Ligar] Robert McCanary found, 1 foot under the surface of a small gravel hill in 1833, a large gold gorget which weighed 1 oz. 4 dwt. He sold it to Robert Leslie Ogilby of Dungiven, Esquire, in May 1836 for 7 pounds; see drawing in the appendix.

Parish of Desertmartin

Within 7 yards of the same place another was discovered some time previous and was sold to a watchmaker in Magherafelt for 1 pound 6s 8d. It was much smaller than the one sold to Mr Ogilby.

Copper Article

A curious copper article was found in 1832 in the townland of Carncose, beneath the surface of the ground. It is in the shape of a hollow cone with a base of 2 and a half inches and 1 inch high, with a small round hole at the top. The interior has been well gilded and the outside covered with a coating of enamel of different colours, and each colour forming a certain figure. Much of it has been broken off from the copper and there are small holes and vacant spaces where some precious metal or gems appear to have been carefully picked out; see drawing in the appendix.

Chamber or Cove

In the townland of Iniscarn a subterraneous chamber or cove was found in 1828 and since destroyed. It was built of rough stones similar to the other coves described and was 6 feet long.

Cross and Coins

A silver cross and 3 pieces of silver coin were found in 1828, in the townland of Iniscarn. They have been given to a lady in Moneymore (Mrs Rowley Miller).

Miscellaneous Discoveries

An ancient urn with carvings on the outside was found in the townland of Iniscarn, but fell to pieces when lifted out of the ground.

Francis Sweeny, when cutting turf in the townland of Annagh in 1834, found, 12 feet under the surface, 12 brass spearheads and a quantity of brass rings, similar to those described in the parish of Magherafelt and varying in diameter from half an inch to 5 inches. He sold all to the Belfast museum.

2 brass instruments resembling chisels, but most probably used in war, were found in the townlands of Moneysterling and Brackagh Slieve Gallion; see drawings in the appendix.

2 arrowheads, one of brass and the other of flint, were found in the townlands of Annagh and Durnascallon. These implements of war, so different in material, would lead to the supposition that they had been used by distinct races of people, or the same race at very different stages of civilization; see drawing in the appendix.

Giant's Chair

On the south west side of Slieve Gallion, in the townland of Iniscarn, there was formerly a giant's chair. It appeared to have been formed partly by nature and partly by art, but nothing remains at present of it but the large rocks on which it stood.

Giant's Grave

Within a short distance to the west of this chair, on the summit of the mountain, there are the ruins of a carn of stones called the Giant's Grave. The carn is 4 feet high and 14 yards in diameter at the base. It was opened in 1825 by the Revd Francis Quinn P.P. of Omagh, when a grave of 8 and a half feet in length was found enclosed on the sides by large stones and covered by others of still larger dimensions, one of them being 5 and a half feet long, 3 and a half broad and 1 and a half thick.

On the west side of this grave there is another carn of stones which has been used for one of the stations for the Ordnance Survey, and is said to have been formed by the persons visiting the mountain for the sake of performing stations and seeing the prospect which it commands, who each brought a stone and laid it to the heap. It is called the Tummock. This was an ancient custom but is not now followed.

The following tradition is in connection with the Giant's Grave, where one Teag More or "Big Teag" is said to have been buried.

When St Patrick was building the cathedral of Armagh, he was so much annoyed by a large black bull who came every day and destroyed the work, that St Patrick was obliged to allow the workmen to relinquish their task; but hearing of Teag More, a man of courage who lived at the foot of Slieve Gallion, he sent for him and endowed him with great strength and, after blessing him, left him alone to guard the rising edifice. The bull came tearing on as usual, when Teag, seizing an ash tree in his hand, made at him and, after seizing him by the tail, belaboured him so heartily with the ash tree, which he handled like a benweed, that the animal took over the Blackwater and Bann, and made for the top of Slieve Gallion, where he fell into a bog hole and was killed by his enemy.

Teag, feeling an appetite after his exercise, fell to work on the bull and had him nearly devoured before the crowd, who watched him in his journey, reached the mountain. They were so frightened with Teag's strength that they prayed to the saint to reduce him down to his former powers, which he did, and in consequence Teag immediately died and was buried in the grave now called the Giant's Grave.

The saint had either not known or had forgotten the great dinner his friend Teag had made and when he reduced the strength of his body, the strength of the stomach also followed and he died of indigestion.

Social Economy

Early Improvements

[J. Boyle] It would be difficult to say as to when the earliest improvements took place in this parish, as the popular tradition [is] that the village of Desertmartin, from which the parish takes its name, was at one time the assizes town of the county and that the neighbouring country was inhabited by a class of persons infinitely more powerful and important than its present humble occupiers.

It may be probable that the most permanent and important change which took place in the morals or habits of the people was at the time when the county was apportioned by James I to the London companies. About one-half of this parish is included in that portion of the county allotted to the Drapers' Company and this comprises its southern and more mountainous district, most of which is still occupied by the descendants of the native Irish, who seem to have retreated before the invaders of their country. The lower and more fertile parts are occupied by a much more independent, comfortable and enlightened class, who are all either of English or Scottish descent.

The very great difference which formerly existed between the inhabitants of these districts as to civilisation has been nearly obliterated, owing to the very spirited exertions of the Drapers' Company, who spare no expense in promoting the civilisation and improvement of their tenantry.

It was not until the year 1817 that the company came into actual possession and occupation of their estates in this county, and that year may be dated as the era of a total revolution in the morals, customs and general civilization of that part of the parish in their possession.

Progress of Improvement

4 large schools were established, 2 for males and 2 for females. Upon these 260 pounds are annually expended and the children educated gratis. Roads were cut at their expense through every part of their estate to the summit of the mountains, opening communications with districts hitherto almost unknown and shut out. Since, freestone quarries were opened for supplying the various works and buildings in progress, and these afford employment and support to many.

Illicit distillation, which was formerly carried on extensively here, was totally checked by their exertions, as by a clause in their regulations any tenant guilty of a breach of the revenue laws is subject to expulsion from their estate; and few acts of theirs could tend more to the civilisation of their tenantry.

Farming Societies

A great improvement in husbandry has been the result of the establishment of farming societies. This, however, applies to the entire parish, the lower part of which is principally connected with that in Magherafelt, while that part of it in the Drapers' estate is connected with its own.

In the lower parts of the parish the improvement in husbandry has been remarkable. Green crops, which a few years ago were scarcely thought of, as also wheat, are now abundantly and successfully cultivated. Ploughing, which formerly could not be done without the assistance of a driver, is now performed by 1 man with reins. There is also a great improvement in their cars and implements of husbandry.

Clergy

There are perhaps few parishes where the clergy of all denominations devote themselves more assiduously to their flocks than this. The consequence is that "sheebeen" houses, which formerly abounded in the lower parts and were the most fruitful sources of immorality, have now been eradicated. Party processions or assemblages are discountenanced. Against these the priest has decidedly set his face and refuses to administer the rites of his church to such of his flock as are concerned in them.

Weaving

Another matter of importance to the people of this parish has been the introduction of weaving linen from mill-spun yarn, which affords constant employment and steady wages to the manufacturing class; and as each cottager generally possesses from 2 to 3 acres of ground, the elder member of the family generally minds the farm while the others pay the rent with what they can earn by weaving.

Obstructions to improvement: none.

Parish of Desertmartin 59

Local Government

There are neither magistrates nor police, manor courts nor sessions, the petty sessions for this district being held on every alternate Wednesday in the town of Magherafelt.

There have not been any outrages committed in this parish for a long time. Illicit distillation has been totally stopped for some years, as before stated.

There are few, if any, fire or life insurances.

Dispensary

The health of the people has been improved by the establishment of dispensaries in the neighbouring parishes, to which they are admissible. There is not a dispensary in this parish. The people are and have been comparatively healthy, nor is there any disease particularly prevalent.

Schools

Schools are gladly resorted to and have produced very beneficial effects on the rising generation. Few parishes possess the same advantage in the gratuitous education of the poor than this, as will be seen by a reference to Table of Schools.

Poor

There are not 30 resident poor in this parish. Except the usual collections on Sundays, there is no regular provision for them; neither is it required, as the people possess sufficient voluntary charity to support them, as their assistance in a "gowpen" of meal or a lap full of potatoes is never withheld from the beggars at their door.

Religion

By the revised census of 1834, there are in this parish 835 Episcopalians, 1,108 Presbyterians, 2,788 Roman Catholics and 203 of other denominations. The rector is supported by his tithes, which amount to 400 pounds per annum, a glebe of 326 acres 1 rood 17 perches and a farm attached to the Glebe House. The Protestant curate has 75 pounds per annum.

The Seceding clergyman receives his stipend of 40 pounds per annum and regium donum of 50 pounds per annum. He also receives annually from the Drapers' Company 10 pounds.

The priest holds the parish of Kilcronaghan in union with this one. He receives 105 pounds from the two. He has a curate to whom he pays one-third of his receipt or 35 pounds. The Roman Catholic clergy do not live at their lodgings more than one-third of the year, but are entertained by their flocks when on stations and other calls.

Houses

The cottages of the peasantry in this parish are inferior in comfort or appearance to those in the adjoining parishes, many of them (particularly near the edges of the bogs) being constructed of mud. This, however, is chiefly owing to the scarcity of building stones, the soil being for the most part gravelly and the stones small and pebbly.

They are nearly all thatched and rather low and small, generally consisting of 2 small apartments, one used as a kitchen and the other for sleeping. Their furniture is not plentiful nor of a very good description. They are lit by generally 2 small windows. Their external appearance is not neat nor prepossessing, as the use of lime seems (though it is abundant) to be little known, and there are few of them that want the usual accompaniment of a heap of manure before the door. Internally, however, they are rather cleanly.

Food

The people of this parish are pretty well-off for milk, as there are few of them who do not possess a cow. This, with potatoes, salt herrings and a little bacon at Easter or Christmas, principally constitute their food. Tea is more in use, as is also bread, than formerly. Very little meal is now made or used as they prefer selling the raw corn.

Habits of the People

The people are considered as honest, peaceable, sober and industrious, and though not quite so affluent as the inhabitants of some of the neighbouring parishes, they are all above want and many of them in the lower districts very comfortable. There are in this parish some tolerably extensive farmers who have got very neat and comfortable residences, but except the clergy there are no resident gentry.

A considerable portion of the male population are engaged in the manufacture of linen. The females spin linen yarn but not so generally since the introduction of mill-spun yarn. All possess a little land, usually about from 2 to 3 acres, which grazes a cow, grows their potatoes, besides a little flax or corn.

Turf is their only fuel and it is very abundant.

Their dress, except in the mountainous districts where it is not so neat nor of so good a description, differs little from that of the inhabitants of the neighbouring parishes, it being neat, comfortable and of an excellent description.

Longevity and Marriage

There are generally to be found in each townland persons of from 70 to 80 years old. They are in general rather long lived. Last year (1835) a man named Thomas McChrystal (in the townland of Tirgan) died at the very advanced age of 116.

They marry rather early, particularly in the mountains, but there are not any remarkable instances of early marriage.

The average number in a family is 5 and a half.

Amusements

Their favourite amusements, dancing, cock-fighting, horse-racing and card-playing, which were formerly very frequent, have within the last 3 or 4 years almost totally been stopped by the interference of their clergy.

Easter used formerly to be observed by their assembling on Easter Monday and Tuesday in a green or field but this is now observed only by children.

Cammon playing (a sort of hurling) was the favourite game at Christmas but it is now given up and there are merely a few idle days at these festivals.

Traditions

The Catholics have their usually numerous patrons and patrons' days but have not any traditions. They are in general superstitious and implicitly believe in fairies, ghosts. They have not any local customs peculiar to themselves. The children burn fires on St John's Eve but they cannot assign any reason for doing so.

They have not any ancient music, nor peculiarity of costume.

Emigration and Migration

About 20, on an annual average, emigrate in spring to Canada. They are mostly of the poorer class and they are generally from the Drapers' estate where cottiers are not permitted; few, if any, return.

Upwards of 100 go annually to the Scottish or English harvests. They are generally men who have a little land of their own or are agricultural labourers, all of whom return in time to reap their own harvests.

See appendix for a list of the exact numbers who have emigrated in 1834 and 1835, and the exact number from each townland who migrate.

Remarkable events: none.

Table of Schools

[Table contains the following headings: name, situation and description, when established, income and expenditure, physical, intellectual and moral education, number of pupils subdivided by age, sex and religion, name and religion of master and mistress].

Parish school, in an excellent 2-storey house built for the purpose by subscription, contiguous to the village of Desertmartin, established 1835; income: 10 pounds per annum from the Honourable Revd Mr Pomeroy, the rector, 1 pound per annum from the curate, [total] 11 pounds, from pupils 13 pounds; intellectual education: books of the Sunday School Society; moral education: visits from the Protestant clergy, Authorised Version of Scriptures and catechisms daily; number of pupils: 8 under 10 years of age, 20 from 10 to 15, 4 above 15, total 32, all male, 26 Protestants, 6 Presbyterians; master Charles Kane, Protestant.

Female school, under the London Hibernian Society, in the upper storey of the above house, in an excellent schoolroom, established 1835; income: 5 pounds per annum from Lady Garvagh, 3 pounds per annum from John Boyle Esquire, [total] 8 pounds, from pupils 9 pounds; intellectual education: sewing, books of the London Hibernian Society; moral education: visits from the Protestant clergy, Authorised Version of Scriptures and catechisms daily, and Sunday school; number of pupils: 28 under 10 years of age, 5 from 10 to 15, 10 above 15, total 43, all female, 14 Protestants, 18 Presbyterians, 11 Roman Catholics; mistress Mary Riley, Protestant.

Under the Worshipful the Drapers' Company, in an excellent house containing apartments for the teacher built by the Drapers' Company in the townland of Iniscarron, established 1819; income: supported wholly by the Drapers' Company, who expend annually the sum of 130 pounds between the male and female schools in this townland; expenditure: to the master 50 pounds, to the mistress 35 pounds, with a free house, garden, a cow's grass to each; intellectual education: the females learn sewing, spelling and reading; the boys learn spelling, reading, writing and arithmetic, books and cards of the Sunday School Society; moral education: visits from the clergy, Scriptures daily; number of pupils: 73 under 10 years of age, 47 from 10 to 15, total 120, all male, 6 Protestants, 14 Presbyterians, 100 Roman Catho-

Parish of Desertmartin

lics; master John Conlan, mistress Margaret Lennox, Protestants; the master and mistress each spend 3 days in each week in the schools in this townland and in those mentioned below in the townland of Cranny.

Under the Worshipful the Drapers' Company, female school, in the same house as above but in a separate schoolroom, established 1819; number of pupils: 69 under 10 years of age, 52 from 10 to 15, 9 above 15, total 130, all female, 6 Protestants, 18 Presbyterians, 106 Roman Catholics.

Under the Worshipful the Drapers' Company, male school and female school, in an excellent house built for the purpose by the Worshipful Drapers' Company in the townland of Cranny, in the same house but in a separate schoolroom, established 1819; income: supported wholly by the Drapers' Company, who expend annually the sum of 130 pounds between the male and female schools in this townland; number of pupils: males, 69 under 10 years of age, 51 from 10 to 15, 120 total males; females, 82 under 10 years of age, 78 from 10 to 15, 160 total females; total number of pupils 280, 26 Protestants, 107 Presbyterians, 147 Roman Catholics.

National school, in a house kept for the purpose in the townland of Grange, established 1833; income: from the Board of National Education 8 pounds, from pupils 8 pounds; intellectual education: books of the Board of National Education; moral education: visits from the priest, all versions of the Scriptures at stated hours; number of pupils: males, 10 under 10 years of age, 9 from 10 to 15, 4 above 15, 23 total males; females, 9 under 10 years of age, 6 from 10 to 15, 2 above 15, 17 total females; total number of pupils 40, 14 Presbyterians, 6 Roman Catholics, 20 other denominations; master Hugh Mullan, Protestant.

National school, in a house kept for the purpose in the townland of Knocknagin, established 1834; income: from the Board of National Education 8 pounds, from pupils 15 pounds; intellectual education: books of the Board of National Education; moral education: visits from the priest, all versions of Scriptures at stated hours; number of pupils: males, 23 under 10 years of age, 19 from 10 to 15, 8 above 15, 50 total males; females, 19 under 10 years of age, 14 from 10 to 15, 3 above 15, 36 total females; total number of pupils 86, all Roman Catholics; master Mr McCartney, Roman Catholic.

[Subtotals]: income from public societies or benevolent individuals 295 pounds, from pupils 45 pounds; expenditure in salaries 85 pounds; number of pupils: males, 183 under 10 years of age, 146 from 10 to 15, 16 above 15, 345 total males; females, 207 under 10 years of age, 155 from 10 to 15, 24 above 15, 383 total females; total number of pupils 831 [sic], 78 Protestants, 197 Presbyterians, 464 [sic] Roman Catholics, 20 other denominations.

Private school, in a house the property of the teacher in the townland of Killyboggan, established 1825; income from pupils 22 pounds; intellectual education: reading, writing, arithmetic, book-keeping, mensuration, the works of no particular author; moral education: Authorised Version of the Scriptures, Church and Presbyterian catechisms daily; number of pupils: males, 11 under 10 years of age, 9 from 10 to 15, 6 above 15, 26 total males; females, 9 under 10 years of age, 5 from 10 to 15, 14 total females; total number of pupils 40, 8 Protestants, 24 Presbyterians, 8 Roman Catholics; master Richard Marow [insert correction: Morrow], Presbyterian.

Benevolence: Establishments for the Indigent

[Table contains the following headings: name, object, management, number relieved, funds, annual expense of management, relief afforded, when founded].

8 schools wholly or partly supported by charitable societies or individuals; object: the removal of ignorance; management: by individuals or sundry societies; numbers relieved: 831 children daily receiving instruction; funds from public bodies: 260 pounds annually from the Drapers' Company, 16 pounds from the Board of National Education, [total] 276 pounds, from private individuals 19 pounds annually; salaries: the teachers receive a sum paid by the scholars, besides 85 pounds; relief afforded: school requisites; when founded: at sundry periods.

PRODUCTIVE ECONOMY

Trades and Occupations in Desertmartin

Blacksmiths 1, carpenters 1, grocers 3, nailers 1, millers 1, schoolmasters 1, spirit sellers 2, shoemakers 1, wheelwrights 1, tailors 1, total 13.

ANCIENT TOPOGRAPHY

Drawings by C.W. Ligar

Stake of the oak piles supporting the island of Shillin, dimensions 3 feet 9 inches high [by J. Stokes].

[Decorated lunula] copied from a drawing made by the person who found the gorget. This drawing was made from a gold gorget which was found in

1833, 1 foot under the surface of a small gravel hill in the townland of Rosegarran, <Rosegarland>, parish of Desertmartin, county Londonderry, by Robert McCanary, who sold it in May 1836 to Robert Leslie Ogilby of Dungiven, Esquire, for 7 pounds; weight 1oz. 4 dwts. Castle Dawson, 21st June 1836.

A copper article found in Carncose, underground, in 1832, full size, side view and view from above. 31st August 1836.

A silver coin in the possession of Alexander McCanary, townland of Rosegarland. The black spot is a hole through the coin. 20th June 1836.

Hollow copper hatchet, side view and section drawing, full size, found in the townland of Moneysterling.

Brass hatchet, side view and section drawing, full size, found in the townland of Brackagh Slieve Gallion.

Flint spear or arrowhead found in the townland of Annagh.

Brass spear or arrowhead found in the townland of Durnascallon, both full size.

Emigration

The following is a list of persons who emigrated to America from the parish in the years 1834 and 1835.

Males: 15 in 1834, 12 in 1835; females: 5 in 1834, 1 in 1835; total 20 in 1834, 13 in 1835.

Males under 5 years of age: 1 in 1834; males 15 and under 20: 1 in 1835; males 20 and under 25: 11 in 1834, 7 in 1835; females 20 and under 25: 1 in 1834, 1 in 1835; males 25 and under 30: 2 in 1834, 4 in 1835; females 25 and under 30: 4 in 1834; males 50 and upwards: 1 in 1834; total 20 in 1834, 13 in 1835.

Protestants: 6 in 1834, 2 in 1835; Presbyterians: 3 in 1834, 3 in 1835; Roman Catholics: 11 in 1834, 8 in 1835; total 20 in 1834, 13 in 1835.

To Quebec: 11 in 1834, 8 in 1835; to St John's: 4 in 1834, 1 in 1835; to New York: 4 in 1834, 2 in 1835; to Philadelphia: 2 in 1835; to New Orleans: 1 in 1834; total 20 in 1834, 13 in 1835.

Migration

The following is the number of persons who migrate to England and Scotland for harvest work.

Rosegarran <Rosgarran>, 5 to England. Grange, 5 to England, 6 to Scotland. Luney, 12 to England. Annagh, 5 to England. Moneysterlin, 4 to Scotland. Knocknagin, 4 to Scotland. Ballynagown, 8 to Scotland. Rusure, 7 to Scotland. Curr, 1 to Scotland. Stranagard, 6 to England. Durnascallon, 3 to England. Motalee, 4 to England. Longfield, 4 to England. Cullion, 6 to England. Brackagh Slieve Gallion, 6 to Scotland. Dromore, 3 to Scotland. Iniscarn, 8 to England. Boveagh, 5 to Scotland. Cranny, 2 to England. Carncose, 1 to Scotland. Gortanewry, 3 to Scotland. Total 60 to England, 48 to Scotland.

Office Copy of Draft Memoir

NATURAL FEATURES

Hills

The ground falls gradually from the top of Sliabh Gallion mountain until it loses itself in the low flat country east of Desertmartin village.

Lakes and Rivers

Lakes: none.
Rivers: none of any consequence.

Bogs

In the eastern direction there is a considerable quantity of cold boggy land; more westerly the soil consists of sand, loam and micaceous gravel. There is a large bog in the townland of Grange, which is every day becoming more valuable for fuel.

Woods

The Drapers' Company have made great improvements in this part of the parish by planting all the rough and before useless ground.

MODERN TOPOGRAPHY

Towns: Desertmartin

Desertmartin is a dirty little village on the road from Moneymore to Maghera and Dungiven, in the townland of Stranagard, belonging to Lord Garvagh. It contains about 50 houses. There is no market: the inhabitants attend the markets of Maghera and Magherafelt. There is a patent for holding 8 fairs in the course of the year but no one in or about Desertmartin remembers to have seen more than 2 held in the year, viz. November 7th and December 27th; none at all have been held during the last 9 years.

[Insert addition: No fairs have been held since 1821. The inhabitants boast that this was once an assizes town. They show the site and remains of the gaol and note the adjacent height of Knockagin (the hill of heads) as the place of execution].

Parish of Desertmartin

Public Buildings

There is a small neat church situated on the Glebe, a Roman Catholic chapel in the townland of Annagh and Moneysterlin, and a Presbyterian meeting house in the townland of Lecumpher.

Communications

The only roads of any consequence are those leading from Magherafelt and Moneymore through Desertmartin and on to Tobermore. They are kept in tolerably good order and, as far as the Drapers' estate goes, they are very good. They are repaired with river gravel and whinstone broken small. There is no communication by public conveyances to any part of the parish. The nearest places at which jaunting cars etc. may be hired are Maghera, Magherafelt and Moneymore.

Parish of Kilcronaghan, County Londonderry

Memoir by J. Stokes, 1837

NATURAL FEATURES

Hills

The surface of the parish of Kilcronaghan is formed by the descending features of Sliabh Gallion. Its highest point is situated on the western side of the summit of that mountain and from it the ground falls in a series lying south and north. These become more and more broken and irregular as they approach the River Moyola.

The highest point (that already spoken of) is at the altitude of 1,091 feet above the sea. The lowest, the western extremity of the townland of Tobermore, is 130 feet in altitude. The summits named on the maps are: Donelly's hill, 336 feet high; Brackaghlislea, 465 feet; Mormeal, 358; Bonfire hill, 337; Todd hill, 201; Calmore hill, 268.

Lakes

There are 16 small lakes in Brackaghlislea, Tullyroan, Gortahurk and Mormeal, from 2 perches to 5 perches in breadth and from 10 to 20 feet deep. This is but a surmise as no one has ever sounded them.

Rivers

The parish is watered by numerous small rivulets rising in the flank of the mountain. These on the eastern side all pass into the parish of Desertmartin, but on the western they fall into a stream that falls into the parish of Ballynascreen. It rises in the most western part of Brackaghlislea and, after a course of 2 and three-quarter miles, passes into that parish. It forms the boundary between Kilcronaghan and Ballynascreen. Its fall in the lower grounds is 176 feet in the mile. It is a broad brisk stream.

There are abundance of springs and also a good spa well in the townland of Mormeal.

Bogs

Nothing but oak is found in the small bog of Coolsarragh. Blocks are the most plentiful. The sticks found have fallen from south to north and are of good quality; some have been found 30 feet long. Some appear as if the half had been burned away thus: [drawing of pointed wooden stick]. The blocks and sticks are all on the same line or level and are apparently of the same growth. Their average depth is 2 and a half feet below the present surface. Blocks have been often found resting on sticks. The depth of this bog is at present about 14 feet. The bottom is of clay and sand.

The flow bog in the townland of Clooney was originally 10 feet deep. 5 feet of it have been cut away. The imbedded timber consists of fir and oak, the largest sticks 2 feet in diameter. They have fallen from west to east.

The flow bog in the glen between Tullyroan and Gortahurk is nearly all cut out but no imbedded timber has been found in it worth notice. The quantity was small.

Woods

The natural wood of the parish of Kilcronaghan consists of oak, ash, birch, alder, hazel and holly, with thorns. There are about 20 acres of it in the townland of Gortahurk and 4 acres in the townland of Mormeal, at the sides of the stream that separates this parish from Ballynascreen. It is all of but little value.

A large oak called the Royal Oak, which grew near the castle of Calmore, is still remembered in the parish. It is said to have been so large that 2 horsemen on horseback could not touch one another with their whips across it, after it had been cut down. From this vague description it may be conjectured that it was about 10 feet in diameter or 30 feet in circumference. It was drawn away by bullocks to Killymoon near Cookstown.

There was another oak tree which, from its tallness and straightness, was called the Fishing Rod. The former grew near the parish church, the latter near the small bog in which Mr Knox's canoe was found (see Ancient Topography). The tradition is that the whole of the lowlands were once covered with a magnificent wood of oak.

Climate

The general character of the climate is the same as that of the parish of Ballynascreen. See Productive Economy for particulars as to the ripening of crops. No meteorological register has been kept.

MODERN TOPOGRAPHY

Towns: Tobermore

Tobermore is a village situated between Maghera

Parish of Kilcronaghan

and Magherafelt, Castledawson and Draperstown. It is 2 and a half miles statute from the first town, 5 and a half from the second, 6 and a quarter from the third and 3 and a half from the fourth. The long street in which it is arranged is 75 feet wide.

Its general appearance is not prepossessing, most of the houses being merely thatched cabins with dirty fronts and dilapidated roofs. They are nearly all of brick and in bad repair. The reason of this, their neglected state, is the dispute about the proprietorship of the townland. It is in the hands of the court of chancery, who have appointed Messrs Rowley Miller and John Rowley Miller their agents; see Obstructions to Improvement.

Its name, Tobermore, had its origin from a large well that stood at the western end of the street; it has since dried up. The oldest house is inscribed "J.M. 1727." This was James Moore, for particulars of whose family see Ancient Topography.

At the period of the transfer of the fair from the Gort of Kilcronaghan to this place, the time of which is unknown, the village was composed of this house and a few adjacent huts of mud. The fairs had been formerly regularly held upon the Gort at the parish church, but at length, upon being disturbed by a party of robbers from the mountains, they removed to Tobermore, since which time many more houses were built in it, particularly since the year of the Union. The removal of the fair was also produced by the influence of a parish priest of Desertmartin called Grimes.

It contains 146 houses, of which 10 are 2-storey high and 120 are 1-storey high. For trades and occupations, see the following pages.

PRODUCTIVE AND SOCIAL ECONOMY

Trades in Tobermore

The following are the trades and occupations: labourers 26, farmers 14, tailors 8, nailers 8, weavers 8, publicans 6, grocers 5, publican and grocer 1, pensioners 5, hucksters 6, poor widows 8, blacksmiths 2, postmaster and leather cutter 1, apothecary and surgeon 1, blacksmiths 2, carpenters 2, shoemakers 4, widow and pensioner 1, tinkers 2, old maids who live by spinning and knitting 8, wheelwrights 2, slater 1, schoolmasters 2, schoolmistress 1, dressmakers 2, dress-

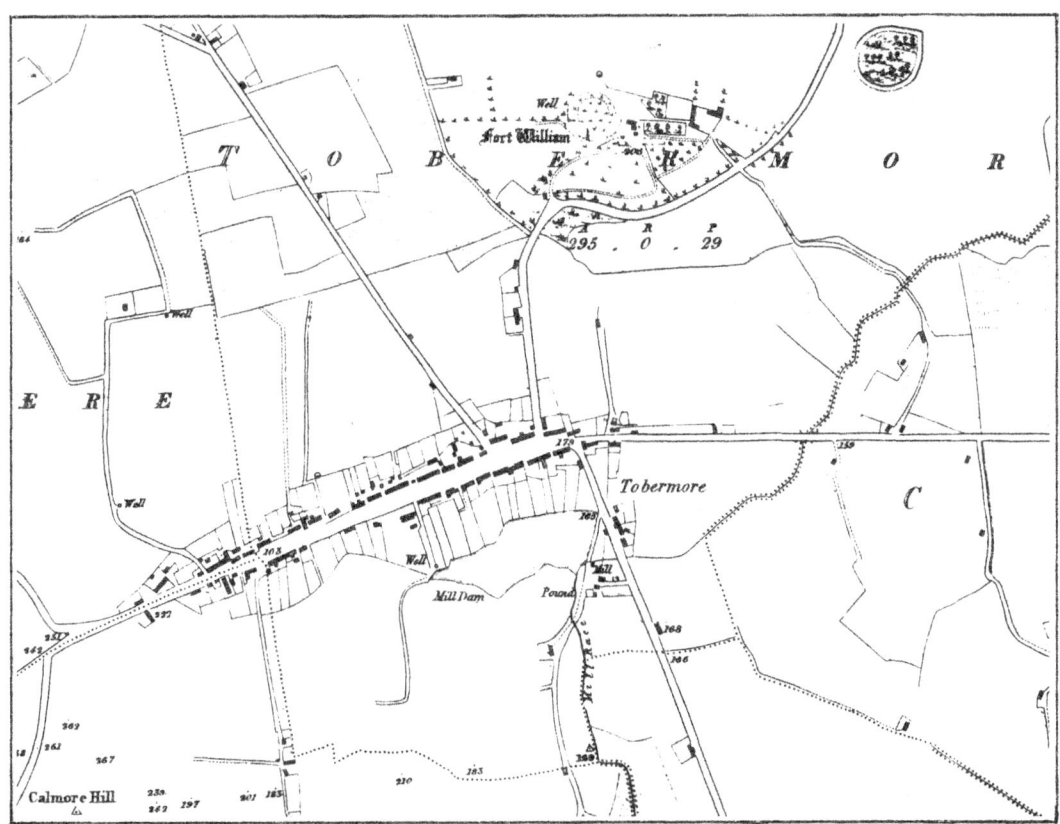

Map of Tobermore from the first 6" O.S. maps, 1830s

maker and haberdasher 1, grocer and haberdasher 1, baker and grocer 1, lodging house keeper 1, dealer in hardware 1, weaver and blue dyer 1, sexton to meeting house 1, sawyers 2, watch and clockmaker 1, hacklers 3, painter and glazier 1, thatcher 1, carmen 2, butchers 2, gentlemen's servants who occupy houses 3, [insert addition: small farmers 119, cottiers 47].

Conveyances

There are 2 cars for hire in the village. 2 coaches pass daily through it, one from Coleraine to Dungannon, the other from Dungannon to Coleraine, the first at half an hour p.m. and the other at 11.30 a.m.

MODERN TOPOGRAPHY

Parish Church

The parish church is prettily situated among some groups of trees to the north of the road leading from Draperstown to Desertmartin. It is close to the minister's house and is a rectangle 42 and a half feet by 25 feet, all in good repair except as to the pews inside which are in a dilapidated state. Over the inner door is the following inscription: "Rebuilt 1806, Revd William Bryan, rector, James Stevenson Esquire and Thomas Jackson, churchwardens."

In the interior there is a flagged aisle and sittings for 100 adults. There is light from 3 small lancet-shaped windows, of which 2 are on the southern wall and one on the east end. The pulpit and reading desk are not in good repair. There is a baptismal font of cut freestone. The cost of rebuilding was about 350 pounds.

The Ecclesiastical Board, it is expected, will soon build a new church. The present one is too small for the congregation, the increase of population in the last 30 years having, with other causes, increased its former numbers. The following Latin inscription was formerly in the interior but on its repair was transferred to the churchyard and placed in front of a wall built purposely for it: "Hic jacet Elizabetha Moore uxor rev. de domini Andrew Henderson, rector de Ballynascreen. Generosa praeclara virtutis et pietatis e familia de Rowallan apud Scotas qua obit vicesimo 8tava die Maie anno domini 1715. Prope jacet Fredericus Henderson eorum natus Ecclesia Anglicana presbyter qui obit vicesimo obito anno suae aetatis nomine eximii ingenii specimine una elim [?] Andrea et Elizabetha eorum natus qui deces [?] serunt in pueri libus [?] annus." Of this Henderson, nothing more is known than that he was rector of Ballynascreen.

Before this church was rebuilt service was performed in the house of the rector. It was at first quite large enough for the accommodation of the congregation. When the present rector, the Revd James Spencer Knox, was first inducted into the parish of Kilcronaghan, the number of the congregation was usually 5, 6 or 7. He has now, by his active exertions, increased it to 120.

Presbyterian Meeting House

The Presbyterian meeting house, situated in the centre of the village of Tobermore, was built in the year 1728. It is a plain white building with a slated roof and is 69 feet by 24 feet inside. It is lighted by 21 rectangular windows. The pews in the interior are in tolerable repair. The aisle is of earth and the roof is not ceiled. There is accommodation for 450 adults.

In 1825 this house was nearly new roofed and 2 buttresses were put to the back wall to prevent its falling. The seats were all repaired in 1831 at the expense of the Drapers' Company and at the cost of 50 pounds.

Mr Carson's Meeting House

The meeting house of the Revd Alexander Carson was built in 1814 at the expense of the congregation. The cost, however, cannot now be ascertained. It is a low, slated rectangular building of coarse stone with the gable towards the street and is 65 feet by 25 feet in the clear. There is a very small sessions room attached to the western side. The interior is in good repair with sittings for 270 adults, including the galleries, of which there is one at each end of the building. There are 8 square windows, of which 5 are on the eastern, one on the western and one at each gable.

There is no yard attached but there are materials collected on the ground for the purpose of surrounding the meeting house with a wall. It stands near the western end of the street of Tobermore.

Catholic Chapel

There is no Catholic chapel at present in this parish.

Gentlemen's Seats

Fort William, the residence of John Stevenson Esquire, is situated on a rising ground a quarter of a mile to the north of the village of Tobermore and

Parish of Kilcronaghan

on the road from it to Maghera. It was built in the year 1795 and takes its name from an ancient fort which stands at the rear. [Insert footnote: This fort was called after William III by a Mr Jackson, the first proprietor of this place]. It is surrounded by a plantation of fir, ash, sycamore, beech and alder. The oldest of the trees are a century old but the greater part is between 20 and 30. The house is 2-storey high with garrets etc., and from its elevated situation completely commands the village of Tobermore.

Solitude, the residence of the Revd Alexander Carson, is in the townland of Coolsarragh and on the leading road from Tobermore to Magherafelt. It is a prettily situated farmhouse. It is here noticed on account of its very fanciful name.

The Glebe House, at present the residence of Mr Knox's curate, stands close to the churchyard and was built about 30 years ago. It is not in good repair. There is a small plantation round it.

Gortahurk, the residence of Robert Bryan Esquire, stands on a by-road in the townland of that name. It is of 2-storeys and was built in 1721. It is now quite in a neglected state. There is some artificial planting around it with a small natural growth of oak, ash and hazel. It is in a picturesque situation among the ravines and small valleys that abound at the foot of Sliabh Gallion.

Mills

A new flax mill will shortly be completed in the townland of Moneyshanere. It is not yet finished.

A corn mill formerly stood in the townland of Gortahurk, but was destroyed by fire at night and has not been rebuilt since.

A corn mill stands near the village of Tobermore, in the townland of Calmore. The interior is in bad repair. For further particulars relating to this mill, see Fair Sheets attached.

There is nothing to prevent any extension of mills or machinery.

Communications: Roads

The following main lines of road pass through this parish: from Tobermore to Draperstown, three-quarters of a mile; from Tobermore to Magherafelt, 2 miles; from Tobermore to Maghera, three-quarters of a mile; from Tobermore to Dungiven, 1 and three-quarter miles; from Draperstown to Desertmartin, 2 and a half miles; from Tobermore to Desertmartin, 2 miles.

400 perches of the road between Maghera and Magherafelt through Tobermore is contracted for for 7 years at 8d per perch, beginning from 1835.

The road from Tobermore to Desertmartin through the townlands of Killytoney, Cloughfin and Coolsarragh is contracted for at 2d a perch for 7 years from 1834.

The remaining part of the mail coach road between Maghera and Magherafelt above mentioned is contracted for [for] 7 years from 1834, at 3d farthing per perch.

All the main roads are 21 feet wide.

From the sandy and gravelly nature of the hills here, the roads are always disposed to be dry and clean.

Bridges

The bridge over the Moyola, on the road from Tobermore to Maghera and at the parish boundary between the townlands of Drumcrow and Lisnamuck, has 3 arches, each of them 18 feet in span. The roadway is 18 feet wide, with parapets 4 feet high. The bridge was destroyed 3 times by floods. In 1834 it was repaired at the expense of the county but is at present not in good repair.

The Old Forge bridge, as it is called, in the townland of Moybegkirly and at the parish boundary, is on the road from Tobermore to Dungiven. It spans the Moyola with 4 arches, each of 21 feet 6 inches. The roadway is 15 and a half feet wide, with parapets 4 feet high. It was built 2 years before the new style commenced and is in good repair. It is said that shortly after its erection violent floods destroyed almost all the bridges in the county of Londonderry and that this was one of the very few that remained.

The bridge on the parish mearing, and on the road from Magherafelt to Draperstown, has 2 arches, each 20 feet in span. The parapets are 3 feet high and roadway 20 feet broad. All is in good repair.

There is nothing to prevent the erection of bridges or other improvements in communications.

ANCIENT TOPOGRAPHY

Ecclesiastical Remains

The parish church is an ancient church. There are the remains of a window in the western gable. It is built up on the outside but a view of it from the interior is given in the drawings. The Gothic pillars at the side of the present doorway were brought thither from the old door, the situation of which had been in the southern wall. They are represented in the drawings and are 5 feet high.

No part of the old church was incorporated with the new one but the western gable and the northern wall. It was a rectangle, 62 and a half feet by 25 feet, being 20 feet longer than the present one. The other parts of the old building were pulled down, being in an unsound state.

In the churchyard there are 3 gravestones cut into the form of crosses. Could these have formerly stood round the old building or was it only fancy that provided this form? They are drawn in the margin grouped together and are all 2 feet high. Their dates are between 1700 and 1720. [Drawings of 3 crosses in the churchyard of Kilcronaghan].

The following names appear on the tombstones: Martin, Connor, Clark, Ferguson, McGowan, Coar, Cerny, Quigly, McDavan, McCristal, Cassidy, Magee, O'Kelly, Rowan.

According to tradition, this church was founded by St Cronaugh, a bishop and son to a king of Munster. It was then called Kille Cronaughan and afterwards Kilcronaghan. It is likewise said that there had been a nunnery close to it.

Military Remains

Nothing remains of Calmore Castle but a part of the wall which was 3 feet thick and which is now the side wall of a cabin. It was the residence of the Rowley family at the breaking out of the rebellion of 1641 and was burned by a party of Irish in the year 1690. The last male inhabitant was Henry Rowley Esquire. It seems to have been the successor to a stronger and more ancient castle belonging to the O'Hagans and it stood close to the village of Tobermore, on the south east side. About the year 1814 an ancient cellar or dungeon was discovered on the site of this castle.

The traces of Mr Rowley's house cover a rectangle 40 feet by 50 feet in the clear. It was defended by a fortified arched gate with holes for musquetry on each side. This was the part of the building that remained the longest and it is well recollected by the oldest inhabitants of Tobermore. In digging on the site some bottles with the initials H.R. were found.

There is a tradition that 2 years after it was burned, the very man who was the leader of the party that surprised it, and who was the first to throw the sheaf of burning straw into the rooms, came back begging to the windows, the place being then partly repaired. He was recognised by one of the servants and he was immediately stabbed in the avenue by Mr Rowley himself.

The site is about 100 perches south east of the village, in the townland of Calmore. It is said that it was formerly surrounded by a magnificent growth of oak and other timber. It seems to have been built at the period of the Plantation settlements.

Ancient Lease

Extracts from a memorandum of a lease granted by the Rowley family. The following extracts from the memorandum of a lease in the possession of Charles Moore of Tobermore is inserted here, as it throws some light upon the subject of this castle and also confirms the traditions relating to it and the military events of the parish.

Memorandum. "That it is this day agreed upon between Mary Rowley of Cullmore in the county of Londonderry, widow, Elizabeth Rowley, Sarah Rowley and Catharine Rowley, all of Cullmore in the aforesaid county, gentlewomen, on the one part and Jane Moore, widow, and William Moore, son to the said Jane Moore, of Moneyshanere in Drappers' mannor, according to the present marches of ye whole town as it is now possessed by them, John Knox and Thomas Meck, ye third part being now in the possession of the said Jane Moore and William Moore, to have and to hold ye said third part, now in their occupation from Alsaints last part for and during ye natural life. She, ye said Jane Moore, and him, ye said William Moore, and William Moore, the third son of Samuel Moore, yielding and paying yearly and every year during the said time 3 pounds 6s 8d, they or such as shall hold the same under them shall hold the same and shall pay yearly during his and their holding the same, 1 bole of good sufficient seed oats, old measure, 4 fat hens and 4 days' work of a man and horse; and also upon the death of every life aforesaid they, the said Jane Moore and they that are possessed of the premises, shall rectifie and pay 1 half year's rent, and another life to be put into the grant in lieu of the life that shall be so deceased and so successively for ever."

Then follows a prolix clause binding them to "divide the land into well-arranged parks" and to build "sufficient houses," and also to bring their corn to ground at the landlord's mill.

"And they, the said Jane Moore and William Moore and such as shall hold the same under them, will keep up the third part of this dearpark pails just so far as it marches with Monishanere and shall give equal helps of work to ye said Mary, Elizabeth, Sarah and Catharine Rowley, their heirs or either of their heirs or assigns, when within this county and do suit and service its mills and courts." Then succeeds penalties for nonpayment.

Parish of Kilcronaghan

"And that the said Mary, Elizabeth, Sarah and Catharine Rowley, their heirs and assigns, will perfect a deed of lease in parchment. Indented according to the above covenants such as a council shall advise within 5 years, in which there shall be a farther clause and covenant that ye said Jane and William Moore, or such as derives under them, shall vote for the choice of such persons as shall be knight of the shire for parliament successively as the said Mary, Elizabeth, Sarah and Catharine Rowley, their heirs or either of their heirs or assigns shall desire.

In witness whereof, the said parties have herunto interchangeably set their hands and seals this 13th of June 1707. Signed, sealed and delivered in the presence of Edward Hall, John Knox, Mary Rowley, Elizabeth Rowley, Sarah Rowley, Catharine Rowley, Jeane Moore, William Moore." From the clause binding them to divide the land into well-arranged parks and to build sufficient houses, it would appear that the townland was in a waste and desolate state at the time the memorandum was made.

The "dearpark pails" mentioned in the second extract were the wooden pails that surrounded the deerpark or ornamental grounds of the house. This lease never was perfected.

Family Traditions

There is a tradition relating to the Moore family as follows: Sir Phelim O'Neill, when he was encamped upon Brockagh in the parish of Kilcronaghan, had granted a pass or warrant of safety to James Moore, an English trumpeter who had settled in the district. However, 6 of his own men came to him, James Moore, one day and, having decoyed him out with a pretended message from Sir Phelimy, they fell upon him in a retired hollow of the country and killed him. Their commander, as in honour bound, hung all the murderers upon a stone that projected out of the wall of Kilcronaghan church. Moore's wife immediately fled in dismay towards Coleraine. She was overtaken by the pains of labour on her journey and her son, the ancestor of the present family, was born in the snow on the top of the Car hill near Garvagh. A passer-by, hearing her moans, took them into his house and sheltered them until the country became more tranquil.

This Mrs Moore and her child are the Jane and William Moore of the foregoing memorandum with the Rowleys.

Castles

O'Hagan's castle was, according to the local tradition, built by Shane More O'Hagan. He was succeeded by William O'Hagan, his son, and then by Owen Roe O'Hagan. It is said to have been burned on a fair day of Kilcronaghan.

The only members of the family at present existing are 5 farmers in the south of the county and the Revd Edward O'Hagan, parish priest of Tobermore.

This castle was afterwards inhabited by the Rowleys and altered according to a more modern taste. It became Calmore Castle.

The site is a picturesque one and is capable of being much improved as to its beauty by judicious planting. If a mansion house is ever erected in the neighbourhood of Tobermore, on the contested estate spoken of under the head Obstructions to Improvement, it would be a very good situation to choose. See Habits of the People for some motives which would even make it popular.

Miscellaneous Discoveries

The drawings represent the different specimens in the collection of Mr Knox, the rector. An old brass spur of large size was found several years ago in some flow bog in Moneyshanere, 1 and a half feet under the surface, by Robert Moore. He sent it to the Dublin museum.

There is a tradition that a battle was fought at that townland between the O'Hagans, who then ruled at Tobermore, and the O'Neills of Tyrone, who had come ravaging down the country from Ballynascreen.

An ancient Irish gold ornament was also found in this parish and is now in the possession of William Stewart Esquire of Killymoon near Cookstown. Also an old felt hat, shapeless but with a very broad leaf, found in a bog, 15 feet under the surface and now in the cabinet of the Revd James Spencer Knox. It is yellow and of the usual dimensions of a hat.

2 poles, as thick as a spade shaft, with the form of a cross cut on the top of each, were discovered 2 feet under the surface of a flow bog in the townland of Mormeal. They are, however, now lost.

An ancient brass spearhead of the usual form, found in a cut-away part of the bog in the townland of Coolsarragh, is represented in the drawings. Along with it is represented a flint arrowhead from Tobermore, cut with remarkable symmetry and precision. It is drawn full size.

In a little flat, partly covered with bog, in the townland of Calmore, containing 5 acres Cunningham measure, which had been formerly a lake, there was found in April 1835 a canoe or

Ancient boat from Calmore

flat-bottomed boat of oak and hollowed from the trunk of a tree. The bottom of the boat was 4 feet from the surface of the bog, in which the turf-cutters have gone down 11 feet without coming to the substratum. The ground round the edge of the lough is sandy.

No nail or iron work is visible anywhere in the workmanship of this boat. It has been altogether hollowed out from the trunk of a tree. Some decayed oak boards were found that had apparently served as seats, as there are small ledges left in the sides to support them on. An oar was also found, of the form represented in the margin and having the dimensions of an ordinary oar [drawing of an oar].

About 50 years ago the grandfather of the farmer on whose land this place is situated found, 200 feet to the north east and on the same flat, another canoe, in the same form and made in the same manner but much smaller.

60 years ago this bog is remembered to have been a very shallow lake full of wild ducks. Fir and oak piles have been found driven down along the shore, apparently to prevent it from crumbling down, and in the interior fir and oak blocks and sticks have been found at different depths and in various directions.

There is a small round hole at the bottom filled with a wooden peg, by which the boat seems to have been scuttled and sunk at different times. It is now in the possession of the Revd J. Spencer Knox, rector of the parish, and will be soon covered by him with a shed from the influence of the wind and weather. From the smoothness with which it is hollowed out it would appear that the tools used were not of so primitive a construction or so early a date as would naturally be inferred from its rude formation. It is believed by the country people to have been either a pleasure boat or fishing boat belonging to the Tobermore Castle.

MODERN TOPOGRAPHY

General Appearance and Scenery

The most attractive characteristic of the general appearance and scenery of this parish is the endless variety produced by the numerous hills with which its surface is broken. This produces so many changes that, though none of the prospects

Parish of Kilcronaghan

partake in the least degree of the grand or magnificent, yet by their multiplicity, combined with their general resemblance to one another as to farmhouses and their attendant fields, there is produced on the whole a pastoral and pleasing character. The mountain Sliabh Gallion is constantly seen to the south overtopping all. It has, though not a bold, a picturesque outline and consequently contributes greatly to the ornament of the parish.

SOCIAL ECONOMY

Early Improvements

Kilcronaghan has been affected with respect to the progress of its improvement by the same causes as the neighbouring district of Desertmartin. Though separated by a parochial division, yet in matters not ecclesiastical they are similar. From Desertmartin westward, this head of the Social Economy does not begin to change until the valley of the Moyola is approached, that is, until an entry is made into the parish of Ballynascreen, in which district the Irish preponderate to a greater degree.

The Drapers' Company have been the most useful of the landlords.

There are no cattle shows or premiums for agricultural instruments. The inhabitants find a ready vent for their produce in the neighbouring fairs and markets of Draperstown, Magherafelt and their own village of Tobermore.

Obstructions to Improvement

The chancery lawsuit which has been going on between Ball and Company of Dublin and Sir George Hill has operated as an obstruction to the improvement of the village of Tobermore, which stands upon the estate disputed. The tenants for a length of time refused to pay rent at all to any person, giving it as their reason that they had not sufficient security in their receipts against a repetition of the demand for the same year's rent. Now, however, they pay to Rowley Miller Esquire, agent to the Drapers' Company, according to the direction of the court and are gradually improving the exterior appearance of their houses.

There are no other disputes or obstructions.

Local Government

John Stevenson Esquire of Fort William is a magistrate firm and respected by the people. There is no police, either revenue or constabulary, nor are there any manor courts. Illicit distillation does not prevail. There have been no outrages for many years, except a few assaults in the street of Tobermore on the persons of those who came to collect rent.

Dispensaries

There is no dispensary. The people resort to Ballynascreen or Maghera for medicine and advice. The parish is healthy.

Schools

See tables for particulars of schools. The good effect of Sunday schools has been made evident to disinterested individuals by the good effect, in a religious point of view, produced in the minds of their parents by those children who were in habit of attending at them.

Poor

There are no charitable institutions or legacies for the poor of this parish. They receive relief from the poor box collection at church, which amounts to 8 pounds 10s per annum at an average. This does not include the contributions of the rector or curate. It is distributed at Christmas and Easter.

There are but 8 actual paupers known within the parish of Kilcronaghan. Those who receive alms at the houses of the wealthier inhabitants are, except these 8, all strangers; but though the paupers are few, the poor are many. 20 names are on the church poor's list. The cause of the small number of these paupers or beggars is the feeling of respectability which pervades all classes and hinders them from wandering when reduced to poverty.

With respect to the comparative poverty and wealth of different townlands, it may be stated that Brackagh Rowley is the poorest and Drumballyhagan the wealthiest. In the latter there are the largest farms and in the former the greatest proportional number of tenants.

Of the names on the church list, all but 2 are females. The majority are Church Protestants. The number is never allowed to exceed 20, but those for whom there is no room on the list are allowed a small trifle notwithstanding. Old age and the death of husbands are the general causes of each individual case. None have been reduced to poverty by drunkenness. One of the men was admitted on account of his having accidentally broken his legs in a limestone quarry.

The churchwarden states that there were more applicants to get on this list 10 years ago than there are now. In 1826 there were 8 applicants for admission, in 1836 only 3. The several vacancies produced in the list by death or otherwise are filled up from these extra names.

The comparative scarcity of applications in 1836, when coupled with their absence in intermediate years, seems to indicate a diminution of poverty in the district.

Religion

In this parish there are 505 of the Established Church, 1,343 (Synod of Ulster) Presbyterians, 1,785 Roman Catholics, 553 other Protestant Dissenters, [total] 4,186.

Presbyterians

The Revd William Brown's Presbyterian congregation of Tobermore is composed of persons from the parishes of Kilcronaghan, Ballinderry, Maghera, Termoneeny, Ballynascreen and Desertmartin. From the first and second there are 1,125, from the third 72, from the fourth 47, from the fifth 382 and the sixth 18, making in all a total of 1,644 members.

The Ballynascreen part will soon be detached and formed into a distinct congregation with a permanently settled minister from the Synod of Ulster.

Roman Catholics and Seceders

The Roman Catholics and Seceders resort to places of worship in the adjoining parishes.

Baptists

The congregation of the Revd Alexander Carson, minister of the commonly so called Baptist Church at Tobermore, is composed of persons from the parishes of Kilcronaghan, Ballynascreen, Termoneeny, Maghera, Killelagh, Ballinderry, Magherafelt, Desertmartin and a few from the town of Portglenone.

Mr Carson separated from the Synod of Ulster in 1805. He had been minister of the Presbyterian congregation of Tobermore from 1798 until that year. His tenets are peculiar and an explanation of them will be found in his works, of which there is a list added to this head.

There are 302 communicants in Mr Carson's congregation. These constitute his church and no new members are allowed to join them until they give evidence that they are influenced by the Spirit. The form of admission is similar to that of asking the banns of matrimony in the Church of England. When the day comes and no objection is made, Mr Carson admits the new members into his church by advancing from the pulpit and shaking hands with them.

This congregation does not wish to take any sectarian name. They desire to be distinguished only as the "Church at Tobermore," as the churches of the New Testament are usually designated. They are commonly called Baptists, but this name they reject as they do not refuse admission to those Christians who differ from them on the subject of baptism. Their order of worship, when they meet, is as follows: 1st, they meet by salutation according to the apostolical command, 2 Corinthians XIII chapter 12; 2nd, prayer; 3rd, singing; 4th, reading the Scriptures; 5th, prayer; 6th, singing; 7th, eating the Lord's Supper; 8th, singing; 9th, collection for the poor; after this in summer there is an intermission for 15 minutes; 10th, then singing again; 11th, prayer; 12th, exhortation by the brethren; 13th, preaching; 14th, prayer; 15th, singing, after which the church separates.

Income of the Clergy

The rector, the Revd James Spencer Knox, receives 350 pounds tithe composition from this parish.

The Presbyterian minister, the Revd William Brown, receives 75 pounds regium donum and 60 pounds stipend with 20 guineas annually from the Drapers' Company.

The income of the Revd Alexander Carson is derived from the voluntary contributions of his congregation. It fluctuates at and about 40 pounds per annum. The Drapers' Company present him with the rent of his farm, amounting to 10 pounds per annum, and the rector with his tithe and bog.

Habits of the People

The houses of the parishioners are of superior kind to those of the adjacent parish of Ballynascreen. On the Drapers' estate they exhibit at least an external cleanliness, from the punctuality with which they are obliged by their landlords to whitewash the walls. The farmhouses in the neighbourhood of Tobermore appear to be the most comfortable. They are all of stone with 2 rooms in general and a clock. Their food is good and their dress respectable but rather tawdry, especially among the Presbyterians. Longevity is not remarkable among the people, neither are early marriages.

The lower orders are very well instructed in religious subjects and indeed are generally intel-

Parish of Kilcronaghan

ligent and well informed. The following is a dialogue that accidentally took place between a stranger and a little boy of about 14, one of the parishioners. He addressed him thus: "I will give you a pear if you tell me where God is?" Answer: "I will give you 2 if you will tell me where he is not." "Can you tell me, is God big?" Answer: "He is that big, that he fills the whole world; and he is that wee that none of us can see him." The gentleman then asked him his religion, which was a Catholic, and gave him a shilling for his answer.

Traditions and Superstitions

The Bonfire hill (see Natural Features) has been so called on account of its being the usual place for burning fires on at St John's Eve.

There seems to be a great fondness for the memory of Calmore Castle. It probably originated from the beauty of the place.

The inhabitants have not a great deal of either legendary or traditionary stories among them. They believe in the occult virtues of the Ballynascreen bell and relate some instances of persons who suffered in consequence of swearing falsely upon it.

Payment of Rent

The inhabitants of Tobermore displayed a very unruly disposition with respect to the payment of their rents to Mr Miller of Moneymore. They resisted the pounding of their cattle, executed by him, with pitchforks and sundry other primitive implements of warfare. When they found that resistance was useless, they employed Mr Costello, one of the orators of the Corn Exchange, to litigate their cause at the Magherafelt sessions, but as may have been expected, their efforts in this way were unsuccessful also. It has been remarked that, though they were so long free of rent, none of them became, in the end, the least degree richer. Their rent money which, if saved every year, would have secured some of them a comfortable competence, found its way to the whiskey shops of the village and neighbourhood.

Emigration

The following are the number of persons who have emigrated to America from the parish of Kilcronaghan during the years 1834 and 1835.

1834: 1 male and 2 females under 10; 3 males and 1 female 10 and under 20; 8 males and 10 females 20 and under 30; 5 males and 1 female 30 and under 40; 1 male 40 and under 50; total 32.

1835: 1 male under 10; 3 males and 1 female 10 and under 20; 1 male and 2 females 20 and under 30; 2 females 30 and under 40; total 10.

2 males, the one 22 and the other 35, emigrated in 1835 to Van Diemen's Land.

Migration

There are of persons in the habit of migrating to England and Scotland from Brackagh Rowley 27, Mormeal 9, Tobermore 5, Tamnyaskey 4, Keenaght 3, Granny 2, Calmore 2, Moybegkirly 1, total 53. Of these, there are 11 Presbyterians and 6 Protestants of the Established Church.

Remarkable events: none.

Table of Schools by J. Bleakly

[Table contains the following headings: name, situation and description, when established, income and expenditure, physical, intellectual and moral education, number of pupils subdivided by age, sex and religion, name and religion of master and mistress].

Tobermore, situated in the village of Tobermore and held in a room which was formerly a public house, and thatched, 18 feet by 17 feet, in tolerable repair, established 1817; income: from the London Hibernian Society 6 pounds, from the Revd J. Spencer Knox, rector, 5 pounds, 6 pounds from pupils; expenditure: house rent paid by the master, 3 pounds 3s; physical education: none; intellectual education: books published by the London Hibernian Society with *Thompson's and Gough's Arithmetic* and *Murray's English grammar*; moral education: visited by the clergy of the Established Church, Authorised Version of Scriptures is taught and catechism on Saturday; number of pupils: males, 20 under 10 years of age, 15 from 10 to 15, 2 above 15, 37 total males; females, 6 under 10 years of age, 2 from 10 to 15, 8 total females; total number of pupils 45, 14 Protestants, 13 Presbyterians, 10 Roman Catholics, 8 other denominations; master Andrew Davidson, Established Church.

Tobermore Presbyterian school, held in the session house in the rear of the Presbyterian meeting house, established 1835; income: in connection with the Synod of Ulster, has yet received no salary from the synod, 5 pounds from pupils; physical education: none; intellectual education: *Universal spelling book and primer*, and *Gough's Arithmetic*; moral education: visited by the Presbyterian clergy only; number of pupils: males, 5 under 10 years of age, 19 from 10 to 15, 24 total males; females, 6 under 10 years of age, 6 total females; total number of pupils 30, 2 Protestants,

27 Presbyterians, 1 Roman Catholic; master William Milligan, Presbyterian.

Parish school, in the townland of Granny, on the leading road from Tobermore to Draperstown Cross, a good house, slated, 30 by 16 feet, 3 Gothic windows, 2 in front and 1 on the back, established 1825; income: 10 pounds from pupils; intellectual education: books published by the Kildare Place Society, *Murray's English grammar, Thompson's Arithmetic, Gough and Knowles*; moral education: visited by the clergy of the Established Church and Presbyterian clergy occasionally, Authorised Version is taught; number of pupils: males, 21 under 10 years of age, 19 from 10 to 15, 3 above 15, 43 total males; females, 15 under 10 years of age, 10 from 10 to 15, 2 above 15, 27 total females; total number of pupils 70, 28 Protestants, 20 Presbyterians, 2 Roman Catholics, 20 other denominations; master James Wass, Established Church.

Killytoney national school, on the old leading road from Tobermore to Desertmartin, a good house of stone, thatched, 15 feet by 14 feet, connected with the National Board since 1833, established 1826; income: from the National Board 10 pounds, 10 pounds from pupils; physical education: none; intellectual education: books published by the National Board; moral education: visited by the Roman Catholic clergy; number of pupils: males, 34 under 10 years of age, 6 from 10 to 15, 40 total males; females, 16 under 10 years of age, 3 from 10 to 15, 1 above 15, 20 total females; total number of pupils 60, 3 Protestants, 40 Presbyterians, 5 Roman Catholics, 12 other denominations; master John Allen, Presbyterian. Report for July 1836.

Sunday Schools

[Table contains the following headings: name, situation, when established, superintendent, number of teachers, number of scholars subdivided by sex and religion, hours of attendance, societies with which connected, observations].

Kilcronaghan Sunday school, held in the day schoolhouse, superintendents the Revd J. Spencer Knox, the rector, and the Revd John Thomas Paul, curate; 4 male and 2 female teachers, total 6; number of scholars: 50 Established Church, 33 Presbyterian, 3 Roman Catholic, 15 other denominations, 51 male, 47 female, total 98 [sic], 48 exclusively Sunday school scholars; hours of attendance: from 10 o'clock a.m. to 12 at noon; societies with which connected: books published by the Sunday School Society for Ireland; commences with prayer.

Tobermore Baptist or Independent Sunday school, held in the meeting house, established 1832, superintendents the Revd Alexander Carson, the minister, and John Wallace, farmer; 6 male and 6 female teachers, total 12; number of scholars: 8 Established Church, 10 Presbyterian, 4 Roman Catholic, 113 Independent, 55 male, 80 female, total 135, 39 exclusively Sunday school scholars; hours of attendance: from 10 till half past 11 o'clock a.m. and in the evening from half past 4 p.m. till 7 o'clock; societies with which connected: Sunday School Society for Ireland give books free, carriage excepted; commences with singing and prayer and concludes with the same.

Tullyroan Sunday school, held through the houses in the neighbourhood; superintendents: some of the teachers; 5 teachers, all male; number of scholars: 19 Established Church, 22 Presbyterian, 3 Roman Catholic, 8 Independent, 32 male, 20 female, total 52, 10 exclusively Sunday school scholars; hours of attendance: from 6 o'clock p.m. till 8 in summer and from 9 till 11 a.m. in winter; societies with which connected: the Sunday School Society for Ireland give books at a reduced price; commences with singing and prayer and concludes with the same.

Mormeal Sunday school, held through the neighbouring houses, established 1827, superintendent John Johnstone; 4 teachers, all male; number of scholars: 18 Established Church, 16 Presbyterian, 6 Roman Catholic, 16 male, 24 female, total 40, 30 exclusively Sunday school scholars; hours of attendance: from 7 o'clock till half past 9 a.m.; societies with which connected: the Sunday School Society gives books at a reduced price; commences with singing and prayer and concludes with the same.

Moneyshanare Sunday school, held through the houses in the townland, established 1824, superintendent Thomas Wallace; 2 teachers, both male; number of scholars: 6 Presbyterian, 5 Roman Catholic, 19 Independent, 15 male, 15 female, total 30, 15 exclusively Sunday school scholars; hours of attendance: from 6 till 9 o'clock p.m.; societies with which connected: Sunday School Society for Ireland gives books; commences with singing and prayer and concludes with the same.

Granny Sunday school, held through the neighbouring houses, established 1832, superintendent John Neilson; 3 teachers, all male; number of scholars: 7 Established Church, 20 Presbyterian, 23 other denominations, 40 male, 10 female, total 50, 13 exclusively Sunday school scholars; hours

Parish of Kilcronaghan

PRODUCTIVE ECONOMY

Mills

[Table] Near the village of Tobermore, built of stone and thatched, proprietor Andrew Wisner; breast wheel, fall of water 6 feet, diameter of water wheel 12 feet, breadth 1 foot 6 inches, diameter of cog wheel 6 feet 6 inches, single geared, wooden machinery, in bad repair; this mill can work all seasons of the year but in summer only 3 hours each day, on stream from Slieve Gallion mountain.

ANCIENT TOPOGRAPHY

Drawings by J. Stokes

Door of Kilcronaghan church showing pillars; view from the interior of the window, now filled up, in the west gable, 4 feet wide.

Brooch and stone rings from the collection of Revd J.S. Knox: 2 views of brooch, 2 and half inches long; 2 views of stone rings, depth three-quarters of an inch, width 1 and half inches, three-quarters of an inch thick.

Felt hat found in a bog, from the collection of the Revd J.S. Knox.

Part of an ancient stone bowl with an ornamented handle, in the collection of the Revd J.S. Knox, side and overhead views.

Spearhead found in the townland of Coolsarragh, 4 inches long; arrowhead, side view and section.

Ancient boat found in the townland of Calmore, side and overhead views, 23 feet 9 inches long, 3 feet wide.

MODERN TOPOGRAPHY

Bridges

The bridge at Fort William, and on the road from Tobermore to Maghera, has 4 arches, each 25 feet in the span. The parapets are 5 feet high and in good repair. The roadway is but 13 feet 8 inches broad. About 41 years ago the middle arch was swept away by an inundation of the river. At those times the water runs over the road at each end of the bridge.

Memorandum: in the Kilcronaghan Memoir a "Fort William bridge" has been already described. Let its name be changed to "the bridge over the Moyola, in the townland of Drumcrow."

Office Copy of Draft Memoir

NATURAL FEATURES

Hills

The highest part of the parish is at the south western extremity, in the townland of Gortahurk, 1,246 feet above the level of the sea, from which elevation it slopes gradually off towards the north east into the low gravelly hills which indent and diversify the greater portion of the parish.

Rivers

The Moyola river flows at its northern extremity, into which a few small rivulets fall which water the parish.

MODERN TOPOGRAPHY

Village of Tobermore

The village of Tobermore is situated in the north of the parish. It is a post town and has 9 fairs in the year but has no market; is very capable of improvement.

Communications

The principal roads crossing the parish are those from Moneymore and Magherafelt to Maghera and Dungiven. They are kept in good order, the materials for their construction and repair being everywhere in abundance.

Fair Sheets by Thomas Fagan, August and November 1836

HISTORY AND ANCIENT TOPOGRAPHY

Mrs Jane Moore

Mrs Jane Moore, wife of the late William Moore of Monishenare, who was at a former period waylaid and murdered by some of Phelim Roe O'Neill's army, in Falakeran within the above parish, was the Jane Moore who, on her flight to Coleraine, was delivered of a male child on the Fair hill, Maghera, or better known by Windmill hill. On hearing of her husband, the above Mr Moore, being murdered as aforesaid, she thought proper to fly to Coleraine where she might be protected from the relentless hands of a deadly enemy; but on getting the length of Maghera she was suddenly taken by travail, as above stated, safely delivered and conveyed safe to her intended destination, herself and child, by an old trustworthy servant, who betimes carried them both on his back. She is likewise the Jane Moore alluded to by Mr Stokes. 8th November 1836.

Ancient Castle

There is no local certainty of a second castle having been raised in Calmore, or occupied by any family, but that the castle locally said to have been founded by the O'Hagans and locally called Calmore ancient castle was subsequently occupied by the Rowley family.

Discoveries in Calmore Castle

There are some vestiges of this castle still to be seen, but in raising a portion of its ruins from time to time there have been several articles of iron, brass and copper found beneath the ruins. These articles were employed in some parts of the castle fixtures. Informants William and Charles Moore, John Campbell and others.

Ancient Church

Local tradition says that the ancient church of Kilcronaghan <Kilcronohan> was founded by a St Cronaugh, a bishop and son to a late king of Munster. The church and burial ground was subsequently dedicated to the saint's name and called in the Irish language Kille Cronaughan, but subsequently changed to Kilcronaghan, and gave name to the parish. It is likewise said that there was a nunnery beside the old church.

However, at the period of this church being overhauled and reduced to its present size, on raising tombs and ancient graves that stood in the interior, there were several skulls raised out, with silk skull caps on them, completely cemented to the skulls by time. There was also found in the same graves a number of gold rings and other jewels, supposed to have been worn by the nuns and buried with their remains in the body of the church. There was also found in one of the graves an ancient book, but the print quite defaced by time and damp. All these articles were again deposited with the skulls and other bones, by orders of the late Revd Mr Bryans, who was rector of the parish at the time.

There was an ancient water font in the church which has been taken away to his own place by Mr Robert Bryans of Gortahurk at some former period and where it is said to be at present. The old church was roofed with oak, timber and shingles, and the oak of so good a quality and in so good preservation that it was purchased by weavers for looms. Informants John Campbell, Francis Higgins and others.

History of Kilcronaghan and Tobermore Fairs

Local tradition says that there were 9 fairs annually held at, or in the neighbourhood of, Kilcronaghan old church, for which fairs there was a patent obtained and were for a series of years published in the almanacks, under the title of the "church town fairs;" but the dates of the year on which held is not in the recollection of the local inhabitants. However, at some former period the proprietors of Tobermore and its neighbourhood purposed to change the fair to the last-mentioned town; but such efforts on their part proved fruitless for many years till taken up by a Revd Roger Grimes, who was parish priest of Kilcronaghan and Desertmartin at that period.

How he established the fair, was to solicit the attendance of the parishioners of the 4 neighbouring parishes to the town of Tobermore, on each of a number of retrenched holy days, on which days the town was well supplied in eatables and drinkables. This attendance of the people continued to increase, till at length cattle and other commodities were brought to the town on these days and a regular fair established.

This Roger Grimes is interred in Desertmartin old churchyard. He died aged 101 years, 20 of which years he was captain in the army, 20 years seneschal <seniskel> of a manor court and 41 years parish priest of Kilcronaghan and Desertmartin. He was married previous his to ordination and had issue, one daughter. This gentleman retained his title in the army to his last moments and was locally called the Revd Captain Grimes. Informants Francis Higgins, Arthur Otterson and others, 9th November 1836.

Brass Ring and Discoveries

The above draft [drawing] represents the size, and approaches to the shape, of a brass ring found in 1836 about 5 feet beneath the surface, in the remains of an ancient lough in the townland of Calmore. The part extending above the circle only shows the size of an article suspended on the ring.

In the above remains of a lough, which at present is cut out for bog, there have been found from time to time several wooden vessels of odd shape but decayed when found. There was also

Parish of Kilcronaghan

found in the same bog in 1836 a large boat, constructed out of a solid oak stick, dimensions not given, as it stands at the Revd Spencer Knox's house at Maghera and can be accurately inspected. Informants James Atkinson and John Peden.

Brass Halbert

The annexed draft [drawing] approaches to the shape of a brass halbert found beneath the surface in the above parish and neighbourhood of Slieve Gallion in 1820. It measures 15 inches in length, as described by the finder. The Revd Francis Quin, parish priest of Omagh, has it at present in his possession, together with other brass instruments found from time to time in the above parish. Informants Henery Higgins and others.

False Swearings

A man of the name of Higgins, who lived in the townland of Gortahurk, was at some former period accused of stealing some articles from a neighbouring farmer, in the event of which accusation he procured the ancient bell that fell at Ballynascreen ancient church, in order to clear himself of the charge of theft brought against him. However, the result was that he brought the bell to the scene of accusation and made oath on it that he was innocent of the crime of which he was accused; but immediate mental derangement was his fate, in which state he continually suffered during the remainder of his life, as does also 2 of his offspring who live within the above parish at present.

There is also in the above parish at present a woman suffering from mental derangement for many years past, in consequence of having made a voluntary, but unlawful, oath on the aforesaid bell, in the event of being accused of pregnancy.

All the aforesaid misfortunes are locally attributed to false swearing on the bell. Informants Michael Kelly, Francis Higgins and others, 10th November 1836.

Ancient Castle

The ruins of Calmore ancient castle stands about 300 yards from the town or village of Tobermore. Local tradition says that the above castle was built by Shane More O'Hagan, who was at some former period the proprietor of the Drapers' proportion, together with other tracts of land, within the above county. The castle was subsequently inhabited by Sir William O'Hagan, son of the above Shane More O'Hagan, and afterwards by Owen Roe O'Hagan Esquire, likewise by some of the Rowley family. However, at some period subsequent to the rebellion of 1641 the castle was consumed on a fair day of Tobermore.

The only members of the family of the above O'Hagans at present known in this part of the above county are 5 farmers and the Revd Edward O'Hagan, parish priest of Drumachose. Information obtained from Daniel O'Hagan, Michael Otterson and others, 3rd August 1836.

Artificial Island and Discoveries

In the remains of the ancient lough that stood in Calmore, near to the site of the ancient castle, and which remains has been cutting out in turf for some years back, there have been discovered beneath its surface at some former period the ruins of an artificial island, constructed on an oak frame composed of large logs and planks bound together by mortices and wooden pins. The frame approaches to a circle and of a tolerable large size, and enclosed by long poles standing upright and fastened in the frame by mortices.

There is a portion of the frame remains yet unmolested, but in raising parcels of it from time to time, there was found in the ruins several wooden vessels resembling small barrels, also a number of wooden bowls, in size sufficient to contain half a bushel, and various other articles made of wood, but all of these rudely constructed and in such a state of decay that on being removed they crumbled down into small pieces, but the frame and upright poles in so perfect a state that they were found most valuable for various purposes and brought high prices to those who lifted them.

There was also discovered beneath the surface, and seeming to lead from the dry land to the aforesaid island, a road made of small flinty limestones that must have been carried from some distant quarry. The road lies some feet beneath the surface and exceeding 12 feet in breadth, but partly destroyed. Informants James Hanna, John Campbell and others, 15th November 1836.

Executions at Old Church

Local tradition says that during the time that the assizes of the county was held in the town of Desertmartin, that all persons condemned to die were executed or hung from a stone that projected out some inches over the door of the old church of Kilcronaghan; likewise, during the rebellion in which Phelim Roe O'Neill was engaged, and even at subsequent periods that Kilcronaghan old church was the scene of executions. This stone remained in its original berth till the period of the church being overhauled and reduced to its present size. In this stone there was a gutter cut to embrace the rope or prevent it from slipping off the stone during the executions.

The blood of some of the persons executed at the above old church remained on the walls to a very late period; but for what design the aforesaid stone was originally placed in the church wall is not locally known, though it has been subsequently devoted to the aforesaid purpose. Information obtained from John Campbell, Francis Higgins and others. [Signed] Thomas Fagan, 11th November 1836.

Fair Sheets by J. Bleakly, July 1836

NATURAL FEATURES

Lakes

There are 24 small lakes in the townland of Brackagh Rowley, situated on small gravelly hills. The inhabitants are supplied with water from these lakes which are never dry. Information obtained from Robert Bryan Esquire and Patrick Kelly, 29th July 1836.

Bogs

The flow bog in the townland of Clooney was originally 10 feet deep but was all cut away, and is now cutting a second time and is 5 feet deep. The imbedded timber consists of fir and oak, the largest 2 feet in the [?] face in diameter and found with the top towards the east.

The flow bog in the glen between Tullyroan and Gortahurk is nearly all cut out, but no imbedded timber is found in it worth notice.

The small flow bog in the townland of Tamnyaskey and Culmore is 6 feet deep and consists of small oak and fir, and so rotten from the spring of water in the bog as to render them useless.

The flow bog, which is very small, in the townland of Gortamney is 10 feet deep. Small oak and fir is found in it but not worth notice. Killytoney flow bog is 6 feet deep. The imbedded timber consists of fir and oak, the largest 3 feet in diameter, point towards the north east. From Thomas Henry and Alexander White, 3rd July 1836.

MODERN TOPOGRAPHY AND SOCIAL ECONOMY

Roads

The leading road from Tobermore to the Cross is 21 feet broad clear of drains and fences, and in good repair, made by presentment and kept in repair by contract for 7 years at 1d ha'penny per perch by Thomas McKenna, assisted by Philip Kelly.

The road leading from Tobermore to Magherafelt is 21 feet clear of drains and fences, and in good repair by contract for 7 years at 8d per perch. Information obtained from Jackson Hessan, publican. 6th July 1836.

The leading road from Tobermore to Dungiven is 21 feet broad clear of drains and fences, and in good repair, made by presentment and kept in repair by contract for 7 years, at 2d ha'penny per perch by Michael McKenna of the parish of Maghera. This road, from its various windings, makes it much longer than it appears and which might be much improved, if the proprietors of the land would allow it, by making it further down; but the land being freehold property, the occupiers would not allow it to pass through the good part of their land at the time it was made.

The leading road from Magherafelt to Draperstown Cross is 21 feet clear of drains and fences, and in good repair, kept in repair by contract for 7 years by Loughlin McNamee of the Cross, at [blank] per perch. 12th July 1836.

The old leading road from Tobermore to Desertmartin is stopped up since 1830; and in order to avoid the hill at Bernard McGurk's house, a new line of road was made round the hill the same year, 1830, at the expense of the county, by presentment, and is 21 feet clear of drains and fences, and in good repair.

The road leading by the church from Magherafelt to Draperstown Cross is 21 feet clear of drains and fences, and in good repair at the expense of the county.

The by-road leading from the Tobermore road to the top of Brackagh Rowley mountain is from 15 feet to 30 feet broad, for the conveyance of turf from the mountain bog, part made by the county and part by the inhabitants, and in middling repair.

The leading road from Moneymore to Dungiven over the Old Forge bridge is 21 feet broad clear of drains and fences, and in good repair, made by presentment of the grand jury but kept in repair by contract for 7 years, at [blank] per perch by Loughlin McNamee and others.

Also the by-road from the above road through the townland of Moneyshanere and is 15 feet clear of drains and fences, part by the county and part by the Drapers' Company, and in good repair.

Parish of Kilcronaghan

The leading road from Tobermore to Curran is 21 feet clear of drains and fences, and in good repair, made by presentment 33 years ago and kept in repair by presentment of the grand jury.

The by-road leading from the church to the Magherafelt road is 15 feet broad clear of drains and fences, and in good repair, made by presentment at the expense of the county and for the accommodation of the inhabitants.

The road leading by the house of Robert Bryan Esquire through the townland of Gortahurk is now a by-road leading to the quarry, and kept in repair at the expense of the county.

The by-road leading to the mountain bog from the Moneymore leading road through Gortahurk is 15 feet broad clear of drains, and in good repair, made at the expense of the Drapers' Company.

The leading road from Moneymore to Draperstown is 21 feet clear of drains and fences, and in good repair, made by presentment but kept in repair by contract for 7 years, at 2d per perch by Loughlin McNamee.

The by-road leading from the Magherafelt road through Killytoney townland is 15 feet clear of drains and fences, and in good repair, made by presentment and kept in repair by contract by Loughlin McNamee.

Bridges

The bridge which divides Drumcrow from Lisnamuck in the parish of Maghera has 3 arches, each 18 feet in the span across the Moyola. It is 18 feet broad on the top; the walls are 4 feet high and 18 inches thick. This bridge, from the rapidity of the flood, was destroyed 3 times, in the rebuilding of which 3 men were accidentally killed. In 1834 it was repaired at the expense of the county and is at present only in a middling state of repair, as the walls are cracked in several places. 11th July 1836. [Insert marginal note: To be transferred; mem. to write to McGann].

The bridge called the Old Forge bridge spans the Moyola with 4 arches, each 21 and a half feet in the span and 15 and a half feet broad on the top. The walls are 4 feet high and in good repair at the expense of the county. This bridge divides the townland of Moybegkirly, parish of Kilcronaghan, from Drumconready, parish of Maghera, and was built 2 years before new style commenced; late repair on the walls 2 years ago. 14th July 1836.

Village of Tobermore

Tobermore is a small village situated between Maghera and Magherafelt, Castledawson and Draperstown, 2 miles from Maghera, 4 from Magherafelt, 4 from Castledawson and 3 from Draperstown. The street is 75 feet wide and contains 130 houses, 10 2-storey high and 120 1-storey high. The oldest stone wall house at present standing is opposite the Independent meeting house and was built in 1727.

Presbyterian Meeting House

The Presbyterian meeting house is situated in the centre of the village of Tobermore and was built in 1728. There are 2 rows of windows, oblong, each 2 and a half by 4 feet, 14 on the lower part of the meeting house, viz. 6 on the front, 8 on the back, and 7 on the gallery. The lower part contains 35 pews, 3 of which are double, each 9 feet by 5 feet, the other 32 single pews, each 9 feet by 3 feet. The gallery contains 30 single pews, each 11 and a half by 3 feet, all in tolerable repair. The roof is not ceiled. The aisle is 5 and a half feet wide, not flagged but of earth. There are 3 doors on the lower part, oblong, each 3 and a half feet broad. The entrance to the gallery is outside by stone steps with 2 doors, 1 on each end, 3 feet wide, arched on top with glass.

On a stone over the front door is the following inscription on the front [drawing of tablet]: "R.H. Esq. 1728 H heciss B." There is an iron gate 9 feet wide. The wall is only at the front and at the east end, and is 6 feet high. The oldest gravestone is dated 1803. The pulpit is at the centre of the meeting house.

The Presbyterian meeting house was nearly new roofed in 1825 and 2 abutments put to the back side wall to prevent it falling. The seats were all repaired in 1831 at the expense of the Drapers' Company, and cost 50 pounds. This is the first Presbyterian meeting house in Tobermore. From Jackson Hessan, publican, and Andrew Davidson. 8th July 1836.

Original Presbyterian Clergy

The following are the original Presbyterian clergy of the parish of Kilcronaghan: 1st, the Revd Wray; 2nd, the Revd Turretine; 3rd, the Revd James Whiteside; 4th, the Revd Alexander Carson, who commenced in 1698 [1798] or '99 and continued until 1805, when he separated from the Presbyterian congregation and formed an Independent congregation in the village of Tobermore. From 1805 till 1810 the congregation was without a stationed minister, during which interval the congregation was supplied with ministers by the Synod of Ulster. 5th, the Revd William Brown, who commenced in 1810 and still continues, and whose residence is in the parish of Ballynascreen and townland of Duntybrian.

The Worshipful the Drapers' Company gives to the Presbyterian minister, the Revd William Brown, 10 guineas per annum.

Presbyterian Congregation

The Revd William Brown's congregation is composed of persons from the following parishes, viz. Kilcronaghan and Ballinderry 1,125, Maghera 72, Termoneeny 47, Ballynascreen 382 and Desertmartin 18, total 1,644. 19th July 1836.

Independent Meeting House

There is an Independent meeting house at the upper part of the village, which was built in 1814 at the expense of the congregation and cost [blank] pounds. [Insert note: The cost of building the Independent meeting house cannot be ascertained as part was by manual labour]. It contains 45 pews at the lower part, 2 of which are double, each 9 by 5 feet, and 43 single pews, each 9 by 2 feet 4 inches, all in good repair. The aisle is only 2 feet 9 inches wide. There are 8 windows, each oblong and 2 and a half by 5 feet, viz. 5 on the front, 1 on the back and 1 on each end of the gallery.

The pulpit is at the centre of the back side, with a small door leading to the small session room. There are 2 oblong doors, viz. one on the end next to the street and the other on the side, each door 2 feet 3 inches by 6 feet 3 inches. The gallery is at each end with stairs leading from the aisle inside. There are 10 single pews at each end, i.e. each gallery, each pew 8 and a half by 2 and a half feet; total pews on the gallery 20.

The pews of the gallery are nearly level with the side walls, which renders it unpleasant for those who sit at each end of the pews, as they cannot sit erect from the lowness of the roof. Necessity, from the crowded congregation, compelled them to erect these galleries: an additional aisle would have been much better. Total dimensions outside 65 by 25 feet in the clear. The materials are at present on the ground to build a wall round the meeting house but no yard attached.

This is the first Independent meeting house known in this parish.

Income of the Clergy

The income of the Revd William Brown, Presbyterian minister, is 75 pounds regium donum and 60 pounds stipend. His residence is in the townland of Duntybrian, parish of Ballynascreen.

The income of the Revd Alexander Carson, Independent minister, is fluctuating and depends entirely on the liberality of the congregation, as he receives nothing but from the congregation.

Kilcronaghan Church

Kilcronaghan church is situated near the minister's house in the townland of [blank] and is very old, but was rebuilt in 1806, i.e. a new roof and an east gable, but was formerly 21 feet longer at the east end. The church contains 8 double pews, each 7 by 8 feet, the aisle 4 feet wide. There are 3 Gothic windows, 2 on the front, each 4 feet wide, and 1 on the east end 5 and a half feet wide, and 2 doors on the west end, 1 on the porch and 1 inside, each 3 and a half feet by 6 feet; total dimensions outside is 42 and a half by 25 feet, all in middling repair. The pulpit and reading desk is at the east end, 1 at each end of the communion table, with a baptismal font of cut freestone; the aisle is flagged. 13th July 1836.

A cross similar to that on the Glenn Roman Catholic chapel is on the east gable and was put up by order of the Revd William Bryan, who was then rector of the parish, as it formerly stood on the same end of the old church. There is a bell and belfry on the west end but no steeple. The outside door is of the Gothic style and formed of cut stone in 4 columns of very ancient appearance.

Over the inside door is the following inscription: "Rebuilt 1806, Revd William Bryan, rector, James Stevenson Esquire and Thomas Jackson, churchwardens."

Monument at Church

An ancient monument which formerly stood inside the church before it was rebuilt, but is now outside at the east end, and erected to the memory of the members of the Henderson family in 1715, and written in Latin, and which appears to be the oldest in the graveyard. The wall is only at the front and is 4 feet 3 inches high with an iron gate and piers.

Income of the Rector

The income of the rector of the parish of Kilcronaghan, the Revd J. Spencer Knox, from the parish of Kilcronaghan, is 350 pounds tithe composition and 150 pounds glebe house and land, total 500 pounds.

Parish of Kilcronaghan

Income of the Curate

The income of the Revd John Thomas Paul, curate of Kilcronaghan, amounts to 80 guineas per annum, paid by the rector, the Revd J. Spencer Knox, with a good house, 2-storey high, and 3 acres of a gort attached a few yards from the church.

Collection for the Poor

The average collection for the poor in the church of Kilcronaghan amounts only to 2s each Sunday.

Baptist Meeting House

The Worshipful the Drapers' Company gave towards the building of the meeting house the first grant 20 pounds, second grant 25 pounds, Robert Holden Esquire, Edinburgh, 10 pounds, from friends in Letterkenny 5 pounds, the remainder by local subscription of the inhabitants. 15th July 1836.

Baptist Congregation

There are 302 persons who break bread or communion together in the Baptist congregation. The meeting house is crowded every Sunday and contains about 570 persons. The remainder, from 302 to 570, are nominal members, who are not admitted into the church until they are influenced by the Spirit, which is generally known by their walk and conversation. The form of admission is like calling or publishing the banns of matrimony in the Church of England, and are proposed by some one or more of the members of the church in the presence of the congregation.

"The above congregation, of which the Revd Alexander Carson is pastor, does not wish to take any sectarian name and desires to be distinguished only as the Church at Tobermore, as the churches in the New Testament are usually designated. They are usually called the Baptist church but this designation is not proper as they do not refuse admission to the Christians who differ from them on the subject of baptism, and a church of Christ should not be designated from any [blank], none but such as are employed in the Holy Scriptures."

Catalogue of Works

The following is a catalogue of the works published by the Revd Alexander Carson.

1. Reasons for separating from the General Synod of Ulster, 1806.
2. Remarks on a late pastoral address from the ministers of the Synod of Ulster to the people under their care, 1806.
3. Reply to Mr Brown (of Scotland's) "Vindication of the Presbyterian Form of Church Government," 1807.
4. Answer to Mr Ewing's attempt towards a statement of the doctrine of Scripture on some disputed points respecting the constitution, government, worship and discipline of the Church of Christ, 1809.
5. A view of the Day of Judgement as delineated in the Scriptures, 1818.
6. The truth of the gospel demonstrated from the character of God manifested in the atonement, 1820, second edition 1826, in a letter to Mr Richard Carlile.
7. Remarks on the late miracles of Prince Hohenlohe, in a letter to Doctor Doyle, 1822.
8. Strictures on the letters of J.K.L., entitled "A Vindication of the Religious and Civil Principles of the Irish Catholics," addressed to His Excellency the Marquis Wellesley K.G., Lord Lieutenant General and General Governor of Ireland, in a letter to the same nobleman, 1823.
9. The right and duty of all men to read the Scriptures, being the substance of a speech intended to be delivered at the meeting of the Carlow Bible Society, containing a refutation of several facts of a late pamphlet of J.K.L., entitled "Letters on the State of Education and Bible Societies," 1824.
10. The doctrine of transubstantiation subversive of the foundation of human belief; therefore incapable of being proved by any evidence or of being believed by men under the influence of common sense, 1825, second edition 1836.
11. A letter to the Right Revd [Hon.] William C. Plunket, His Majesty's Attorney-General for Ireland, containing strictures on some facts of his late speech on the Roman Catholic question in the House of Commons, touching the Cavan Reformation, 1827.
12. The incompetency of the Revd Professor Lee of Cambridge, for translating or correcting translations of the Holy Scriptures proved and illustrated in a criticism on his remarks on Doctor Henderson's appeal to the Bible Society, 1829.
13. Answers to the letters of the Revd Professor Lee, in reply to the proof and illustrations of his incompetency for translating or correcting translations of the Holy Scriptures.
14. A treatise on the figure of speech, 1827.
15. Review of the Revd Doctor J. Pye Smith's defence of Dr Haffner's preface to the Bible and of his denial of the divine authority of part of the

canon and of the full inspiration of the Holy Scriptures, 1827.

16. The theories of inspiration of the Revd Daniel Wilson (now Bishop of Calcutta), Revd Doctor Pye Smith and the Revd Doctor Dick proved to be erroneous, with remarks on the *Christian Observer* and *Eclectic Review*.

17. Reply to Doctor Drummond's essay on the doctrine of the Trinity, in a letter to the author.

18. Refutation of the review in the *Christian Guardian* for January 1832 of Mr Carson's work on the inspiration of the Holy Scriptures, 1832.

19. Baptism or its mode and subjects considered, and the arguments of Mr Ewing and Doctor Wardlaw refuted, 1831.

20. Answer to the article in the *Edinburgh Presbyterian Review* on Mr Carson's refutations of Mr Ewing and Doctor Wardlaw on baptism, showing the incompetency and ignorance of the reviewer, 1832.

21. Review of the Revd Mr Brown's work on baptism, 1834.

22. Defence of the review of Mr Brown's work on baptism, 1835.

23. Review of the discussion on the Unitarian controversy, between the Revd John Scott Porter and the Revd Daniel Bagot A.M., held in Belfast on April 4th 1834 and the 3 following days, 1834.

24. History of Providence as unfolded in the Book of Esther, 1833, second edition 1836.

25. The God of Providence, the God of the Bible, or the truth of the gospel proved from the peculiarities of its progress, 1835.

26. Examination of the principles of biblical interpretation of Ernesti, Ammon, Stuart and other philologists, 1836.

Income of Minister

The income of the Revd Alexander Carson, Baptist minister of Tobermore, is supposed to amount to about 40 pounds per annum paid by the congregation, who are chiefly poor persons, which is the reason why the minister is so poor and could hardly support his family except by his writings. The Worshipful the Drapers' Company make him a present of 10 guineas per annum of his rent. Also Mr Knox makes him a present of the tithe and bog.

The congregation is composed of persons from the parishes of Kilcronaghan, Ballynascreen, Termoneeny, Maghera, Killelagh, Ballinderry, Magherafelt, Desertmartin and a few from Portglenone. Information obtained from the Revd Alexander Carson, minister, and John Wallace, farmer. 21st July 1836.

Baptist Meeting House

The pews in the Baptist meeting house are free to the hearers' roll.

Residence of Minister

The residence of the Revd Alexander Carson, Baptist minister, is in the townland of Coolsarragh and is called Solitude, near the leading road from Tobermore to Magherafelt. Solitude is a name given to it by the proprietor.

Revd Brown's Books

Books written by Revd William Brown, Presbyterian minister of Tobermore.

1. Baptism by pouring or sprinkling, together with infant baptism, vindicated by William Brown, minister of Tobermore, 1833.

2. A refutation of Mr Carson's review of the Revd Mr Brown's work on baptism by William Brown A.M., 1834.

3. Remarks on Mr Carson's defence of his review by the Revd William Brown, Tobermore, 1835.

New Meeting House

There is a new meeting house in contemplation in parish Ballynascreen which, when erected, will considerably reduce the Presbyterian congregation of Tobermore. From the Revd William Brown, Presbyterian minister, and Jackson Hessin, publican. 27th July 1836.

Houses in Tobermore

The reason why the houses in the village of Tobermore (which are nearly all built of brick) are in so bad repair is chiefly owing to its not having a head proprietor, but is in the hands of the court of chancery, and who have appointed Messrs Rowley and John Rowley Miller agents. 26th July 1836.

2-Storey House

The 2-storey house on the leading road from Magherafelt to Draperstown was built this year, 1836, by Arthur Auterson.

Flax Mill

There is a new flax mill at present in operation in the townland of Moneyshanere by Samuel Walker, and will be shortly finished.

Corn Mill

A corn mill formerly stood in Gortahurk about 12

Parish of Kilcronaghan

years ago, but was maliciously burned by night and has not been rebuilt since, on the farm of George Orr. Information obtained from Robert Bryan Esquire and Robert McBride. 28th July 1836.

Fort William

Fort William is the residence of John Stevenson Esquire. The house is 3-storey high, built in the year '95, situated near the village of Tobermore, about 2 miles from Maghera and takes its name from a fort which is at the rear of the dwelling house, planted with forest trees. The planting consists of fir, ash, sycamore, beech and alder, the oldest upwards of 100 years planted, the general planting between 20 and 30 years planted.

Residence of Robert Bryan

The old 2-storey house on the by-road in the townland of Gortahurk was built in 1721 by Captain Boyde but is now the quite neglected residence of Robert Bryan Esquire, whose father was the former rector of this parish. The artificial planting consists of fir, beech, ash, birch and all manner of forest trees, planted 1810. The natural consists of oak, ash, hazel and birch.

Fort William

Fort William is the residence of John Stevenson Esquire. The house is 3-storey high, situated near the village of Tobermore and about 2 miles from Maghera. The fort from which the place takes its name is situated at the rear of the house and all planted with forest trees, circular and 139 feet in diameter. The parapet is 6 feet high, the trench is 14 feet wide and well fenced.

PRODUCTIVE AND SOCIAL ECONOMY

Trades and Occupations: Tobermore

The following are the trades and occupations: publicans 6, grocers 5, shoemakers 5, tailors 5, weavers 8, dressmakers 8, coopers 1, wheelwrights 2, slaters 1, flax dressers 4, blue dyers 1, watchmakers 1, glaziers and painters 2, bakers 1, surgeons 2, post office and leather store 1, pensioners 4, painter and glazier 1, barbers 1, hucksters 4, schoolmasters 2, schoolmistress 1, cottiers 47, small farmers 119, Presbyterian meeting house 1, Independent meeting house 1, nailers 5, blacksmiths 2, butchers 2, thatcher 1, medical repository 1.

Post Office

The post office was established about 50 years ago and is a daily general post; arrivals from Dublin at 11.30 a.m. and from Coleraine at 1 o'clock. From James Christy, postmaster, and others. 7th July 1836.

Conveyances

There are 2 post cars and 2 horses for hire, when called on, in the village of Tobermore. The mail coach passes through the village from Dungannon to Coleraine daily, one up and the other down.

Fairs

There are 9 fairs held annually in Tobermore, viz. one on 17th January, 17th February, 28th March and one on the Monday before New May, and one on 31st May, 5th July, 12th August, 19th October and one on 11th December, for the sale of black cattle of all sorts, viz. horses, cows, sheep, pigs, goats, yarn, delph and fruit in the season, a little mutton, soft goods of all sorts and some hardware.

There is no custom paid at these fairs. The custom ceased at the same time it ceased in Maghera. As there was no legal authority for collecting it, the people very justly refused to pay it.

Census of the Parish

Established Church 505, Presbyterians 1,343, Roman Catholics 1,785, other Protestant Dissenters 553, total 4,186.

Encroachment of River

A plan to prevent the Moyola from encroaching on the land is in operation for the last 7 years, and was introduced by John Stevenson Esquire of Fort William near Tobermore in this parish and by Smylie Paul of the parish of Maghera, and is at present in operation by Hugh Lyle of Clooney in this parish and on his farm, by making what is called creels, composed of stakes driven into the river and projecting so far as to prevent the rapidity of the flood from taking away the good land. Sods of clay and bushes are put between those stakes and are generally commenced above the windings, and continued so far as the stream is likely to encroach on the land, and those creels are placed a short distance from each other, so as to break off or lessen the rapidity of the stream. Hugh Lyle has for the last 8 days gained about 2 square perches of land to his farm from the river. Many of the inhabitants lose a considerable quantity of land from neglect of this practice.

Superstitions of the People

The Roman Catholics of this country at large do not think an oath taken on the Bible so binding as if taken on their own manual or prayer book.

The superstitious do not mix the milk of one quarter with that of another quarter, lest their cows should be blinked, as it is believed that mixing the milk is the reason of so many cows being blinked. Not even a single drop of the last quarter milk will be mixed with that of the next, in any one way, either sweet milk or buttermilk.

Social Meetings

There is a social meeting held in the townland of Mormeal thro' the houses in that townland, and consists of an unlimited number of members, 5 years established and held on Sunday evenings only.

There is also another social meeting held in the townland of Granny and consists also of an unlimited number of members; established 3 years.

There is also one held in Coolsarragh, 3 years established, and also consists of an unlimited number of members. From John Johnstone, schoolmaster.

Emigration in 1834

List of persons who have emigrated from the parish of Kilcronaghan during the year 1834. [Table contains the following headings: name, age, religion, year left the country, townland, port to which emigrated].

Jane Gilmour, 23, Nancy Gilmour, 20, Established Church, from Tobermore to Quebec.

Eliza McKeever, 18, Presbyterian, from Tobermore to Quebec.

Sara Wright, 21, Presbyterian, from Tobermore to Quebec.

Hannah Laird, 22, Presbyterian, from Tobermore to Quebec.

John Hughs, 34, Presbyterian, from Moyesset to Quebec.

Anne Devlin, 20, Roman Catholic, from Killynumber to Quebec.

Thomas Neely, 25, Presbyterian, from Cloyfin to Philadelphia.

Sarah Clarke, 20, Presbyterian, from Tamnyaskey to Philadelphia.

Archy Campbell, 22, Charles Campbell, 17, Robert Campbell, 25, Presbyterians, from Granny to Quebec.

William McKee, 18, Presbyterian, from Granny to Philadelphia.

Jane Espy, 20, Sarah Espy, 22, David Espy, 19, Presbyterians, from Granny to Philadelphia.

James McCartney, 30, Roman Catholic, from Tullyroan to Philadelphia.

Thomas Hart, 24, Mary Hart, 30, Presbyterians, from Mormeal to Philadelphia.

William Sheagog, 25, Established Church, from Brackagh Rowley to St John's.

Matthew Clarke, 45, Independent, from Drumballyhagan Clarke to St John's.

Michael McKeever, 35, Margaret McKeever, 37, Mary Ann McKeever, 5, Catherine McKeever, 3, John McKeever, 1, Roman Catholics, from Moybegkirly to New York.

James Higgins, 24, Roman Catholic, from Keenaght to Philadelphia.

Denis Regan, 33, Roman Catholic, from Keenaght to Philadelphia.

Sarah Higgins, 24, Roman Catholic, from Keenaght to Philadelphia.

Bridget Kearney, 21, John Kearney, 28, Roman Catholics, from Keenaght to Philadelphia.

John Lyle, 35, Independent, from Tullyroan to Philadelphia.

Henry George McKee, 20, Independent, from Tullyroan to Philadelphia.

William Stewart, 20, Independent, from Tullyroan to Philadelphia.

Emigration in 1835

Emigration from parish of Kilcronaghan in 1835.

[Crossed out: William Lesly, 23, Established Church, from Granny to Glasgow.

John McCart, 36, Established Church, from Mormeal to Glasgow].

James McWilliams, 19, Roman Catholic, from Mormeal to Philadelphia.

John McShane, 35, Roman Catholic, from Mormeal to Van Diemen's Land.

Patrick Henry, 22, Roman Catholic, from Mormeal to Van Diemen's Land.

[Crossed out: William Stewart, 28, Established Church, from Granny to Glasgow].

Matthew Stewart, 22, Jane Stewart, 25, Robert Stewart, 1, Established Church, from Granny to Glasgow.

Sarah McCart, 30, Established Church, from Granny to Glasgow.

Ellen Stewart, 20, Established Church, from Granny to Glasgow.

Sarah Neil, 30, Mary Neil, 28, James Neil, 17, John Neil, 19, Mary Neil, 15, Roman Catholics, from Drumsamney to Quebec.

Migration

List of persons who migrate annually from the parish of Kilcronaghan.

Parish of Kilcronaghan

James Hagan, 20, Patrick Hagan, 30, Roman Catholics, from Brackagh Rowley to Merryport in England.

John Murphy, 22, Roman Catholic, from Brackagh Rowley to Merryport.

Andrew Kelly, 20, Patrick Kelly, 22, Roman Catholics, from Brackagh Rowley to Merryport.

Patrick Carny, 27, Felix Carny, 35, Roman Catholics, from Brackagh Rowley to Merryport.

Peter McNamee, 35, Roman Catholic, from Brackagh Rowley to Merryport.

Michael Hagan, 30, Roman Catholic, from Brackagh Rowley to Merryport.

Michael McKeever, 25, Frank McKeever, 35, Roman Catholics, from Brackagh Rowley to Merryport.

Frank McGuician, 35, Patrick McGuician, 25, Roman Catholics, from Brackagh Rowley to Merryport.

Frank McGuigan, 32, John McGuigan, 30, Daniel McGuigan, 38, Roman Catholics, from Brackagh Rowley to Merryport.

Frank Magowan, 21, Roman Catholic, from Brackagh Rowley to Merryport.

James Trainer, 27, Roman Catholic, from Brackagh Rowley to Merryport.

Patrick O'Neil, 22, Roman Catholic, from Brackagh Rowley to Merryport.

Edward McBride, 23, Roman Catholic, from Brackagh Rowley to Merryport.

Michael McCristal, 40, Roman Catholic, from Brackagh Rowley to Merryport.

Michael Galligher, 35, Roman Catholic, from Brackagh Rowley to Merryport.

Patrick Kelly, 30, Andrew Kelly, 32, Roman Catholics, from Brackagh Rowley to Merryport.

James McGuigan, 45, Roman Catholic, from Brackagh Rowley to Merryport.

James Henry, 22, Roman Catholic, from Brackagh Rowley to Merryport.

Charles McCann, 38, Roman Catholic, from Brackagh Rowley to Merryport.

Daniel McKeever, cattle jobber, 35, Roman Catholic, from Gortahurk to Merryport.

Henry Bryan, cattle jobber, 25, Roman Catholic, from Gortahurk to Merryport.

Michael McWilliams, 28, Roman Catholic, from Keenaght to England.

James Bryan, cattle jobber, 28, Andrew Bryan, cattle jobber, 24, Roman Catholics, from Keenaght to England.

James Hannah, 35, Presbyterian, from Tobermore to Glasgow.

Peter Devlin, 25, Presbyterian, from Tobermore to Glasgow.

Ambrose Convery, 21, Presbyterian, from Tobermore to Glasgow.

Frank Callighan, 30, Presbyterian, from Tobermore to Glasgow.

Charles Colgan, 24, Presbyterian, from Tobermore to Glasgow.

Andrew Stewart, 40, Established Church, from Granny to Glasgow.

Hugh Toner, 30, Roman Catholic, from Mormeal to Glasgow.

James Crilly, 26, Roman Catholic, from Mormeal to Glasgow.

William Campbell, 25, Presbyterian, from Mormeal to Glasgow.

William Burnside, 25, Presbyterian, from Mormeal to Glasgow.

John Melon, 20, Presbyterian, from Mormeal to Glasgow.

George McCart, 26, Established Church, from Mormeal to Glasgow.

Patrick Toner, 50, Roman Catholic, from Mormeal to Glasgow.

Owen Hara, 20, Roman Catholic, from Mormeal to Glasgow.

James Stewart, 19, Established Church, from Mormeal to Glasgow.

John Devine, 40, Established Church, from Granny to Glasgow.

William Peady, 30, Established Church, from Tamnyaskey to Glasgow.

William Gibson, 25, Roman Catholic, from Tamnyaskey to Glasgow.

David Lyle, 36, Presbyterian, from Tamnyaskey to Glasgow.

William Perry, 32, Established Church, from Tamnyaskey to Glasgow.

John McCalister, 27, Roman Catholic, from Moybegkirly to England.

Thomas Bryans, 20, John Bryans, 22, Presbyterians, from Culmore to England.

ANCIENT TOPOGRAPHY

Forts

There is a fort of earth on the farm of James Fowler in the townland of Drumcrow, but is long since demolished, in the digging of which a quantity of Danes' pipes were found.

There is another fort of earth on the top of Mormeal hill, on the farm of Frank McKane. The fort is circular, 112 feet in diameter and about 8 feet high, but all sown with corn. Near this fort is a small lake and about 20 perches farther is another small lake in the same townland. A trigonometrical station is on the top of the fort. Rabbits have their burrows in this fort.

There is a fort of earth in the townland of Killynumber, on the farm of John Johnstone, but all demolished.

The fort of earth on the farm of John Payne in the townland of Coolsarragh is circular and 129 feet in diameter, and very high, i.e. on a high hill; the parapets are well fenced with hawthorn, entire east and west all sown with corn.

There is a fort of earth in the townland of Moneyshanere, on the farm of Thomas Wallace, on a hill in the rear of his house, which is circular and 75 feet in diameter but all planted with potatoes, and is 15 feet high with 2 trenches.

About 30 perches north west of the above fort there is another fort of earth in the same townland and is nearly circular, 75 feet in diameter. Part of the parapet is taken away for manure and is 10 feet high, on the farm of Samuel Sinclair. Information obtained from the proprietors.

Forts

There is a fort of earth in the townland of Brackagh Rowley, called the Black Fort, and is very high and nearly circular, 100 feet in diameter, on a very high hill. On the top is a trigonometrical station and undisturbed, on the farm of Andrew Kelly.

There is another fort of earth a considerable distance from the above, and in the townland of Tamnyaskey, in the rear of William Lyle's house and on his farm, near the church, and is nearly of an oval shape, 45 by 30 yards and all planted in the centre with young fir trees. The parapet and trenches are planted with large trees many years ago, but part of the trench is taken away for manure.

There is a fort of earth in the flow bog near the verge on a clay bank on the farm of Robert McDowell, in the townland of Clooney, and is nearly circular, 120 feet in diameter and perfect; the parapets are very low.

There is another fort of earth in the same townland, on the farm of Hugh Lyle, but is all demolished and houses built on it near the roadside, a short distance from the above fort. 25th July 1836.

There is another fort of earth in the townland of Tullyroan, on the farm of Henry James Ferguson, but all long since demolished.

There is a fort of earth and stones in the townland of Gortahurk, on the farm of Robert McBride, which is circular and 45 feet in diameter, but little parapet and all grown over with black and whitethorn.

There is a fort of earth in the same townland, a few perches from the house called Lissan and in the midst of a wood. This fort is circular and contains an English rood of land. The parapet is 5 feet high outside, on the farm or property of Robert Bryan Esquire.

There is another fort of earth in Brackagh Rowley, on the farm of Patrick Kelly, which was circular and 65 feet in diameter, but now only one-half remains undisturbed.

There is a fort of earth in the townland of Gortamney, on the farm of John Porter, which is circular and 100 feet in diameter, near the house and sown with clover.

There is also a fort similar to the above in the townland of Drumsamney, on the farm of Thomas Henry, and is also circular and 100 feet in diameter.

There are 2 forts in the townland of Killynumber, one on the farm of John Johnston but all demolished, and the other on the farm of Alexander Henry and is 100 feet in diameter.

There was a fort of earth in Killytoney, on the farm of Alexander White, but all demolished; also one on the farm of Samuel Black, but demolished, in the townland of Moyesset; also one on the farm of Samuel McElree but all demolished, in the townland of Moneyshanere.

Brass Spur

An ancient brass spur of unusual size, 7 inches wide at the bow and 5 inches long at the level, or from the bow to the roller, and as thick as a switch whip, would fit the thigh of the largest man in the parish, found many years ago in a flow bog in Moneyshanere, 1 and a half feet under the surface by Robert Moore of the same townland, who sent it to the Dublin museum.

Miscellaneous Discoveries

An ancient Irish gold ornament found in the parish of Kilcronaghan, but is now in the possession of William Stewart Esquire of Killymoon near Cookstown. Also an old felt hat, broad leaf but without shape, found also in a bog, 15 feet under the surface in this parish, but now in the cabinet of Revd J. Spencer Knox.

Deer Traps

The pointed stakes found in the bogs were used in ancient times in taking the deer.

Culmore [Calmore] Castle

Nothing remains of this ancient castle but a part of the wall, which was 3 feet thick and which forms

Parish of Kilcronaghan

the side wall of a cabin. The last inhabitant was Henry Rowley Esquire. This old castle was burned in 1690, at William's war, by the Irish. Culmore means "a large hazel" and was so called from a large hazel which grew near the castle. A large oak called the Royal Oak formerly grew (with many others) near the castle and was so large, when cut lying on the ground, that 2 horsemen could not touch each other with their whips across it. Part of it was taken to Killymoon near Cookstown, drawn by 8 bullocks to make mill axles. A few ash trees only remain.

Some bottles were discovered in digging up the cellar in the ruins, on which was the initials H.R., by James Millican, a publican, with a few ancient silver coins, a few years ago.

The ruins is about 100 perches south east of Tobermore, in the townland of Culmore, on the farm of William Young. Total dimensions of the castle when standing 40 by 50 feet in the clear; the mortar, like that of similar buildings, very coarse. 20th July 1836.

A draw-well was near to the castle but 40 years ago closed up. There was also an artificial lake or fish pond but also closed up.

There was a fort of earth near the ruins of Culmore Castle, on the farm of William Young, but all demolished and sown with flax.

Discoveries

An old buff or felt hat was discovered in 1834, 15 feet under the surface, in a flow bog in the townland of Moyesset, by Alexander Porter and is now deposited in the cabinet of Revd J. Spencer Knox.

Ancient Bell

The ancient bell, the property of John Stevenson Esquire of Fort William near Tobermore, was found by one of his labourers about 60 years ago, in digging near the old house, and is of brass or a composition of brass with other metals, and is supposed to have been used [as] a sheep bell, and was used as such by the proprietor Mr Stevenson. An antiquarian passing that way heard it ring on the neck of the sheep and stopped to see it, and offered the herd, an old man, 5 guineas for it. However, it will not be sold. Information obtained from Hugh Lyle, farmer, and Robert McDowell. 22nd July 1836.

Ancient Altar

Mass was formerly celebrated in a whinny glen near the new Roman Catholic chapel in the townland of Keenaght. This spot, though nothing more than a whinny glen, is still revered by the Roman Catholics.

Discoveries

2 poles, as thick as a spade shaft, with the shape of a cross cut on the top of each, discovered 2 feet under the surface of a flow bog in the townland of Mormeal by George McCart, but now lost.

School Statistics by J. Bleakly

SOCIAL ECONOMY

Table of Schools

[Table contains the following headings: name, situation and description, when established, income and expenditure, physical, intellectual and moral education, number of pupils subdivided by age, sex and religion, name and religion of master and mistress].

Brackagh Rowley national school, on the road leading from the Cross to Tobermore, i.e. the byroad, a good house, thatched, 21 feet by 14 feet, established 1833; income: from the National Board 8 pounds, 6 pounds from pupils; expenditure: house built by the teacher and cost 7 pounds; intellectual education: books by the National Board only; moral education: visited by the Roman Catholic clergy only; number of pupils: males, 20 under 10 years of age, 8 from 10 to 15, 28 total males; females, 20 under 10 years of age, 6 from 10 to 15, 6 above 15, 32 total females; 60 total pupils, 4 Presbyterians, 56 Roman Catholics; master Allen John Sheil, Roman Catholic.

Brackagh Rowley Irish male school, situated at the foot of the mountain, 3 miles south west of Tobermore, established 1835; income: from the Irish Society for the last quarter 1 pound 15s; expenditure: teacher's house; intellectual education: books by the Irish Society only; moral education: visited by the inspector from the Irish Society; number of pupils: 29 from 10 to 15 years of age, 25 above 15, 54 total males, all Roman Catholics; master Patrick Murray, Roman Catholic.

Moneyshanare national school, on the leading road from Draperstown Cross to Tobermore, a good house, of stone, slated and cost 51 pounds 7s 7d, viz. from the Kildare Place Society 42 pounds and 9 pounds 1s 7d from the inhabitants, from the Revd J. Spencer Knox, rector, 2 pounds, Revd Edmond Knox 10s; house 30 feet by 18 feet, walls 11 feet high; since 1833 in connection with the

National Board; income: from the National Board 8 pounds, 6 pounds 6s from pupils; intellectual education: books published by the National Board, with *Thompson's and Gough's Arithmetic, Lennie's English grammar*; moral education: not visited by any but the inspectors from the National Board; number of pupils: males, 9 under 10 years of age, 28 from 10 to 15, 7 above 15, 44 total males; females, 5 under 10 years of age, 7 from 10 to 15, 12 total females; 56 total pupils, 13 Presbyterians, 32 Roman Catholics, 11 other denominations; master William McWilliams, Roman Catholic.

Evening adult class, private, held in the session room of the Presbyterian congregation, only held 2 evenings in each week, established December 1835; income from pupils 4 pounds 16s; intellectual education: English grammar is only taught; moral education: visited by the Revd William Brown, the Presbyterian minister; number of pupils: 4 from 10 to 15 years of age, 10 above 15, 14 total pupils, all male, 12 Presbyterians, 1 Roman Catholic, 1 other denomination; master Henry McNally, Presbyterian. Report for July 1836.

Female Schools

Mormeal female school, near the leading road from Kilcronaghan church to the Black hill or Desertmartin, a room in a farmhouse, established May 1836; income: 25 pupils at 1s per quarter; intellectual education: *Universal spelling book and primer*, and Sunday school books, plain and fancy needlework, knitting; number of pupils: males, 3 under 10 years of age, 3 total males; females, 15 under 10 years of age, 5 from 10 to 15, 2 above 15, 22 total females; 25 total pupils, 8 Protestants, 3 Presbyterians, 11 Roman Catholics, 3 other denominations; mistress Eliza McCart, Presbyterian.

Tobermore female school, near the village, on the leading road from Tobermore to Magherafelt, a small room in a dwelling house, in good repair, established 1829; income: from the London Ladies' Society 8 pounds, from London Hibernian Society 4 pounds, 4 pounds from pupils; intellectual education: books published by the London Hibernian Society, plain and fancy needlework and knitting; moral education: visited by Mrs Stevenson, Authorised Version of Scriptures; number of pupils: 7 under 10 years of age, 24 from 10 to 15, 12 above 15, total 43, all female, 14 Protestants, 6 Presbyterians, 15 Roman Catholics, 8 Independents; mistress Matilda Burns, Established Church.

Tobermore female school, held in the day schoolhouse near the church, attended by the mistress of the Tobermore school on every Saturday only, assisted by Mrs Paul and Miss Holmes, established May 1836; income from Mrs Paul 2 pounds 12s; intellectual education: nothing but needlework, knitting and writing; moral education: visited by Mrs Paul and Miss Holmes; number of pupils: 4 under 10 years of age, 14 from 10 to 15, 5 above 15, total 23, all female, 17 Protestants, 4 Presbyterians, 2 Roman Catholics; mistress Matilda Burns, Established Church.

Female Irish school, held in the townland of Brackagh Rowley, near the mountain, in a private house, held on Thursday, Friday and Saturday only, established May 1836; income: from the Irish Society 1 pound 6s 4d; intellectual education: books by the Irish Society, and only in the Irish language, and all the Douai Version of Scriptures with the *Irish primer*; moral education: visited by the inspector from the Irish Society and the Presbyterian clergy, Douai Version of Scripture; number of pupils: 17 from 10 to 15 years of age, 17 above 15, total 34, all Roman Catholics and female; mistress Sarah Murray, Roman Catholic.

Parish of Lissan, County Londonderry

Memoir by J. Stokes, 1836

NATURAL FEATURES

Hills

This part of the parish extends over the south eastern and south western sides of the mountain Slieve Gallion. Its descending features are broken up into a surprising number of very small hills, which are studded over the surface of its flanks and fall towards a little stream that issues out of Lough Fea. Round that lake the mountain slopes gradually and the ground is much more level and more unbroken. The top of Slieve Gallion is here 1,750 feet above the level of the sea.

Lakes

Lough Fea is 3 miles in circumference; for dimensions see the maps. It contains some very picturesque headlands but no islands. Its depth has not yet been ascertained. Among the small hills spoken of in the preceding head there is a small piece of water called Lough-na-Muck, from a number of pigs that were formerly drowned in it. It is in a flow bog. Its depth is about 15 feet.

Rivers

The stream that issues out of Lough Fea divides this part of the parish from the county of Tyrone and bounds it on the south for 5 miles statute. It flows from west to east with a broken rapid current, but [does] not at present work any mills within it. It afterwards becomes the Ballinderry river. It is liable to sudden floods.

There is a plentiful supply of springs.

Bogs

There is but little bog of importance. The mountain is encrusted with thin heathy turf and in the lowlands there are a few small patches now nearly cut away. Of these, the most important is the small flow bog of Coltrim and Dunnabraggy. It has been cut away from 10 feet in depth to 5, and contains very little wood of any kind.

Woods

None, except on a fort in Drumard and a few small spots. [Insert marginal note: Query about woods].

Climate

The same as Desertlyn, except that round about Lough Fea it is a little colder.

MODERN TOPOGRAPHY

Public Buildings: Parish Church

The parish church is situated in the townland of Tullynure. It contains accommodation for 240 persons and is 70 feet by 16 in the inside. The aisle is flagged and the eastern window ornamented with stained glass. All is in good repair. All the windows, of which there are 4 including the eastern, are plainly arched, i.e. with semicircles. The architecture in every part resembles that of the parish church of Coleraine.

There is neither tower or steeple. The original roof was of shingles, which in 1807 was taken off and one of slates substituted. There are still a few of the original pews, made of solid oak, and the door, which is of oak, appears very old. On the south angle of the west wall there are 2 vertical sundials, the gift of the Revd William Martin, 1732. [Insert footnote: He was rector of Lissan at that time].

Presbyterian Meeting House

The Presbyterians have no place of worship within this part of the parish: they go to Moneymore and Cookstown. There are some Covenanters but neither have they any.

Roman Catholic Chapel

The Roman Catholic chapel is situated at a short distance from the church, in the townland of Tullynure. Its dimensions on the inside are 72 feet by 37; it is slated. In the interior there are no pews or forms and the floor is earthen. It is lighted by 13 lancet-shaped windows and has a respectable appearance from the road.

It was begun in 1803 and finished in 1833. The amount of money expended on it was 520 pounds, obtained by subscription. 10 guineas and half an acre of land for the site were granted by Sir Thomas Staples' father. In 1834 the average congregation was 1,357 persons. It is nearly the same still.

Close to the church is a large and handsome schoolhouse, 2-storey high and slated. It is 47 feet by 20 feet in the interior with apartments. It was established in 1814.

Gentlemen's Seats

Grouse Lodge, the seat of Captain Rowley Miller of Moneymore, is prettily situated in the townland of Ballybriest <Ballybrist>, at the head of a long glen and in the immediate neighbourhood of the mountain scenery of Lough Fea. A stream from that lake passes by. Plantations 19 years old surround the house, which is slated and of 2-storeys. It is at present undergoing repair. It stands adjacent to the high road from Dungiven to Cookstown. It is 6 and a half miles statute from Moneymore and was built in 1800 by [blank] Wright Esquire.

The Glebe House, at present the occasional residence of the Revd John Molesworth <Moulsworth> Staples, is a large castellated house on considerably too great a scale for a rectory. It was begun in 1806 and finished in 1811 at the cost of 6,000 pounds, which was supplied from the rector's private fortune and resources.

There are 60 acres of land attached, which is rented by John Watt Esquire, who also occupies the house. The planting is from 30 to 5 years old and it is 2 and a half miles from Moneymore, on the Cookstown road. The architecture of the front of it has a heavy Dutch character and is rather uninteresting, but that of the back part is more peculiar and is represented in the drawings. The upper tier of arches are formed by an open lattice work of wood.

Drawing: east view of Lissan Glebe House.

Mills

There was formerly a bleach mill in the townland of Clagan which ceased working in 1806. It had been the property of Messrs William and John Ramsay. The only remaining house is now a corn mill.

There was another in the townland of Ballybriest which ceased in 1831. It originally belonged to William Wright Esquire, who let it to an undertenant. Nothing remains of it but a few ruined houses. For further particulars about mills, see Fair Sheets attached.

[J. Bleakly] Corn mill, situated in the townland of Clagan, on the road leading from Moneymore to Londonderry. The mill is of stone and lime, thatched, but was formerly slated; proprietor Matthew Conlon rents it from Mr John Ramsay of Clagan; breast wheel, fall of water 10 feet, diameter of water wheel 13 feet 6 inches, breadth 2 feet 2 inches, diameter of cog wheel 7 feet, single geared, wooden machinery. This mill can work all seasons of the year and was originally a bleach house. The stream on which it is situated takes its source chiefly from an excellent spring called Anna's Well near Grouse Lodge, in the townland of Ballybriest.

[J. Stokes] There is no obstruction to the further erection of mills and machinery. The site of the second bleach mill above mentioned is very well adapted to the purpose, as there is an excellent stream from Lough Fea having a fall of about 30 feet to the mile.

Communications

The following high roads pass through this part of the parish: 1, from Moneymore to Cookstown, 2 and a half miles; 2, from Moneymore to Arboe, three-quarters of a mile; 3, from Cookstown to Dungiven, 2 and a half miles.

The first is 21 feet broad clear of drains and fences. There is a footpath at present to the distance of 1 mile from the town of Moneymore. The county surveyor is taking measures to extend it the whole length and he will also soon have the whole line, with all the others also, in complete repair by means of contracts which, however, have not yet begun. It passes through the district in a direction from north east to south west and has hitherto been kept in order by presentments.

The second passes through from north to south. It is 21 feet broad clear of drains and fences, and is kept in repair by presentments.

Bridges

The bridge in the townland of Ballyforlea, and on the mearing of the county of Derry, has 2 arches, each 20 feet in span. The roadway is 19 feet broad, the parapets 4 feet high, all is in good repair.

Also the bridge which is in the townland of Rossmore, and on the mearing of the county of Derry, has 1 arch 20 feet in span. The roadway is 18 feet broad and the parapets nearly broken down. It is not in good repair. These are the 2 only important bridges in that part of the parish belonging to the county. The rest are of small and insignificant dimensions. There is nothing to prevent any further improvement in communications.

ANCIENT TOPOGRAPHY

Ecclesiastical Remains

It is affirmed by many of the inhabitants of the townland of Clagan that an ancient church formerly stood in it. The stones of it were taken away by Mr William Magill of Creeve to build a bleach mill with. Many human bones were dug up by labourers when tilling the field in which the graveyard had been. There is nothing at present on the spot but an old hawthorn bush. The field is still called the Church Field and it is situated on the farm of John Ramsay. It is more than probable that this was the old parish church.

Military: none.

Pagan Remains

The district is also scantily, and in some parts completely, without any pagan remains, i.e. forts. This is owing to the long settlement of it and the greater destruction that has consequently taken place. There are still a few forts, for the dimensions of which see the maps.

Giant's Grave

There is a giant's grave close to Lough-na-Muck. It is, properly speaking, an oblong cairn of small stones 125 feet long and from 20 to 30 feet broad. It lies nearly from west to east. At one end there is a stone lying in a horizontal position, 9 feet by 4 feet and 2 feet thick. Close to it there is another 5 feet by 3.

This grave is in the townland of Ballybriest. It is believed to be the burial place of a chief called Kallan More, who was killed at the south west end of a mountain then called Slieve Iniver and in view of a lake then called Lough-na-Cuin, now Lough Fea. The shores of this lough was, it seems, a favourite place for hunting among the ancient chiefs. From that circumstance it took the name of the Greyhound lake or Lough-na-Cuin. The mountain was also called Slieve Kallan, afterwards Slieve Gallion, but why the name of the lake is changed to Lough Fea is not known among the inhabitants.

On the borders of Ballynascreen they still say in Irish "Kallan More, the son of the king of the silent country, lies entombed on the north of the glen. His head lies towards Slieve Iniver and his feet towards the Greyhound lake."

Gold Ornament

An ancient gold ornament was found a long time ago in the townland of Dunnabraggy, in the ditch of a Danish fort. Nobody at present knows what has become of it.

Names on Gravestones

Note, the following names are in the churchyard: Wilson, Conyngham, Custre, Kirgan, Magill, Logan, McGlone, Donelly, Doris, McKeirnan, Mullon, Conlon, McCann, Conelly.

Modern Topography

General Appearance and Scenery

The general appearance and scenery of the lowlands of this district resembles that of the parish of Kilcronaghan. It is, however, much richer, from the greater abundance of trees as well as the larger size of the hills. Yet it partakes of the same pastoral character.

The mountain Slieve Gallion ornaments it in the same way, by overtopping in every direction the landscape of the lowlands. It has here not quite so rugged an aspect and there is also much more of it to be seen than in Kilcronaghan.

That landscape changes its character altogether after passing Grouse Lodge, which is situated, as it were, on the hip or shoulder of the mountain. It is then wild and dreary: Lough Fea first appears, with its shores (except that part of it near the above seat) destitute of trees and surmounted with some small fantastically shaped hills. A high flattened country then succeeds, covered with low ridges and dangerous bogs and quagmires. It extends into the county of Tyrone, is uninhabited, and is separated from the low country by the Slieve Gallion ridge, which rises upon both sides of Lough Fea, and also by the Sixtowns glen which is in the parish of Ballynascreen <Ballinascreen>.

It was formerly much resorted to by wolves, and certainly the character of the scene was very suitable to that of the inhabitants.

Social Economy

Early Improvements

The most prevalent names in this part of the parish are Irish. With the exception of Ballybriest, the Irish are more numerous in the mountainous townlands. That part of the Drapers' proportion which is within the district has partaken of the advantages derived by the whole estate from the care and attention of the company. A road is in the course of being made by them from the western side of Slieve Gallion to the parish of Desertmartin, across the property as far as it goes. It is believed that it will be finished by the county and it will have the advantageous effect of opening a ready communication between the western side of that mountain and the most convenient source for the supply of lime, without which agent it cannot be

Progress of Improvement

The decay of the linen trade has been much felt in the townland of Ballybriest, in which there had been formerly a good bleach green. The inhabitants of that place and of several other spots along the mountain side now support themselves in part by making heath brooms. However, they attend to their agriculture also with increased attention and vigour, and in it they have received great help from several excellent by-roads laid out with care and judgement by the Drapers' Company.

A fair was held on the 26th November every year at the parish church. In 1832 it was discontinued by order of W.L. Conyngham Esquire of Springhill in the parish of Artrea <Ardtrea>, on account of the frequent quarrels and riots at it.

Obstructions to Improvement

Within the district there are no agricultural societies. The people find a ready vent for their produce, both in Moneymore and the neighbouring village of Cookstown.

There is a disputed boundary between the townlands of Ballybriest and Mobuoy. There are no other obstructions to improvement.

Local Government

No magistrates or police force of any kind are within this part of the parish. There is no illicit distillation, and offences are few at present. No murders or house burnings have been known to occur. The firmness and vigilance of the magistrates in the neighbouring parishes is a great check. Criminal offences have not yet risen higher than petty larceny, trespass or assaults. The last originates in most cases from drunkenness. When the fair was held at the church it sometimes amounted to riot.

Dispensaries

The health of the people is good. They attend the dispensaries at Moneymore and Cookstown. The neighbourhood of Lough Fea is more healthy than that of Moneymore, but the district is inferior in that respect to Bovevagh, Dungiven or Ballynascreen. Fever this year (1836) prevails to some extent in the lowlands.

Sunday Schools

Schools: see Tables.

Sunday schools are almost the only ones from which a certain and satisfactory conclusion can be drawn relative to the beneficial moral effect of schools in general. From an examination of the subject it appears that: first, they are in a high degree useful, not only to the young persons attending the schools but to a certain degree to their families also; second, but this degree of advantage is proportional to the zeal and attention of the conductors of the school; third, in one of the schools of the parish there is a class of adults (young persons from 15 to 20 years of age) whose information and religious attainments are superior and distinguished, and whose Christian conduct is such as will always be the consequence of that character.

Fourth, Sunday school education has stimulated one of these, a female, to establish in a remote district a Sunday school which, under her own and her brother's exertions and care, is doing remarkably well; and she has for the last 2 years brought forward the children of her school to the annual examination held in Lissan church, when it was gratifying to observe their progress, which but for her would have been nothing, as they were not only at a great distance from the church school but also had not sufficient clothes to attend.

Fifth, these schools form a strong link of mutual affection between the clergyman and the scholars. They become perfectly known to him and the consciousness of this on their part appears to have a good effect. The following anecdote will serve to show the attachment of the young people to the system and the advantage which they think they derive from continued attendance. A young woman, who had for many years attended the school at Lissan church, was lately married. She came to be examined with her class as usual at the annual examination in October 1836, without any advice or recommendation.

There are 2 instances of adults being, at their homes, taught by the little Sunday school children to read.

National Schools

There are the foundations of a national schoolhouse 105 feet north of the Roman Catholic chapel and within the boundary of the chapel yard. Money was collected at the chapel for its erection and the foundations were cleared out and partly built upon, when its further progress was stopped by Sir Thomas Staples, the lord of the soil. A stable had been marked off in the ground plan for the accommodation of the priest's horse.

Parish of Lissan

[Insert footnote: Sir Thomas had not been consulted on the subject].

Hibernian Schools

The manner in which the schools attached to the London Hibernian Society appear to have worked in this neighbourhood is similar to that of the Sunday schools, but not so conspicuous. The people themselves are anxious for instruction and improvement.

Habits of the People: Poor

The following information relates to the whole parish of Lissan. There are 32 poor persons' names on the church list receiving the poor box money of the parish church. Of these, 12 are of the Established Church, 3 Presbyterians and 17 are Roman Catholics. The general cause of their poverty is old age and infirmity. 4 are nearly idiots and one was brought to poverty by the misconduct of her husband who was a drunkard.

There are also 8 poor pensioners receiving among them 4 pounds 17s per quarter from Sir Thomas Staples Bart, and 2 poor pensioners who receive 6d per week from the same baronet. One of the first-mentioned 8 receives 30s per annum from a former curate of the parish, the Revd Hugh Hamilton. The average amount of the poor box collection annually is 7 pounds.

The poorest townland in the whole of this part of the parish is at present considered to be Ballybriest.

Income of Clergy

The annual income of the rector, the Revd John Molesworth Staples, is 500 pounds British of tithe composition. That of the parish priest, the Revd Bernard Murphy, is 85 pounds from the congregation and 10 guineas from the Drapers' Company. That of the Presbyterian minister, Revd William Moore, now superannuated, is 100 pounds regium donum. The Revd John Barnett preaches but will not receive the regium donum until the death of Mr Moore. He receives the stipend; see Memoir of Artrea.

Superstition

The following are the habits of the people peculiar to this part of the parish. There is an excellent spring situated near the schoolhouse at Grouse Lodge and called Crockanna Well, from a little fairy of the name of Anna Corr who is always heard crying before any misfortune is about to happen to any of the inhabitants. The hill at which the well is situated is called after her also.

Anna Corr, it seems, was an old woman who lived near it. A man one morning offered her a ride on his horse to the fair of Moneymore, but, after crossing the top of the hill, neither Anna, man or horse were ever heard of again. Many other stories are told about her, but most of the parishioners are ashamed to acknowledge them. The hill and well are in the townland of Clagan.

The stump standing in the water near the edge of Lough Fea is called Charley's Ghost, from a man called Charley Devlin who was nearly drowned there about 20 years ago. It was put up by William Wright Esquire, to whom the townland then belonged, as a warning to others.

The superstition about "gentle bushes" is as prevalent here as in the more mountainous parishes of Ballynascreen or Dungiven. Fairy bushes are numerous.

Superstition regarding Arrowheads

The ancient arrowheads of flint so frequently found are also much regarded for their supposed virtues in the cure of cattle. The following is the recipe: all the arrowheads that can be got (the greater the number, the greater the virtue and the more expeditious the cure) are put into salt and water, along with 3 ha'pence and a piece of silver, generally sixpence. The cure is then performed by rubbing the salt and water on the cow with the hand, beginning from the top of the tail and proceeding to the nostrils. This is done 3 times, during which sundry prayers and charms are uttered. After this, part of the water is put into the mouth and nostrils of the cow and a part also at the foot of some fairy bush; the remainder is put behind the fire.

The people affirm that these arrows are shot from the Danish fort by the fairies and that they pierce the cow through the side. They pretend that they can show the print of the arrow. This superstition prevails as much among the Presbyterians as among the Roman Catholics. This part of the parish is poorer than the other.

Situation and Language

As to the food, comforts etc. of the people, they are very much similar to those of the parish of Desertlyn. The English language is everywhere spoken, except in the mountainous parts immediately on the borders of the parish of Ballynascreen.

Remarks on Superstition

The superstition of this part, although some instances have been described, is not more remarkable than it is in the parish just mentioned, i.e. Ballynascreen, and it is less so than in the parish of Banagher. It may be remarked in general that the nearer a parish is to such rich and populous neighbourhoods, as that of Cookstown, the more weakened is the superstition by the mixture which ensues of industrious and money-making individuals with the mass of the inhabitants. [Insert footnote: These individuals are always to a degree enlightened about such things].

This race is not quite so stunted here as in the more mountainous districts of the county.

Emigration and Migration

The following is the number of persons who have emigrated to America for the last 2 years.

1834: 1 male under 10 years; 3 males 10 and under 20; 7 males and 7 females 20 and under 30; 7 males 30 and under 40; 2 males and 1 female 40 and under 50; 1 male 50 and under 60; total 21 males, 8 females, total 29.

1835: 2 males and 3 females 20 and under 30; 1 male and 1 female 40 and under 50; total 3 males, 4 females, total 7.

14 females and 47 males are in the habit of migrating annually to Glasgow; of these, 54 are Roman Catholics.

Remarkable Events

None: there is a remarkable living character in the person of David Donelly of Moneyhaw, who, though stone blind, can go through all the operations of farming with the greatest accuracy, can weed potatoes, flax. He is 45 years old.

Schools by J. Bleakly

[Table contains the following headings: name, situation and description, when established, income and expenditure, physical, intellectual and moral education, number of pupils subdivided by age, sex and religion, name and religion of master and mistress].

Lissan endowed school is supported from the funds of Erasmus Smith, situated at the parish church in the townland of Tullynure, a good house, 2-storey high, slated, 47 by 20 feet inside, with the master's apartments attached. The under part of the house is vacant since the female school ceased, which was in 1824; established in 1814; income: from the funds of Erasmus Smith annually 20 pounds and of gratuity per annum 10 pounds; physical education: none; corporal punishment is inflicted by means of a pillory which is erected in the schoolroom, through which the head and hands are projected. Intellectual education: the books read are those published by the Kildare Place Society, with *Thompson, Gough* and the national system of arithmetic, *Murray's English grammar, Jackson's Book-keeping* and *Bonnycastle's Mensuration*; moral education: visited by the Revd John Molesworth Staples, rector of the parish, and the Revd William John Irvine, curate, Authorised Version of Scripture is taught and catechisms on Saturday by the master; number of pupils: males, 32 under 10 years of age, 36 from 10 to 15, 2 above 15, total 70; females, 25 under 10 years of age, 20 from 10 to 15, 1 above 15, total 46; total number of pupils 116, 42 Protestants, 20 Presbyterians, 50 Roman Catholics, 4 other denominations: master David Taylor, Established Church.

Grouse Lodge endowed school is also supported from the funds of Erasmus Smith, situated near Grouse Lodge in the townland of Ballybriest and held in a small thatched cottage formerly occupied by the foreman of the bleach green. The schoolroom is attached to the master's dwelling and is only 33 by 12 feet and only 6 feet high, and in very bad repair; established in 1817; income: from the funds of Erasmus Smith per annum 20 pounds and from the funds of Erasmus Smith of a gratuity per annum 10 pounds, from pupils 5 pounds; intellectual education: books published by the Kildare Place Society, with *Thompson and Gough's Arithmetic, Murray's English grammar* and *Jackson's Book-keeping*; moral education: visited by the Revd J. Molesworth Staples, rector, when in the parish, and the Revd William John Irvine, curate, Authorised Version and catechisms on Saturday by the master; number of pupils: males, 28 under 10 years of age, 33 from 10 to 15, 4 above 15, total 65; females, 15 under 10 years of age, 27 from 10 to 15, total 42; total number of pupils 107, 25 Protestants, 30 Presbyterians, 41 Roman Catholics, 11 other denominations; master William Millican, Established Church. Report for September 1836.

Private Schools

Situated in the townland of Dernan, on the road leading from the Moneymore and Londonderry road to the Desertmartin road along Slieve Gallion mountain, and held in a small thatched house 24 by 12 feet, no seats but a few temporary ones of blocks; established in 1829; income from pupils 8 pounds; intellectual education: *Universal spelling book* and *Manson's Primer*, with *Gough and Voster's Arithmetic*; moral education: visited by the Roman Catholic clergy and the Established Church clergy occasionally, Authorised Version of Scripture is taught; number of pupils: males, 12 under 10 years of age, 6 from 10 to 15, total 18; females, 6 under 10 years of age, 11 from 10 to 15, total 17; total number of pupils 35, 6 Protestants, 4 Presbyterians, 25 Roman Catholics; master Phillip Donnelly, Roman Catholic.

Situated in the townland of Moneyhaw, on the leading road from Moneymore to Stewartstown, held in a room of the master's dwelling house, established in 1814; income from pupils 10 pounds; intellectual education: *Universal spelling book and primer*, with *Gough's Arithmetic*; moral education: visited by none of the clergy, Authorised Version of Scripture is taught; number of pupils: males, 6 under 10 years of age, 7 from 10 to 15, total 13; females, 6 under 10 years of age, 1 from 10 to 15, total 7; total number of pupils 20, 3 Protestants, 9 Presbyterians, 5 Roman Catholics, 3 other denominations; master John Larkin, Roman Catholic.

Tintagh national school, situated in the townland of Tintagh, on the road leading from Cookstown to Tobermore. The schoolhouse was a good one but is now out of repair and the school is at present held in a borrowed house in Knockadoo townland; established in 1817 and in 1833 became connected with the National Board; income: from the National Board per annum 8 pounds, from pupils 10 pounds; intellectual education: books published by the National Board with *Thompson and Gough's Arithmetic*; moral education: visited by the Roman Catholic clergy only; number of pupils: males, 15 under 10 years of age, 15 from 10 to 15, 10 above 15, total 40; females, 15 under 10 years of age, 5 from 10 to 15, total 20; total number of pupils 60, 20 Presbyterians, 33 Roman Catholics, 7 other denominations; master James Larkin, Roman Catholic. [Insert marginal note by J. Stokes: This school was dissolved in November 1835].

Coltrim, on the road leading from the Moneymore and Cookstown road to Lissan church, a small house, thatched, built by subscription and 24 by 15 feet inside; established in 1806; income: from the Worshipful the Drapers' Company per annum 5 pounds, from pupils 8 pounds; intellectual education: books published by the Kildare Place Society and London Hibernian Society, with *Thompson and Gough's Arithmetic* and *Murray's English grammar*, and *Jackson's Bookkeeping* if required; moral education: visited by the Revd William John Irvine, curate, and the Revd John Barnett, Presbyterian minister, Authorised Version and catechism is taught by the master; number of pupils: males, 20 under 10 years of age, 10 from 10 to 15, total 30; females, 18 under 10 years of age, 6 from 10 to 15, total 24; total number of pupils 54, 4 Protestants, 22 Presbyterians, 8 Roman Catholics, 20 other denominations; master James Millican, Baptist.

Ballyforlea, on the road leading from the Cookstown road to the Coagh road, a thatched house 21 by 12 feet and in middling repair, built by subscription, established in 1827; income: from the Worshipful the Drapers' Company per annum 5 pounds, from pupils 7 pounds; intellectual education: books published by the London Hibernian Society, with *Thompson and Gough's Arithmetic*; moral education: visited by the Revd William John Irvine, curate of the Established Church, Authorised Version of Scripture is taught; number of pupils: males, 34 under 10 years of age, 7 from 10 to 15, total 41; females, 12 under 10 years of age; total number of pupils 53, 10 Protestants, 30 Presbyterians, 8 Roman Catholics, 5 other denominations; master John Harkness, Presbyterian. Report for September 1836.

Sunday Schools

[Table contains the following headings: name, situation, when established, superintendent, number of teachers and scholars, hours of attendance, societies with which connected, observations].

Lissan, held in the schoolhouse in the morning and in the church after divine service, superintendents the Revd John Irvine, curate of the parish, and David Taylor, schoolmaster; 2 male teachers, total 2; number of scholars: 48 Established Church, 12 Presbyterians, 26 males, 34 females, total 60, 36 exclusively Sunday school scholars; hours of attendance from 10 till half past 11 o'clock a.m. and from half past 2 till 4 o'clock p.m.; connected with Sunday School Society in Ireland; the Society for Discountenancing Vice have given premiums of books to the best answerers.

Grouse Lodge, held in the schoolhouse near Grouse Lodge, established 1817, superintendent the Revd William John Irvine, curate, and the schoolmaster William Millican; teachers: 2 males and 1 female, total 3; number of scholars: 30 Established Church, 30 Presbyterians, 9 Roman Catholics, 48 other denominations, 69 males, 48 females, total 117, 40 exclusively Sunday school scholars; hours of attendance from 3 till 6 o'clock p.m., no school during the winter; the Sunday School Society for Ireland give books free, carriage excepted; this school commences with prayer only and concludes with the same by the schoolmaster and the curate when present.

Claggan, held in an old house which was formerly a dwelling house, established 7th August 1836, superintendent Miss Eliza Ramsay; 1 male and 2 female teachers, total 3; number of scholars: 30 Established Church, 20 Presbyterians, 10 Roman Catholics, 30 males, 30 females, total 60, 58 exclusively Sunday school scholars; hours of attendance from 4 till 6 o'clock p.m.; this school at present is not connected with any society; commences with prayer and concludes with the same by the superintendent; chiefly the Scriptures are used. Report of September 1836.

Derryganard Sunday school, held in the kitchen of the superintendent, established in 1834, superintendent Martha Bodkin, Established Church; 2 male and 2 female teachers, total 4; number of scholars: 33 Established Church, 12 Presbyterians, 20 males, 25 females, total 45, 39 exclusively Sunday school scholars; hours of attendance from 3 o'clock till 7 p.m. during the summer, but none during the winter quarter; the Sunday School Society for Ireland give books at a reduced price; this school closes with singing and prayer.

Since the establishment of the Claggan Sunday school, many of the Presbyterian children have been removed to it, and by order of Roman Catholic clergy the Roman Catholic children have been withdrawn. [Insert note by Stokes: Martha Bodkin was formerly herself a Sunday school scholar and has endeavoured to communicate the good she received from the system under which she was educated].

Fair Sheets by J. Bleakly, September to November 1836

NATURAL FEATURES

Bogs

Coltrim and Dunnabraggy flow bogs were originally 10 feet deep, but now only 5 feet as it was cut away once before. The imbedded timber consists of nothing more than blocks of fir and oak but very little of either. 9th September 1836.

The bogs of the parish consist chiefly of hand or baked turf, except the mountain part which are cut with the spade. The inhabitants consider that bog will be very scarce in the course of some years and is at present scarce near the town of Moneymore, chiefly Moneyhaw townland.

Lough Fea

This lake is situated in the townland of Ballybrist, near Grouse Lodge, and is 3 miles in circumference. Trout are the only fish which this lake produce. At the west end of the lake the channel is black and the trout the same colour, and at the opposite side, where the stones of the channel is whiter, the trout is the same colour, so it is quite evident the fish of both sides do not gender together. 13th September.

Water and Trees

The parish is very well supplied with good spring water, as there is not a townland in which there is not a good spring well, pump or draw-well.

The parish is well sheltered with good hedges and trees, except the mountain district.

River

The river which divides Moneyhaw townland from Springhill produces eels and trout in the season.

MODERN TOPOGRAPHY

Glebe House

The Glebe House is situated in the townland of Muff and was commenced in the year 1806 and finished in 1811, and cost 6,000 pounds at the expense of the Revd John Molesworth Staples, rector of the parish. The house is 2-storey high and of the castellated style, and was insured in 1813. The house is almost secluded in the midst of a planting which was planted by the rector and consists of fir, alder, beech, sycamore, birch, ash and oak. The oldest was planted in the year 1806 and the younger trees in 1831. There are 60 acres of land attached, which is at present rented by John Watt Esquire, who also occupies the house. The proprietor is the Revd John Molesworth Staples, who was appointed to the rectory of this parish in 1800 and whose tithe composition amounts to 500 pounds British. 7th September 1836.

Grouse Lodge

Grouse Lodge is beautifully situated in the townland of Ballybrist and was formerly occupied by William Wright Esquire, now of Limavady, and was succeeded by William Morgan Esquire, now of Cookstown. The house is 2-storey high, slated, but was in a state of dilapidation until Rowley Miller Esquire, the proprietor,

Parish of Lissan

Lissan Glebe House

is now repairing it. The planting consists of fir, ash, oak, beech, alder and birch, oldest 19 years planted and the latest last year, 1836.

Church

The church, which is without a tower or steeple, is situated in the townland of Tullynure, [blank] miles from Moneymore. It contains 26 pews on the lower part, 11 of which are double; 1 is 7 and a half by 14 feet, 5 are 7 by 7 and a half feet, 3 are 4 feet 8 inches by 7 and a half feet and the other 6 are single, 8 by 3 feet. The gallery contains 8 pews, one of which is double, 6 by 6 and a half feet; 3 are single and 13 feet by 3 feet, and 4 are also single and 6 feet by 3; all in good repair except the floor of 2 single pews which are a little broken.

The aisle is flagged and 4 and a half feet wide. The gallery is only on one side of the church. There are 3 arched windows on the side and 1 arched window on the east end, which is of stained glass. The inside door is arched and 5 and a half feet wide, of cut stone, very ancient. The outside door is square and 4 feet wide. Total dimensions inside is 70 by 16 feet.

The original roof was not slated but of shingles. In 1807 it was slated, i.e. at the time Mr Staples became rector. It will accommodate 240 persons, allowing 18 inches to each. [Insert note by J. Stokes: Memorandum, to inspect Sir J. Staples' register].

Sundial and Planting

The sundial at the west end of Lissan church is the gift of the Revd William Martin, rector of the parish, on 1st April 1732. Also in his time the 3 large beech trees, which add so much to the ornament of the churchyard from their branches overspreading so much of the road and wall of the yard, were also planted in 1732.

Roman Catholic Chapel

The Roman Catholic chapel is situated a short distance from the church, in the townland of Tullynure, on the leading road from Moneymore to Londonderry, and was built by local subscription in the year 1803 and cost at present 520 pounds. The first cost was 420 pounds in 1833, the last, which was slating the roof, was 100 pounds in 1835. The total dimensions inside is 72 by 37 feet, of stone and lime, slated with a double roof, but no floor except earth. No pews or forms, as the chapel is at present in course of construction and not yet finished. There are 13 windows, viz. 4 on each side and 1 on each end, with 1 above each door, of the Gothic style and each 4 by 9 feet 8 inches. There are 3 doors, viz. 1 on each end and 1 on the side; each door is 4 feet wide and of the same shape of the windows.

The trees round the chapel yard are of beech and fir planted at the same time the chapel was built. Half an acre of land is attached, granted by Sir Thomas Staples' father, with 10 guineas towards the erection of the chapel. John Staples was father to Sir Thomas Staples. A wall is at present in operation round the chapel yard.

Before this chapel was built, mass was celebrated in the open air through various parts of the parish, and in winter in some empty house. The oldest tombstone is dated 1805. The foundation of a new schoolhouse was laid at the chapel wall and part of it raised at the expense of the congregation, but was opposed by Sir Thomas Staples as it was so convenient to the largest school at the church and would probably decrease its number. 8th September 1836.

Intended Schoolhouse

The schoolhouse which was intended to have been erected at the Roman Catholic chapel is 105 feet north of the chapel. This was intended for a national school, and money collected at the chapel from the Roman Catholics towards its erection, which was commenced and the foundation cleared without consulting the proprietor, Sir Thomas Staples Bart, who immediately prevented its erection, and as it was too near the endowed school at Lissan church. A stable is now building on the site of the intended school for the priest's horse and a wall from the gateway to the west end of the chapel yard, and by subscription of the congregation. From David Taylor, schoolmaster, and Peter Conlon, farmer, at the chapel.

Houses at Ballybrist

There are 38 houses in the townland of Ballybrist, all built of stone and all nearly white outside. All the houses at the lower part of the townland are tolerably clean inside and outside. There are 11 houses at upper or mountain part of the townland which are not kept clean inside, as the inmates are chiefly besom-makers and consequently have their houses at all times irregular. In fact the houses of both Ballybrist and Tintagh are nearly on an equality. The superiority may be given to Tintagh. 12th November 1836.

Houses on the Drapers' Estate

The people have a great desire for improving their houses, particularly those on the estate of the Drapers' Company, as Mr Miller encourages cleanliness as much as possible and will give the poorer tenants lime free. Those who are able must purchase it. Those who will not endeavour to keep their houses clean and comfortable, Mr Millar will make those persons pay a year's rent in advance.

Since the late taxation on houses, many of the farmers are much discouraged and afraid to improve their houses lest they should be taxed. The company prohibit any tenant holding less than 18 or 20 acres of land on their estate from keeping more than one cottier. The cottiers' houses in general are in very bad repair. From James Smith.

2-Storey Houses

There are 12 2-storey houses in the parish of Lissan, i.e. that part of the parish which is within the county of Londonderry. The houses in general through the parish are comfortable except in the mountain district. 19th September 1836.

Bleach Mills

There was a bleach mill in the townland of Clagan which ceased to work about 30 years ago and was the property of Messrs William and John Ramsay. The only remaining house is long since converted into a corn mill.

There was also a bleach mill in the townland of Ballybrist, near Grouse Lodge, which ceased to work in the year 1831 and was at that time the property of William Morgan Esquire, who rented it from William Wright Esquire at 81 pounds per annum, but is now the property of Rowley Miller Esquire whose intention is to re-establish the bleach mill, as the water is abundant and the house in part standing except the roof.

Roads

The by-road leading from the chapel door, intended to run to Tobermore, is only formed for half a mile and by presentment.

Also the road leading from the church to Moneymore is 21 feet clear of drains and fences, and in good repair by presentment.

Also the road leading from the church to Carndaisy mearing is 21 feet clear of drains and fences, made by presentment and kept in repair by

Parish of Lissan

the same and in good repair. Information obtained from the Revd Bernard Murphy, parish priest of Lissan, and Michael Conolan, farmer, and others.

The road leading by the Roman Catholic chapel to Londonderry is 21 feet clear of drains and fences, and in good repair, made by presentment and kept in repair by the same.

The leading road from Moneymore to Cookstown is 21 feet broad clear of drains and fences, with a footpath for the distance of 1 mile from Moneymore which is 4 feet wide, made by presentment of the grand jury and kept in repair by the same, and in good repair by Smith Davison.

Also the by-road leading (from the mail coach road) to Ballyloughran bridge is 16 feet broad clear of drains and fences, and in good repair by presentment and kept in repair by the same by Smith Davison.

The old road leading from Moneymore to Cookstown, i.e. that part leading by Mr Caldwell's 2-storey house on the hill in the townland of Ballyforlea, is 12 years closed up and a new line of road made a little higher in order to avoid the above hill. Other particulars of this road are before described.

The by-road leading from the above, and to Coagh in the county Tyrone through Ballyforlea, is 15 feet clear of drains and fences, made by presentment of the grand jury and kept in repair by the same, and in good repair.

The by-road leading from the Moneymore leading road through the mountain to Ballybrist bog is 15 feet clear of drains and fences. A part is in very bad repair and only formed for the accommodation of the inhabitants to the turf bog, and made by presentment of the grand jury.

Also the road leading from Lissan church through the townland of Drumard is 15 feet clear of drains and fences, and in very bad repair and very hilly, which could have been avoided if the road was made to run west of the hills in the valley. This road leads from Lissan church to Moneymore and was made by presentment of the grand jury, and is kept in repair by the same at the expense of the county.

Also the road leading from the above road to Draperstown Cross is 15 feet clear of drains and fences, and in middling repair, made by presentment and kept in repair by the same at the expense of the county.

The by-road leading from Moneymore to the road leading from the church at Lissan through Drumard townland is 15 feet clear of drains and fences, and in middling repair by the county. 22nd September 1836.

Bridges and Roads

The bridge which divides Dunnan in the county Tyrone from Ballyforlea in the county Derry has 2 arches, each 20 feet in the span and 19 feet broad on the top. The wall is 4 feet high and was repaired 2 years ago at the expense of the county.

Also the bridge which is across the stream which divides Rossmore, county Derry from Drumgrass, county Tyrone has 1 arch 20 feet in the span and 18 feet broad on the top, the walls in very bad repair, nearly level with the road.

Also the road leading to the bridge and to Cookstown is 21 feet clear of drains and fences, and in good repair, made by presentment of grand jury and kept in repair by the same.

Also the road leading from the above road to the church and schoolhouse at Lissan is 21 feet clear of drains and fences by presentment, and in good repair. 11th September 1836.

The road leading from the Moneymore road to the road leading from Cookstown to Derry is 21 feet clear of drains and fences, and in middling repair by presentment.

The leading road from Cookstown to Derry is also 21 feet clear of drains and fences, and in good repair, except parts injured by the late floods, made and kept in repair by presentment at the expense of the county.

Also the road leading from Moneymore to Derry, east of Grouse Lodge, is 21 feet clear of drains and fences, and in good repair except in parts from Mr Ramsay's house through Clagan and Mobuoy, where 2 bridges are very necessary. This road is also kept in repair by presentment.

Also the old road which formerly passed by the demesne from the church at Lissan is now 7 years closed up.

There are 2 small bridges on the leading road from Moneymore to Lissan church, in the townland of Killybaskey, the walls of which are in very bad repair.

There are 2 small bridges on the road between the Glebe House at Muff and the church of Lissan, in the townland of Tullynure, the walls of which are in bad repair, particularly the bridge which is on the stream which runs through Killybaskey townland. 28th September 1836.

ANCIENT TOPOGRAPHY

Gold Ornament

An ancient gold ornament, crescent-like but very thin, was found by Hugh Crawford, farmer, in digging potatoes in the townland of Dunnabraggy

<Donnabraggy>, in the trench of a fort of earth on his farm about 100 years ago. Nobody knows where it is.

Crockanna Well and Hill

This well is an excellent spring situated near the schoolhouse at Grouse, and is so called from an old fairy woman of that name who is heard frequently crying when any misfortune is likely to happen to any of the inhabitants. The hill is situated in the townland of Clagan, between Grouse Lodge and Mr Ramsay's house, and is the property of Mr William Ramsay, who planted it with fir, beech and alder trees in 1827 and in 1829, but was maliciously burned and some of the trees broken in 1833 and 1834 by Samuel and Adam Bennett, who have since emigrated to America.

Many stories were told by the superstitious inhabitants of this part of the parish respecting the above well and hill, but are now, in this enlightened age, ashamed to acknowledge that superstition prevails to any extent. 14th September 1836.

Tradition regarding Anna Corr

Anna Corr was the name of the old woman for whom the hill and well is called, and who resided near the well until a man on a fair morning of Moneymore came riding to the door and asked Anna if she was going to the fair, and said he would give her a ride behind him on the horse, to which she consented. But after riding from the house to the hill, which is a short distance from the house, and for whom the hill is called, neither Anna, man or horse have ever since returned.

Lough-na-Muck

This lake is small but very steep, situated in the mountain flow bog of Mobuoy, and is called Lough-na-Muck from a number of pigs being drowned in it a long time ago. Eels, trout and otters are found in this lake.

Giant's Grave

A few yards from the above lake, on the hill which is a ridge of stones, there is a giant's grave or most likely a druid's altar. The stone over the grave is in a reclined position, 2 feet high from the earth or grave with one end resting on the ground, and measures in length 9 feet by 4 and a half feet high on the east face, and 2 feet thick. Underneath this stone, in the earth of the grave, was found a human tooth of unusual size about 5 years ago, by James McGlone, farmer of Mobuoy.

There is another stone lying almost flat, which appears to have been a part of the altar and was supported by pillars at the edge of the grave. This stone is 5 feet long by 3 feet broad, all on a mountain in the townland of Mobuoy. 15th September.

[Marginal drawing showing alignment of stones with key]. The giant's grave near Lough-na-Muck runs nearly west and north, and is chiefly composed of small stones. The distance between the 2 canopy stones A and B is 2 inches. The largest canopy stone is 2 feet high from the surface, but leaning on one side and 9 feet long. The smaller canopy stone is 1 and a half feet high. The length of the original parallelogram from C to D is 125 feet; breadth of parallelogram at E is 20 feet; breadth of parallelogram at F is 20 feet; breadth of parallelogram at G is 30 feet; height of parallelogram is 4 feet.

Ancient Querns

2 ancient quern stones have been found in the townland of Drumard about 4 weeks ago by Joseph McCullagh, in digging near the house on his farm.

Roman Catholic Clergy

The vault of the Revd Michael Doyle, parish priest of Lissan, is dated 1756, in the churchyard of Lissan.

Forts

There are 2 forts of earth in the townland of Drumrot. One is completely destroyed and the other is converted into a kitchen garden. There are also 2 forts of earth in the townland of Dunnabraggy, one on the farm of Robert Glasgo, partly destroyed, and the other is the garden of Kennedy McCullagh, which is also nearly demolished. A quantity of gold in the form of a cross was found some years ago near the above fort by Hugh Crawford of the same townland, and was taken to Dublin and sold.

There was also a fort of earth on the farm of James McKee in the townland of Moneyhaw, but also demolished.

There is a fort of earth, circular, a little west of the Glebe House, which is planted with forest trees about 30 years and is 110 feet in diameter and 6 feet high.

Also the fort of earth at the Glebe House is circular and 120 feet in diameter. The trees planted in this fort are fir, oak, ash, beech, alder and birch, planted as above. There were 2 other forts in this

Parish of Lissan

townland but long since demolished, all in the townland of Muff.

There is a fort of earth on the top of a very high hill above Ballymully glen in the townland of Tintagh, on the farm of Dennis Haghey, which is nearly circular and 180 feet in diameter but all sown with corn.

There is also a fort of earth on the farm of William Eccless in the townland of Drumard, which is circular and 99 feet in diameter and 6 feet high inside the parapet. The entrance is at the east side and 9 feet wide. The parapet is all covered with a natural growth of oak and hazel. The centre was laboured.

There was also a fort of earth on the farm of Michael Kane in the townland of Tintagh, but all demolished except a part which is a rock.

There was another fort of earth in the townland of Caneese, on the farm of Charles Donnelly, which is also nearly demolished.

There was a fort of earth in Tintagh, on the farm of John Anderson, but long since demolished.

Discoveries

In 1825 in the townland of Tintagh, in a moss near the limestone quarry in the mountain, 2 feet under the surface of the water, was discovered the body of a full-grown female covered with a rug or caddy, not quite decayed, by Bryan Lonnan of the same townland.

Ancient Meddar

The ancient meddar was obtained from Michael Heaney in the townland of Tintagh near the mountain and was handed down from his ancestors, who are Roman Catholics, as it is only the Roman Catholics who preserve those ancient vessels. 23rd September 1836.

Ancient Armour

Part of the ancient armour, consisting of the skeleton of an old helmet, the breast part of the coat of mail, which is of hammered iron, and an excellent sword 2 feet 8 inches long, of the best polished steel and in a good state of preservation, with a basket handle or hilt attached. On the blade of the sword near the handle is written Andre Ferara. The whole armour, consisting of spurs, stirrups, saddle and bridle, have been in the possession of George Harris of Moneyhaw, but only the helmet, sword and breastplate are now in his possession.

The above armour was worn by the French General Mamont at the ever memorable siege of Derry and who was killed at the siege by Mr John McKee of Moneyhaw, who was grandfather to the present Francis McKee of Moneyhaw.

Ancient Pike

There is also an ancient pike in the possession of Miss Crawford, under the roof with George Harris of Moneyhaw.

Ancient Stone

The ancient stone with a hole in the end of it was discovered in the townland of Moneyhaw by John Eccles this year, 1836, in digging near a fairy bush on his farm.

Ancient Sword

Peter Conlon found an ancient brass sword in Tullynure Upper moss in 1833, in cutting turf 3 feet under the surface, and weighed 17 oz. It had 8 sides; the edges of 2 of the sides were very sharp. Sir Thomas Staples purchased it for 4 pounds 3s, where it is said to be at present deposited.

Ancient Church at Clagan

It is affirmed by many of the inhabitants of the townland of Clagan that a church formerly stood in the townland of Clagan, on the farm of Mr John Ramsay. The stones of the walls have been taken away long since by Mr William Magill of Creeve, to build the bleach mills which are now in ruins. Many human bones have been dug up by Mr Ramsay's labourers when digging the field where the graveyard is supposed to have been. There is nothing at present on the spot but an old hawthorn. The field is called the Church Field until this day.

Spade Mill

A spade or plate mill is also said to have stood in the townland of Clagan, on the stream near Mr Magill's house, but long since demolished.

Charley's Ghost

The stump standing in Lough Fea is called Charley's Ghost, from a man named Charley Devlin who was nearly drowned at the spot where the stump stands, in a match of swimming about 20 years ago. The stump was put up by William Wright Esquire of Newtownlimavady, as a warning to others who should venture to swim across the lake. From Alexander Cuddy at the lake and others. 3rd October.

Ancient House

The house now occupied by the Revd Bernard Murphy, parish priest of Lissan, in the townland of Killybaskey, was originally a wooden house built of strong oak, and was rebuilt of stone and lime by James Starrat, who was one of the original Presbyterian settlers who came from Scotland at the time of the persecution of the Presbyterians in Scotland. James Starrat was father to the present Archabald Starrat of Moneymore.

Ancient Mill

The works of an ancient ladle mill was discovered by Robert Glasco of Coltrim townland at the verge of the bog in the same townland in 1818. The buckets of the water wheel was cut or chiselled out of the solid piece of oak, and so curious that millwrights declared that they had never seen anything like it before. From the Revd William Moore, Presbyterian minister, Robert Henderson, farmer, and others. 4th November 1836.

Slieve Gallion

[T. Fagan] The ancient name of Slieve Gallion <Gallen> was Slieve Inivear, till the fall in combat of a chief of the Irish Phoenicians <Phinicians> called Kallanmore, who was killed at the north west end of the above mountain, in view of a lake then called Loughnacuin but at present called Lough Fea <Fee>. The borders of the lough and its immediate neighbourhood along the foot of the above mountain was for a series of years the scene of hunting and various other amusements and competitions, in different actions with these chiefs and their men.

Also they much delighted in competing about the excellence of their grues or greyhounds, which were their chief favourites and which they trained up not only to attend to their various orders but also to compete with each other in swimming from one side to the other of the lough, with as much intent and sagacity as if of the human kind. It is in consequence of these animal swimming matches that the lake was dedicated to them and called in the Irish language Loughnacuin or the "grue or greyhound lake," though from some cause subsequently changed to Lough Fea.

The above mountain was also dedicated to the name of the above chief at the instance of his being interred at the north west end of it, in the townland of Ballybreeve and parish of Lissan, where his remains is enclosed by a number of large columns. The mountain was from that period called in the Irish language Slieve Kallann, but at some after period called Slieve Gallion.

The following epitaph, though not cut or inscribed on Kallanmore's tombstone, yet prevails among the old inhabitants of the neighbourhood, as follows: "Thaa Kallanmore, mack reih thierr an thuaim, nachuillue thieve thoua donn ghlann, thaa chinn ga Slieve Iniver agus a chussa ga Lough Nacuin" or "Kallan More, the king of the silent country's son, lies entombed on the north west side of the glen, his head lies towards Slieve Iniver and his feet towards the grue or greyhound lake."

The subdivision of Ballybreeve in which the above monument stands is locally called Carnbane. It is also locally said that a cock was never known to crow in this subdivision; from what cause is not known by the local inhabitants. Information obtained from Michael McCloskey, Ails McFaull, John McCloskey and others.

Discoveries in Slieve Gallion

There was discovered beneath the surface of the above mountain, and in the parish of Desertmartin, at some former period a quantity of ancient silver coin of various sizes, but letters and figures on them so defaced that it could not be judged when they were coined. These coins have been subsequently sold by weight in Belfast.

There was also found in the same place an ancient pot of very large size, a meat spit and stand of rather odd construction. These last-mentioned articles were subsequently procured by the late Charles Knox of Gortahurk, Esquire. The pot stands at present in John Charles's house in the above parish. Informants John and James Higgins. 12th November 1836.

Discoveries

[J. Bleakly] About 10 years ago a quantity of turned sticks from 1 to 2 and a half feet long were found lying flat, 3 feet deep in the upper moss in the townland of Tullynure, by Peter Conlon, farmer of same townland, but all lost long since.

Also a quantity of butter, which was deposited in a large piece of bark, was found in the same place at the same time, and by the same person, but also lost. From Peter Conlon, James Larkin and others.

PRODUCTIVE ECONOMY

Branch Banks

The introduction of branch banks have been of the

Parish of Lissan

greatest benefit to the people of this part, particularly the weaving class, as they can have from 5 pounds to 100 pounds at 5%. As before, the poor who were obliged to borrow money from the farmers were charged some 1s per pound per month, some 10d per pound per month and some 6d per pound per month. This system left the poor still in poverty.

Ironworks

Ironworks was carried on extensively about the year 1695 by the Staples family in the townland of Lissan. The iron which made the chain which was extended across Lough Foyle as a barrier to prevent the enemy's ships from coming in at the siege of Derry was made from this iron in 1698. 2nd September 1836.

Fair at Lissan Church

There was a fair held annually at Lissan church for business and pleasure until 1832, when it ceased on account of quarrelling by order of Mr Conyngham <Cunningham> of Springhill, as at the last fair, which was in 1832, the mob fired a shot at the magistrat, William Lenox Conyngham Esquire of Springhill, for which reason he had the fair discontinued. It was held on the 26th of November each year, only once a year. The fairs held at Moneymore and Cookstown became so much established that it was also a reason for doing away with the fair at Lissan church.

Planting

The planting on both sides of the road at Coltrim bog consists of fir, oak, ash, birch and alder, and contains [blank] acres planted 14 years ago by the Worshipful the Drapers' Company, who are in the habit of planting the cut-away bog and have planted many patches through the townland of Coltrim.

The planting which is situated near the residence of Sir Thomas Staples in the townland of Rossmore consists of fir chiefly, with some alder and ash. The oldest, which is on the left hand side of the road, is 39 years planted and some beyond it 22 years planted; the younger in the centre is 8 years planted.

Also the planting above the porter's lodge in the same townland consists of fir only and is 12 years planted. All the above is planted at the expense of Sir Thomas Staples Bart.

Also the planting in the townland of Killybaskey consists of fir and alder which is 5 years planted.

SOCIAL ECONOMY

Original Clergy of Church

The first remembered by the oldest inhabitants or by their ancestors was the Revd William Martin; 2nd, Revd Arthur Workman; 3rd, Revd Hugh Stewart; in his time the glebe was changed from Drummeen to Muff, where it now is; 4th, Revd Lodge, who was changed to Armagh; 5th, Revd James Millicut; 6th, the Revd John Molesworth Staples, who still continues. At his commencement the church was improved by studding the walls inside and plastering, in order to render the church more comfortable and dry, and also erected a fireplace and grate inside, and also built the vestry room and porch, the cost of which was 40 pounds. 16th September 1836.

Income of Curate

The income of the Revd William John Irvine, curate of the parish of Lissan, amounts to 75 pounds per annum British currency, paid by the rector, the Revd John Molesworth Staples. The residence of the curate is in the village of Cookstown, county Tyrone.

Religion

There is a Methodist meeting held occasionally in the houses through the townland of Clagan and Derryganard.

There are also a few Covenanters but have no place of worship nearer than the Grange, but hold prayer meetings occasionally in the house of Robert Henderson of Moneyhaw.

The Presbyterians have no place of worship in the parish but go to Moneymore and Cookstown.

Presbyterian Ministers

The residence of the Revd William Moore, Presbyterian minister, is in the townland of Coltrim, in a comfortable house, slated. The place is called Rushfield, a name given to it by the minister. Mr Moore ceased to preach in 1824, or rather was superannuated from infirmity, but still receives the regium donum which is 100 pounds per annum, and was succeeded by the Revd John Barnett, who preaches in the large meeting house at Moneymore but will not receive the regium donum till the death of Mr Moore.

Presbyterian Congregation

Many of the Presbyterians in the above parish, hearers of the Revd John Barnett, have left his congregation since the new meeting house was built, some on account of his endeavouring to impress the necessity of family worship and refusing to give them the rights of the church unless they adopted this system in their houses, as their former minister Mr Moore was not so particular.

Some have also left the congregation from a dispute about seats in the meeting house after its erection. Many have gone to the Established Church and, it is said, through the influence of Mr Miller, who is a great advocate for the Established Church and the most influential person in the country. Some have joined the Seceders and Covenanters. From Adam Eccles and Robert Henderson.

Covenanters

It is upwards of 60 years since the Covenanters first came to the parish of Lissan and was at that time established by the Revd John McKenny, who resided at Drumgrass near Lissan House; but have no place of worship nearer than the Grange in the county Tyrone, but occasionally in the barn of John Eccles of Moneyhaw. Information obtained from John Eccles, Adam Eccles and Robert Henderson, farmers. 7th November 1836.

Roman Catholic Clergy

The first remembered by the oldest inhabitant was the Revd Patrick Doyle, who died in 1756; the second was the Revd Thomas Donnelly; 3rd, the Revd Thomas Conway; 4th, the Revd John Graham; 5th, the Revd Charles Graham; 6th, the Revd Bernard Muldoon; in his time the chapel was built; 7th, the Revd Andrew McGeogh, who came in 1832 and was succeeded by the present, the Revd Bernard Murphy in 1834. NB The above list (except the Revd Andrew McGeogh and the Revd Bernard Murphy) will answer for the parish of Kildress in the county of Tyrone, as the parish of Lissan and Kildress were united until 1822.

Roman Catholic Congregation

In 1834 for 3 successive Sundays the congregation in the chapel amounted on the average to 1,357 persons.

Income of Priest

The annual income of the parish priest, the Revd Bernard Murphy, is 85 pounds from the congregation and 10 guineas from the Worshipful the Drapers' Company. The curate, the Revd James McGeogh, receives 24 pounds per annum from the parish priest. Mr Murphy, the parish priest, resides at private lodgings in the townland of Killybaskey. The curate resides in the townland of Tullynure.

The sum generally paid to the priest for christening a child is 2s; some give more according to their ability.

Offerings at funerals is totally abolished. This was more lucrative than either christenings or marriages.

Marriage by the Priest

The Roman Catholic clergy of this parish charge 1 pound 5s to each couple married by them. The 1 pound is for the bishop and the other 5s goes to the priest. This charge is by order of the bishop.

Superstition: Arrowheads

Thomas Harkness of the townland of Tintagh discovered 4 flint arrowheads, nearly all of the same size and shape, in digging the surface of a road near his house in 1833.

Molly McGarvey and Molly Devlin have also preserved a few of the flint arrowheads which they call elf stones and by which they perform cures on cattle in the following manner.

All the arrowheads (the greater the number, the greater the virtue and the more expeditious the cure) are put into salt and water with 3 ha'pence and a piece of silver, generally a sixpence. The cure is performed by rubbing the salt and water with the hand, beginning at the top of the tail to the nostrils, against the grain of the hair and also round the girth. This is done 3 times, during which prayers are uttered, after which part of the water is put into the mouth and nostrils of the cow and a part at the root of some gentle bush, and the remainder put behind the fire.

The people affirm that those arrows are shot from the Danes' fort by the fairies or some supernatural power and pierce the cow through the side, and pretend to show the print of the arrow. If any of the arrows should fall to the ground, their virtue is supposed to be lost. The people do not wish to part with any of those arrows.

This superstition prevails also among the Presbyterians who reside among the Roman Catholics in the mountainous part of this parish. Information obtained from Thomas Harkness, Molly Devlin and many others. 20th September 1836.

Charm for Toothache

The toothache is generally cured by a charm, of which the following are the words:

Parish of Lissan

"St Peter sat mourning on a marble stone,
By came our Lord and said [to] Peter alone,
What aileth thee? What makes thee shake?
Peter said, 'My Lord, my God, my tooth doth ache.'
Arise up Peter, and behold not you alone,
But all those who shall wear this for my sake,
Shall never be troubled with the toothache."
For the benefit of AB. If for a married female, her maiden name is given.

The above charm is to be sewed in some part of the garment and generally worn about them, and is believed to have had the desired effect when all medical aid failed, except the painful operation of extracting the tooth. The reason why so many persons are afflicted with the pain of the head and toothache is because they comb their hair on Friday and Sundays. There is also a preventive against fever and it is to abstain from fleshmeat on certain fast days.

NB The above charm is well known through many other parishes through the county.

Sprains can be cured by charms and motes extracted from the eyes, although the persons are not present. There are also charms for the fever, ague and falling-sickness.

The priests prohibit their hearers to perform cures by means of charms, as Roman Catholics are generally the persons who are in the habit of performing cures in this way. 21st September 1836.

Custom: The Churn

There is a custom among the farmers of this parish also, that on the evening of the last day of reaping or harvest home those employed assemble at the house of the farmer, where a feast is prepared at the expense of the farmer, consisting of bread, butter, tea and whiskey, and a musician is employed on the occasion, and where the greater part of the night is spent in eating, drinking and dancing. This custom is only practised by the more respectable farmers to any extent, yet the poorer farmers have something like it.

The Calliagh

The word calliagh is Irish and signifies "last," and is the last handful of corn of the harvest. This handful is left standing and plaited 3 plait, when all reapers in the field commence throwing their hooks at it. The person by whom it is cut pulls it up and brings it home to the employer's house, as they say, to choke the mistress if she refuses to give them a treat, or in other words a churn. The handful is left hung up inside the house, perhaps until the harvest following. From Martha Heaney, James Harkness, Adam Eccles, farmers.

Superstitions

James Lunnon of Tintagh (a farmer) declares that on foggy days he has often heard the gentle folk or fairies on the face of the mountain a little above his house, knocking, as it were, 2 stones together and afterwards laughing hearty; and believes with many others of his neighbours that the flint arrowheads (some of which are in his possession) are all made by the fairies and thrown by them at the cattle, which is called by the people elf shooting. From James Lunnan, James Harkness and Martha Heaney.

The Presbyterians are equally superstitious in this parish, which is evident from their desire to preserve the fairy bushes which are in various parts of the parish.

Fairy Bushes

Fairy bushes are very numerous through the parish. The superstition is the same respecting them as in other parishes.

Census of the Parish

Of the Established Church 648, Presbyterians 1,299, Roman Catholics 2,386, other denominations 19, total 4,352. 1st November 1836.

Customs of the People

It is customary for the heads of families at stated seasons, such as Hallow Eve, Christmas and Easter, to invite their children and families (if possible) to spend the anniversary of the above seasons with them. The Episcopalians and Roman Catholics observe new style more than old, the Presbyterians old style more than new style.

It is also a custom among the native Irish to abstain from work if one of their own persuasion dies in the townland, except there is a running stream between them and the corpse.

Gratitude is another feature in the character of the native Irish of this part of the country to their own relations and which is exhibited from their anxiety to remit money from foreign countries to their friends at home. Information obtained from the Revd William John Irvine, curate, the Revd William Moore, Presbyterian minister, and Adam Eccles. 2nd November 1836.

Pride of the People

The desire for dress is very remarkable, as they

will actually live on scanty meals and work hard all the week in order to appear well dressed on Sunday. The Revd Mr Moore states that the Protestants are so proud that they would rather live at home on half-food or emigrate rather than go to service. It is commonly believed that the Roman Catholics make the best servants, as they are more submissive than either Protestants or Presbyterians; chiefly Roman Catholic servants through this parish.

Ancient Families

The oldest and most respectable Roman Catholic family in the parish of Lissan is that of Mr Charles Quinn of Moneyhaw townland.

Prevailing Names

The most prevailing names in the parish of Lissan are Corrs and Conlons.

Surnames on Tombstones in Churchyard

Wilson, Conyngham, Custre, Logan, McGlone, Hutchinson, Donnelly, Doris, McKeirnan, Mullon, Conlon, McCann, Conelly, Kirgan, Magill. Those marked thus "+" [numbers 4–5, 7–12] are Roman Catholics. From David Taylor, schoolmaster, and Peter Conlon.

Irish Language

The Irish language is very little known in this parish, not even in the remotest part on the borders of the parish of Ballynascreen, except by very few persons.

Dispensaries

The people when sick go to the Moneymore and Cookstown dispensary, as there is a dispensary in both places.

Illicit Distillation

Illicit distillation was most prevalent in the parish in 1818 and 1819, and in the mountain parts of the parish, but at present is very little practised.

Malicious Burning

Within the last 2 years some houses and also turf stacks, the property of Owen McCarrigan in the townland of Tintagh, have been maliciously burned.

Richest Townland

Moneyhaw is undoubtedly the richest townland in the parish. The wealth of its inhabitants may be attributed to the extent of their farms and their own industry, viz. one by jobbing in cattle, one by road-making and the remainder by farming. The houses are all very comfortable and clean, both inside and outside.

Poorest Townland

The poorest townland in the parish is Ballybrist. Its poverty is chiefly owing to: the failure in the bleaching trade which, when in existence, gave employment to all the poor of that part of the parish; the poverty of the land, which is all nearly mountain and until of late years very little reclaimed. Many of the tenants have run away twice. The third time they have settled themselves and have become more industrious, and are reclaiming more of their farms and supporting themselves chiefly by besom <bisom> making, the sale of which, with the produce of their farms, enables them to pay their rent when heretofore they thought it impossible to make the rent out by the produce of the land and became careless and idle, and became in arrears <erears> of rent and then ran off. Information obtained from Mr James Smyth, farmer of Dunnabraggy, Mr William Morgan, a former proprietor of Grouse Lodge, townland of Ballybrist, and Joseph Black and many others.

Poor

There are 32 poor persons' names on the church list receiving the poor box money, viz. 12 are of the Established Church, 3 Presbyterians and 17 are Roman Catholics. The general cause of their poverty is chiefly old age and infirmity, except 4 which are almost idiots and 1 woman who had been brought to poverty by the misconduct of her husband, who is a drunkard. There are also 8 poor pensioners receiving amongst them 4 pounds 17s per quarter from Sir Thomas Staples Bart, and 2 poor pensioners who receive 6d per week from Sir Thomas Staples, and 1 of the above 8 who receives 30s per annum from a former curate of the parish, the Revd Hugh Hamilton, now residing at Church Hill, county Fermanagh. The average annual amount of the poor box collection is 7 pounds. Information obtained from David Taylor, treasurer and schoolmaster. 14th November 1836.

Cottiers in Killybaskey

There are only 4 cottiers in the townland of Killybaskey but none so poor as to beg, as they are chiefly employed as labourers to the persons on

Parish of Lissan

whose farms they reside. Killybaskey is churchland property.

Cottiers in Drumard

There are 16 cottiers in the townland of Drumard, none of which can be classed with paupers as they do not go out as such but are chiefly employed as labourers to the persons from whom they have their cottages. Sometimes a few of them are obliged, for want of seed potatoes in spring for their garden, to call on their employers and neighbours for help. Drumard is on the estate of Captain Edmond Staples, a non-resident. Information obtained from Joseph Black, farmer, Killybaskey, John Montgomery, William Eccles, farmers, and James Hogg, Drumard. 9th November 1836.

The Drapers' Company will not allow any cottier on their estate or proportion to beg. If those farmers on their proportion who keep cottiers do not keep their cottiers' houses in good repair, they are ordered to be pulled down. From Adam Eccles, James Smith and Smith Davison, farmers on the estate.

Houses in Tintagh

The townland of Tintagh contains about 32 houses, all built of stone except 2 which are of [mud ?], and with the exception of a few cottiers' houses are all tolerably clean outside. The inside is also middling. NB This being the season for scutching flax, and as few of the inhabitants have barns to scutch or thresh in, and consequently must scutch and thresh the corn in the houses, so the houses do not appear as clean inside at this season as at other seasons, when the above work is not required.

NB In Roman Catholic districts there is more poverty and the houses consequently not kept as clean as in the Protestant and Presbyterian districts.

Derivation of Dunnabraggy

Dunnabraggy or Dunnabrogue took its name from a lump of gold the size of a brogue which was found on the farm of Kennedy McCullagh in the above townland.

Priest

The Christian name of the parish priest of Arboe is John.

Remarkable Living Character

David Donnelly of the townland of Moneyhaw is the son of a labourer, is 45 years of age, and about 14 years ago he was deprived of his eyesight from a hurt occasioned by digging in a fort and is stone blind. This remarkable character can go through all the operations of farming with the greatest accuracy as a man with his eyesight, can weed potatoes, weed flax, dig furrows, thrash corn, bake turf and describe a building and point out any deficiency in the work.

Strong Man

The strongest man in the parish was William Forsythe of Coltrim townland, now 30 years deceased.

William Forsythe before described would lift a large hogshead of flax seed in his arms and throw it from a cart or carry it a considerable distance with ease. From the Revd Mr Moore and others.

Sunday School

There was a Sunday school held in the Roman Catholic chapel which was numerously attended for some time, but was discontinued since the days became short.

Benefit of Sunday Schools

The opinion of Mr Irvine respecting the efficacy of Sunday schools is that they are believed to improve both the moral and religious conduct of the young persons attending them, which is evident from their walk and conversation and from their attention at divine worship, the anxiety of the children to obtain premiums, which is chiefly given in religious books, and from the parents becoming acquainted with the Word of God and from their anxiety occasionally to attend the Sunday schools.

There are 2 living instances of persons in the mountain parts of the parish who have been benefitted much [from] the instruction they have received in Sunday schools; the one a married female and the other a single one, through whose influence many children have been brought to attend the Sunday school, and who have also established branch Sunday schools in their own neighbourhood and who were teachers in the Sunday school at Lissan church.

Another good effect arising from Sunday schools is that it brings the teachers and scholars in contact with the clergy, which they consider a great honour, and also in stirring up a spirit of inquiry among the teachers and adult scholars, which leads them to search the Scriptures and examine for themselves in order to enable them to instruct others. None can be said to have been really converted in the parish through the instrumentality of Sunday schools, but "it is not immediately after the seed is sown that we may expect to reap the produce." From the curate. 9th November 1836.

Schools

Derryganard Sunday school: the circulation of religious tracts are of the greatest benefit to both children and parents, and the desire to read them still greater. There are 2 instances of persons (adults) learning to read at home, instructed by the children. Martha Bodkin, the superintendent of the above Sunday school, was never at a day school: her mother taught her to read.

A night school was established last winter and held in the house of Martha Bodkin, where the Sunday school is held, and was taught by her brother but only for 3 months in winter.

By order of the Roman Catholic clergy the Roman Catholic children were removed from Martha Bodkin's Sunday school. Since the establishment of Miss Ramsay's Sunday school, the Presbyterian children were also removed to Miss Ramsay's Sunday school. Information obtained from Martha Bodkin, 23rd November 1836.

Census

Census of parish of Lissan from the priest. [Insert marginal note by C.W. Ligar: A copy of the census book required].

Tintagh, 222 Roman Catholics, 13 Presbyterians.

Ballyforlea, 43 Roman Catholics, 33 Presbyterians.

Knockadoo, 112 Roman Catholics, 128 Presbyterians, 66 Established Church, 10 Seceders.

Litteran, 136 Roman Catholics, 25 Presbyterians, 8 Established Church.

Dernan, 343 Roman Catholics.

Mobuoy, 234 Roman Catholics, 12 Presbyterians, 44 Established Church.

Killybaskey, 100 Roman Catholics, 78 Presbyterians, 22 Established Church, 31 Seceders.

Tullynure, 310 Roman Catholics, 61 Established Church.

Clagan, 127 Roman Catholics, 33 Presbyterians, 82 Established Church.

Ballybrist, 66 Roman Catholics, 37 Presbyterians, 110 Established Church.

Rossmore, 75 Roman Catholics, 11 Presbyterians, 43 Established Church, 8 Seceders.

Derryganard, 111 Roman Catholics, 20 Presbyterians, 4 Established Church, 7 Baptists.

Lismoney, 48 Roman Catholics, 83 Presbyterians, 3 Established Church, 16 Seceders.

Drummeen, 39 Roman Catholics, 30 Presbyterians, 1 Established Church, 9 Seceders.

Dunnabraggy, 31 Roman Catholics, 17 Presbyterians, 19 Established Church, 47 Seceders.

Muff, 68 Roman Catholics, 32 Presbyterians, 23 Established Church, 21 Seceders.

Moneyhaw, 74 Roman Catholics, 44 Presbyterians, 26 Established Church.

Drumrot, 63 Roman Catholics, 65 Presbyterians, 2 Established Church.

Coltrim, 169 Roman Catholics, 87 Presbyterians, 17 Established Church.

Drumard and Turnaface, 55 Roman Catholics, 85 Presbyterians, 51 Established Church, 36 Seceders.

Caneese, 107 Roman Catholics, 50 Presbyterians, 49 Established Church, 18 Seceders.

Total 2,533 Roman Catholics, 883 Presbyterians, 631 Established Church, 196 Seceders, 7 Baptists.

Emigration

The reason why the emigration from the parish of Lissan is so extensive this year, and chiefly Roman Catholic, because Captain Edmond Staples, who is the proprietor of 7 townlands of the parish, will not allow a Roman Catholic to reside on his property.

Emigration in 1834

List of persons who have emigrated from the parish of Lissan during the year 1834. [Table contains the following headings: name, age, religion, townland in which person resided, port emigrated to].

James Glasco, 29, Presbyterian, from Coltrim to New York.

John Ladden, 40, Sarah Ladden, 20, Bernard Ladden, 6 months, Roman Catholics, from Coltrim to Quebec, returned same year.

Robert McAnana, 22, Roman Catholic, from Coltrim to Quebec, returned same year.

John Devlin, 19, Roman Catholic, from Coltrim to Philadelphia, returned same year.

Margaret McKenna, 29, Roman Catholic, from Dunnabraggy to Quebec.

Mary McCree, 27, Presbyterian, from Dunnabraggy to Philadelphia.

Samuel McCullagh, 34, Presbyterian, from Drummeen to Philadelphia.

John Harkness, 31, Presbyterian, from Drumard to Philadelphia.

Parish of Lissan

Archabald McCullagh, 30, Presbyterian, from Lissan Demesne to Philadelphia.

Francis O'Neil, 40, Roman Catholic, from Tullynure to New York.

James McAnana, 26, Roman Catholic, from Tullynure to Philadelphia.

Sarah Hutchison, 42, Hugh Hutchison, 20, Mary Hutchison, 25, Presbyterians, from Tullynure to Philadelphia.

Nancy Hutchison, 26, Presbyterian, from Ballyforlea to New York.

John Bonnett, 56, Adam Bonnett, 32, Samuel Bonnett, 30, James Bonnett, 10, Martha Bonnett, 25, Roman Catholics, from Clagan to Quebec.

Thomas McCleese, 18, Roman Catholic, from Clagan to Quebec.

Matthew Mills, 32, Presbyterian, from Caneese to New York, returned 1836.

Susan McCann, 23, Roman Catholic, from Tintagh to New York.

Patrick Heany, 24, Roman Catholic, from Tintagh to Baltimore.

Peter Hagan, 27, Roman Catholic, from Tintagh to Dundee.

James McGarvey, 26, Seceder, from Litteran to Quebec.

Peter Campbell, 30, Roman Catholic, from Dernan to New York.

Emigration in 1835

William Glasco, 29, Presbyterian, from Coltrim to New York.

Mary Devlin, 24, Roman Catholic, from Coltrim to Quebec.

Stewart Irwin, 29, Presbyterian, from Killybaskey to Quebec.

Jane McCullagh, 26, Presbyterian, from Drumard to Philadelphia.

Alexander Carson, 40, Esther Carson, 35, Presbyterians, from Knockadoo to New York.

Elizabeth Hunter, 25, Presbyterian, from Knockadoo to New York.

Migration

List of persons who migrate annually from the parish of Lissan.

William McCann, 25, Presbyterian, from Coltrim to Glasgow.

Patrick Devlin, 33, Roman Catholic, from Coltrim to Glasgow.

James Dunsheath, 30, Presbyterian, from Coltrim to Glasgow.

Robert Crawford, 25, Presbyterian, from Coltrim to Glasgow.

Patrick McAnna, 25, Roman Catholic, from Coltrim to Glasgow.

Daniel Ward, 30, Roman Catholic, from Coltrim to Glasgow.

Thomas Cowan, 48, Established Church, from Coltrim to Glasgow.

Jane Devlin, 45, Roman Catholic, from Coltrim to Glasgow.

Bernard Donelly, 45, Roman Catholic, from Muff to Glasgow.

John Greenan, 60, Jeremiah Greenan, 35, William Greenan, 20, Roman Catholics, from Moneyhaw to Glasgow.

John McMaster, 30, Presbyterian, from Moneyhaw to Glasgow.

Hugh Donnelly, 35, Roman Catholic, from Moneyhaw to Glasgow.

Charles Quinn, cattle jobber, 48, Roman Catholic, from Moneyhaw to Glasgow.

Robert Bell, 45, Presbyterian, from Killybaskey to Merryport.

John Toner, 50, Roman Catholic, from Drummeen to Glasgow.

Joseph Wright, 16, Presbyterian, from Clagan to Glasgow.

John Mitchell, 20, Presbyterian, from Clagan to Glasgow.

Edward Sherry, 22, Bernard Sherry, 32, Roman Catholics, from Knockadoo to Glasgow.

John McKernan, 20, Roman Catholic, from Knockadoo to Glasgow.

Christopher McCullagh, 40, Mary McCullagh, 40, Roman Catholics, from Knockadoo to Glasgow.

Eliza Hagan, 21, Roman Catholic, from Knockadoo to Glasgow.

Nancy McCullagh, 18, Roman Catholic, from Knockadoo to Glasgow.

Peter Hagan, 25, Nancy Hagan, 25, Roman Catholics, from Tintagh to Glasgow.

John Doyle, 35, Philip Doyle, 20, Mary Doyle, 32, Margaret Doyle, 17, John Doyle, 15, Roman Catholics, from Tintagh to Glasgow.

John Hogan, 36, Mary Hogan, 26, Roman Catholics, from Litteran to Glasgow.

Martha Devlin, 32, Jane Devlin, 26, Roman Catholics, from Litteran to Glasgow.

Patrick Mullan, 40, Nancy Mullan, 40, Patrick Mullan, 20, Roman Catholics, from Dernan to Glasgow.

John O'Neil, 44, John O'Neil Junior, 24, Roman Catholics, from Dernan to Glasgow.

James Farrell, 45, Roman Catholic, from Dernan to Glasgow.

John Dugan, 30, Roman Catholic, from Dernan to Glasgow.

Michael Mullan, 28, Roman Catholic, from Dernan to Glasgow.

Patrick Campbell, 30 [or 50], Roman Catholic, from Dernan to Glasgow.

John Mullon, 34, Martha Mullon, 40, Peter Mullon, 26, Michael Mullon, 25, Roman Catholics, from Dernan to Glasgow.

Michael Mullan, 32, Roman Catholic, from Derryganard to Glasgow.

John McConway, 30, Roman Catholic, from Derryganard to Glasgow.

Charles McConvery, 32, Roman Catholic, from Derryganard to Glasgow.

Bernard Mullan, 25, Charles Mullan, 30, Margaret Mullan, 50, Roman Catholics, from Derryganard to Glasgow.

Felix O'Neil, 28, Bridget O'Neil, 28, James O'Neil, 26, Bridget O'Neil, 30, Roman Catholics, from Derryganard to Glasgow.

Robert McGlade, 40, Roman Catholic, from Rossmore to Liverpool.

Miscellaneous Papers

Parishes of Ballynascreen, Desertmartin and Kilcronaghan, County Londonderry

Statistical Report by J. McCloskey, 1821

NATURAL STATE

Name and Situation

These parishes are situated in the barony of Loughinsholin, in the county and diocese of Derry. In the ancient civil division of the county the territory of Glenconkyne <Glenconkinn> comprised almost all Ballynascreen <Ballinascreen>, Kilcronaghan and Desertmartin. To the territory of Clandonnell appertained a few townlands in the eastern part of Ballynascreen and in the south eastern division of Desertmartin. The whole formed a part of Tyrone and was in the primitive ecclesiastical division included in the diocese of Rathturig.

Extent and Divisions

Taken as a united district, it is bounded in the north by Banagher, Dungiven and Maghera, on the east by Maghera, Termoneeny and Magherafelt, on the south by Desertmartin and Lissan <Lissane>, on the west by Bodoney in Tyrone and by a part of Banagher. From this description it will be seen that it lies on the south west border of the county, whence stretching northward it rises again to the south east. Its form, allowing for occasional projections and indentations in the boundary line, is that of a parallelogram whose average length is about 9 miles by nearly 6 in breadth; the estimated extent 33,000 acres.

The parish of Ballynascreen is the largest in the district, of which it forms the northern and eastern portion. This parish contains 35 townlands, comprising 22,339 estimated Irish acres, whereof perhaps 12,000 are barren moory pasture.

Its present name, which is also its most ancient known designation, signifies "the town of the library," from an institution of that nature founded therein by St Patrick.

Kilcronaghan (the church of Cronachan) lies to the west and south east of Ballynascreen. It contains 20 townlands, making an area of 5,235 Irish acres; about 2,000 of these are heathy pasture.

Desertmartin occupies the southern and south western portion of the district. There are 24 townlands in this parish. Their computed extent in Irish acres is 5,718, whereof nearly 2,000 are rough pasture lands. Its name is said to signify "the portion or division of St Martin."

NATURAL FEATURES

Hills

This is a mountainous region. The parishes of Desertmartin and Kilcronaghan lie partly on the side of Sliabh Gallion, and partly wind round its base. Ballynascreen, with the exception of its southern side, where it expands into the vale of the Moyola, is girded by lofty chains of hills. It has towards its eastern boundary Evishgore and Craignashoke, bold abrupt headlands terminating the basaltic chain of Benbradagh. On the other 2 sides it reaches respectively to the Sliabh Gallion ridge and to the range of mica slate connected with Sawel and the Tyrone mountains.

River Moyola

From these mountains arises the River Moyola or Minola, which flows through the district from north west to south south east, a course of about 10 miles, receiving in its progress the tributes of the Awain Ban or White Water, the Dhu Glass or Blackwater, and various minor streams. The Moyola now produces only small trout and eels, the ascent of salmon being impeded by the weir at Castledawson. This river often overflows and injures the adjoining holmes, especially in Ballynascreen. If embankments were made and the mounds planted with sallows and oziers, this nuisance might be converted into a benefit.

Surface and Soil

The summits of the mountains are bare, barren and rocky, or clothed with heath and inert mosses, but the sides, especially those declivities which slope to the south and east, are smooth, verdant, covered with bent grass, and showing sometimes sweet little plots of daisies. They form good pasture lands, are well watered, without in general a superabundance of moisture, and might easily be improved by the application of enclosures and drainage. From their unusual depth of soil, cultivation has ascended to a great height, in some instances to perhaps 900 feet above the level of the sea, and it is making annual advances; indeed on the south east side of Sliabh Gallion are yet seen traces of ancient culture to a height of at least 1,100 feet.

The soil of Ballynascreen, with the exception

of a few gravelly swells and moory flats, is clay. That of the eastern side is reddish, being the decomposition of the sandstone which here bassets from beneath the basalt; that of the other parts has been formed by a like process from schistus. The latter varies in colour from bluish to pale grey, but in all its varities it is cold, stiff and retentive.

In the other 2 parishes the surface, particularly on the west side, is broken into hills, sometimes detached, sometimes in groups of various shapes and heights, as if riven from the giant side of Sliabh Gallion by some mighty convulsion of nature. The soil is, of course, gravel with a mixture of gravel and sand; it is light and thin. In the bottoms between the hills are some spots of tolerable depth and proportionate fertility.

Bogs

The red clay appears in the lower grounds. Towards the south east too are many spots of good loam, deep and dark coloured, and throughout the whole district are considerable flats of bog. The principal of these are that between Anagh and Drumsamney, that of Grange, Motalee and near Tobermore <Tubbermore>, with some patches in a few other places. The largest bog in Ballynascreen is that of churchlands. Timber is found in Ballinderry and Grange bogs, and also in that of Ballynascreen. It is mostly fir with some oak found about 4 feet beneath the surface. The trees lie in all directions, one above the other, and large blocks are sometimes found lying above the trees. Some of these trees are charred to a depth of many inches, others bear evident marks of the axe. Nearer the surface are sometimes found acorns, fir cones and even hazelnuts well preserved.

Woods and Planting

The trees which now give ornament and shade to the hamlets and homesteads in the northern part of the district are chiefly birches, alders and a few ash. Holly too is very abundant. The soil of the southern part is more genial to planting: there oak, ash, beech, larch, all the useful and ornamental trees succeed well.

The Glen wood, formerly so famous for the excellence of its oak, which yet stands the antique strength or uncouth ornament of many an old mansion, occupied almost the whole extent of Ballynascreen. This is long gone, and with it, of course, much of the landscape's beauty. Yet few regret the loss. Its place is now filled by a brave hardy race of men, and surely the smoke of one happy hut curling down the glen or floating on the hillside gives to the eye a lovelier image and fills the mind with dearer associations than the loftiest oak that ever spread his arms in the Glen wood.

The great ironworks formerly carried on in this neighbourhood contributed mainly to the destruction of the whole forest. The extension of tillage too made it necessary to clear the grounds. Some old leases remain in which the lessee convenanted to clear a certain number of acres during his tenancy. Yet this rage was pushed too far: many a bare unsightly spot, many a bank useless to man and inaccessible to cattle might have been made to give beauty to the landscape and benefit to its owner, but for this indiscriminate extirpation.

The Drapers' Company have lately made a very extensive and beautiful plantation of forest trees in the glens of Cranny in Desertmartin; it is thriving most luxuriantly. This, with the little coppice wood of Dunlogan, on their property in the north east of Ballynascreen, are sufficient evidences of their wish to restore and replace the far-famed woods of this district.

Among the other recent improvements of Mr Justice Torrens, he planted the last season upwards of 85,000 trees. Mr Bryan has also made a very thriving and fine plantation of larch and other forest trees on his farm of Gortahurk. The neat disposition of the planting, the tasteful advantage which has been taken of the undulating varieties of the surface make the appearance quite romantic.

Some of the farmers too seem not insensible of the beauty and utility to be derived from such improvements. The parish of Desertmartin contains more than 12 of this class, whose dwellings will soon be embosomed in very neat plantations. The table in the appendix shows the names of these respectable individuals to whose taste and spirit our rural scenery will owe this revival of its natural beauty. One of these, John Mairs of Gortanury, has planted upwards of 25,000 trees of various species.

The planting of fruit trees is neglected. There are no old orchards and but few attempts to produce new ones, except here and there in a garden.

Lakes

Loughinsholin, whence the barony derives its name, is a small lake half a mile from Desertmartin, on the west side of the road leading to Ballynascreen. It was formerly of great extent but its waters are now much contracted, not exceed-

Miscellaneous Papers

ing half a mile in circumference; and in the further application of draining to the adjacent bog it will probably be soon dried up. It produces eels and very fine pike. The lake itself and an islet in its centre are said to be artifical and to have been constructed in ancient times as a refuge from enemies. Undoubtedly the lake was enlarged, if not originally formed, by cutting a passage for the little rivulet of Keenaugh. The islet was formed by sinking piles and vast beams.

There is another more spacious lake among the hills in the north west of Ballynascreen. It is called Lough Patrick and is about a mile in circumference.

NATURAL HISTORY

Minerals and Mines

The concurrent tradition of the inhabitants corroborates the testimony of old Dr Boate, who asserts in his *Natural history of Ireland* that gold was found in the rivulet called "Miola which rises in the mountain Sleivgallen." He means the Awain Ban or White Water, one of the tributary streams of the Moyola and which actually rises in Sliabh Gallion. It is said that small pieces of gold have often been found in that stream, as also masses of silver ore.

But whatever may be thought of this report, it is certain that a more useful metal is found in the district. Iron abounds in Sliabh Gallion, both as a bog ore and nearly in a metallic state. It was formerly smelted here to a considerable extent. The works were situated in Moybeg, which has since retained the name of Forgetown, and large heaps of charcoal are to this day dug up in that neighbourhood. The once famous ironworks at Castledawson were also supplied with ore from Sliabh Gallion. The mine was in the townland of Boveagh.

The Moybeg work[s] were first managed by one York, then by Forester, ancestor of the present Mr Forester of Cloverhill, and were finally discontinued, not from any defect in the quantity or quality of the ore, but from the failure of the last proprietor Mr Rainey, whose ruin appears to have proceeded from his having embarked beyond his means in various distant mining speculations.

Coal too is said to have been among the discoveries of this indefatigable miner. 2 deep pits are shown near Gortahurk, whence it was raised by his order. The upper part of these pits shows at present a reddish sandstone. Specimens of coal have often been found after violent floods in the little streamlet of Dunmurry and in Skelly's burn. Both of these brooks fall from Craignashoke; their beds present strata of sandstone. Some indications of coal also occur in Luney.

Geology

Mention of those minerals leads also to a brief consideration to the particular geological structure of the district. In the present instance, as the subject can be but imperfectly treated, the best course will perhaps be to note the strata or substances as they present themselves, beginning with the uppermost.

Basalt

Sliabh Gallion forms the south west limit of the great basaltic region of Ireland, which region is bounded in the east by Belfast Lough, winds along the line of the Antrim and Derry coast, and runs nearly due north and south from Binevenagh <Benevenyagh> by Benbradagh and Craigakeeran to Sliabh Gallion.

This fossil, whose formation has been so much disputed by geologists, appears on the summit of the latter mountain in its tabular form, disposed in large masses irregularly stratafied. The entire deposit is upwards of 160 feet in thickness and shows different varieties of this rock, from the hard coarse-grained basalt in beds, as at the Tummocks, to the loose crumbling trapp in the scaur at Iniscarn. Some fine specimens of zeolite are found deposited on the surface. In other parts of this mountain the trapp alternates into greenstone and iron stone.

At Craigakeeran, on the north east boundary of the district, the basalt appears with a greater tendency to columnar form. Proceeding southwards, Evishgore exhibits a cap of loose zeolitic trapp mouldering away with each successive frost. Onward at Craignashoke the basaltic rock is seen to more advantage. It rises to the summit of this mountain, 1,864 feet. This stratum of trapp is 275 feet thick. Viewed from the road below the whole mountain side appears to have slipped down, a vast avalanche disclosing the front of this lofty barrier of basalt which is here imperfectly columnar in irregular polyhedrous prismoids of coarsely defined joints, standing with a small angle of reclination towards the mass of the mountains.

Limestone

The basalt rest on a fossil of infinite utility, the white limestone. The depth of this deposit is not ascertained, none of the quarries being yet exhausted. It attains its greatest elevation in this district, having ascended, in a course of about 24 miles from the sea beach at Downhill to the quarries on Sliabh Gallion, no less than 1,460 feet. The upper stratum is often covered with clay alone. It is always brittle, shivery and of snowy whiteness, but when long exposed to the action of the atmosphere takes a purplish hue, except where nodules of flint occur. The lower beds rise in large tables vying in solidity and lustre with parian marble.

The heterogenous substances mixed with this limestone are few and only occur in the upper beds. Spars are seen of great beauty and of various textures; some of the finest are disposed in thin horizontal planes which are diagonally intersected so as to form beautiful rhombic crystals. The flints are green, bluish grey and purple. They sometimes assume that organic form known by the name of [?] paramonoid. Belemnites too, echine and terretratutae are found imbedded in the lime.

Steatite is sometimes met: the principal vein of this is seen in Bovevagh, just at the junction of the basalt and the limestone. It is of a dull white colour, is often eat[en] by the herd boys and, boiled in milk, is taken as a remedy for internal bruises.

At the mountain's base, and emerging from beneath a vast mass of calcareous sandstone, appears another and better species of limestone which spreads over all the south eastern portion of the district, where it is accessible in almost every townland. This is the shell limestone, its colour from dusky red to bluish grey. Its upper stratum is friable and choppy, like clay in the act of drying. Further down it becomes very hard and, when broken, shows a close-grained surface covered with small shining particles. This stone produces that white and durable calx so much sought after as the Desertmartin limestone. The strata generally dip north west at angles from 8 degrees to 12 degrees. This fact almost every quarryman knows, yet none avail themselves of it but peversely open in contrary directions, where the limestone soon leaves them or is pursued with great labour and expense.

The organic remains found in this fossil are various species of the conchae anomiae, particularly the tiribratula tribe. At Stranagard it is accompanied by a bed of calcareous marble formerly used for agricultural purposes, but now covered by the fallen bank of a rivulet.

Dr Berger has decided against the existence of limestone in Craignashoke. It certainly does not appear under that range of basalt, but it may be covered by the sinking of the subjacent terrace. Its presence is inferred, from that of the flints apparently covered with a varnish of limestone, from small nodules of lime said to have issued from springs and from the calcareous tinge which they communicate to the sandstone over which they flow.

Sandstone

This valuable fossil, to which, combined with the former, civilized life owes much of its comfort and adornment, is also accessible in many parts of the district.

It is of several hues and of various formation. The calcareous variety, which lies under the white limestone at Iniscarn, is extremely hard and is the whitest in the district. It becomes darker at Keenaught. In Moneyninea the upper stratum is reddish, sometimes white, but becomes grey when exposed to air; the lower strata are harder, more micaceous with a siliceous cement. Westward at the Ess [Ness] or waterfall of the Moneyninea rivulet millstones have been raised. They have also been taken from the Boveagh quarry. At Moydamlaght this stone is yellowish, with siliceous particles, but too soft to be worked till after long exposure to the air. The Mulnavoo quarry contains stone of a fine quality, which forms the spire of Ballynascreen church. But the best specimen of our sandstone is that of the Moybeg quarry, with which all the new buildings of the Drapers' Company at Moneymore are adorned and which their best workmen consider little inferior to the Portland stone.

Granite

In Sliabh Gallion the sandstone is sometimes seen to repose on granite which mutates into a species of granite and again into felspar porphyry. The granite which emerges in the channels of Awain Ban and Altoneill is the coarsest of the species. The finer variety of this rock does not appear within the limit of the district.

Mica Slate

The lofty broken ridges of Dunlogan, Spellchoagh and Derrynoid on the north west boundary is composed of one deep formation of mica slate which varies from ashen colour to light blue.

In the bed of the Moyola at Leabby are some indications of a slate quarry. The colour is deep blue, the surface very soft, but it might be worthwhile to explore the subjacent strata in a district where slates are so costly.

Miscellaneous Papers

A species of blue granular limestone shows itself from beneath the mica slate in a little brook which runs from Dunlogan through Moneyninea. It was once quarried but did not give satisfaction. The stone was of course micaceous. Yet as the lower beds would probably prove to be of a better quality, the expediency of a further exploration should be impressed on the farmers of that backward spot.

Chalybeate Springs

Several chalybeate springs issue from Sliabh Gallion, but they have never been used nor their peculiar qualities analysed.

MODERN TOPOGRAPHY

Village of Tobermore

The village of Tobermore, the capital of the district, is seated in a very commodious position, in the vale of the Moyola and not far from the right bank of the river. It consists of one long and wide street containing 112 houses, mostly built of brick and thatched. Some of these houses are tolerably neat, but many of them are of the most wretched and filthy description, being crowded with labouring poor, who resort thither on account of the cheapness of fuel. The only public buildings are the 2 Presbyterian meeting houses. There is a 3-day post to the village; it is also a fair town and has a few respectable shops.

Tobermore is situated in latitude 54 degrees 48 minutes 43 seconds north, bearing south east from Londonderry 20 and a quarter miles. It is distant 6 and a half miles from Moneymore, 4 and a half from Magherafelt, 5 from Castledawson, 2 from Maghera and 9 from Dungiven.

Gentlemen's Seats

Fort William, the seat of James Stevenson Esquire, the only resident landlord in the district, is within a few perches of Tobermore, on the north side of the Maghera road. It is built in a neat unassuming style of architecture and stands above the Moyola, on a beautiful natural terrace which well merits its Irish appellation of Dunaguny "the sunny height," and which, from its commanding position, makes Fort William indeed "a happy rural seat of various view." The small demesne is tastefully laid out, adorned with some modern shrubbery and sheltered by many fine trees of older growth. In brief, the house and grounds of Fort William are amongst the most pleasing, as they are also the most prominent, objects in the district.

Village of Desertmartin

Desertmartin, 2 and a half miles south of Tobermore, stands also on a very pleasing site. But the houses, of which there are 30, are arranged in the most disorderly manner. 2 of them are licensed, one as a spirit shop, the other for the sale of groceries. The inhabitants boast that this was once an assize town: they show the site and remains of the gaol, and note the adjacent height of Knocknagin (the hills of heads) as the place of execution. Southwards of the houses is a small thriving plantation, and the many natural advantages of the situation seem to invite easy improvement.

Village of Moyheelan

The village of Moyheelan, more usually called the Cross, from the circumstance of 2 roads intersecting each other at the place, is situated about 2 and three-quarter miles west by south from Tobermore. It contains 26 houses built on the declivity and at the foot of a hill, but scarcely adorned by a single tree. It derives an air of importance from the very neat church which stands in it.

There are 1 apothecary's shop, 7 grocers' shops and 3 licensed spirit shops in Moyheelan. It has also a monthly fair and is well entitled to the privilege of a weekly market. It is to be hoped that the Drapers' Company, the proprietors of this little village, may soon turn their attention to its improvement.

Gentlemen's Seats

Derrynoid Lodge, the occasional residence of the Honourable Justice Torrens, is situated about a mile from Moyheelan, on the north side of the road leading to Dungiven. It is a small neat building, surrounded by some improvements, the more valuable as having been effected on a rather unpromising soil. The plantings here are tastefully disposed in belts, screens and clumps, and the whole aspect of the ground is such as to give the eye an agreeable relief from the desolation and poverty that surround them.

Roads

The roads are in general excellent, good gravel being everywhere at hand. The principal lines of road are: that which connects Magherafelt and Moyheelan through Tobermore; that which from the same points leads through Desertmartin; those which connect Tobermore with Dungiven and

Maghera; the road leading by Lecumpher to Moneymore; and the line on the north connecting Cookstown and Dungiven. These are again united by many crossroads which facilitate the intercourse with all parts of the district.

Branches of the Cookstown road also lead over the mountains, one through Glengavna to Newtownstewart and by the Ballymullins to Derry. Another unfinished but very desirable line runs up to the right bank of the Moyola and is intended to lead to Greencastle; a third opens from Moneyninea over the Banagher mountains to Feeny.

Bridges

There are 5 bridges over the Moyola in its course through the district. The uppermost, at Doon on the Cookstown road, is a small bridge with 3 low arches. That near Derrynoid has 2 bold arches of cut freestone. The bridge at Forgetown is of the old construction, high and narrow, as is also the Fort William bridge on the Maghera road. The bridge at Lisnamuck is the prettiest in the district, but is considered rather unsafe though not long built.

There are several bridges over the minor streams and among these such as are of the recent erection are done in no mean style of masonry.

Scenery

Ballynascreen is nearby in the form of an immense amphitheatre. The verdant sides of the hills sink down with a slack or concavous declivity to the narrow arena or terraced plain between the different rivers. The little hamlets are generally clustered together, often in picturesque situations, either on the hill slope or an occasional swell of the plain, and often shaded with lumps [clumps?] of birch or alder. The glens, even now in their denuded state, exhibit beauties of no mean order. The abrupt banks of the Awain Ban glen and of Altoneill, which runs nearly parallel with that of the churchlands, still retain a few lingering remains of their ancient wood and in the rocky course of the rivers are sometimes seen beautiful miniature waterfalls.

The outline of the other parishes is much more diversified and picturesque. Throughout almost their whole extent the surface is of that undulating kind, that beautiful succession of hill and dell which gives the greatest effect to the landscape. The road between Tobermore and the glebe of Desertmartin affords many fine views of this interesting scenery. Here the eye meets many various broken chains of low hills or knolls rising one after another, cultivated all over, and the little meadowy vales between often watered by glassy streamlets.

Here and there appears a nice snow white farmhouse, either pitched on the hillside or retiring in the dell below, while Sliabh Gallion towers aloft in the background. The whole prospect is extremely pleasing and presents a happy union of much that is lovely and all that is wild in the features of rural scenery. Planting is much wanted: it appears indeed in many places, but the generation is yet to arise which shall fully avail itself of the many capabilities of the country that shall invite well-tutored art to lend her helping hand to exhibit and adorn the countless beauties "that nature's boon pours forth profuse, o'er hill and dale and plain."

The view from the Tummocks of Sliabh Gallion presents towards the west and north a scene of the most wild and savage grandeur. Successive chains of dark lofty alps stretch away far and wide, suggesting to the fancy the mountain billows, as it were, of a boundless ocean, arrested amid their tumult and consolidated by the hand of omnipotence. Towards the other points the prospect is more ample and the scenery more cheering. The country below, checkered with its many coloured fields and numerous enclosures, seems one immense tessellated pavement, while the labours and the abodes of man give animation to the landscape.

This view comprehends all the southern portion of the country. The towns of Moneymore, Magherafelt, Maghera, Castledawson and Bellaghy, with the intervening gentlemen's seats, all appear in succession. From the shores of Lough Neagh the eye is carried over the broad and bright expanse of its waters to the distant mountains of Mourne. Again the Bann is seen from its outlet at Toome, along almost the whole line of its silvery course. In Antrim Slemish, rearing its gigantic head, directs the eye to Knocklead, and, far beyond, like turrets dimly seen on the verge of the horizon, appears some mountains in the Western Isles of Scotland.

ANCIENT TOPOGRAPHY

Old Church at Ballynascreen

The old church of Ballynascreen lies on the northern side of the new road leading from Moyheelan to Greencastle in Tyrone and about 3 miles from the former. It was an oblong building about 66 feet by 24 without turret or spire, and (a token of its antiquity) without division between nave and chancel. The gables and north wall are nearly entire. The entrance in the south was spacious and surmounted by a Norman arch. The east window was large and lofty; its arch appears to have been pointed. On the epistle side of the altar is a small niche. It was built of the common landstone, except the coignes which are of a fine-grained cut freestone. The cement is less hard than that of most old buildings, being probably made of the argillaceous lime from Cookstown. Indeed the people have a tradition that all the materials were brought over the Tyrone mountains.

This edifice is said to have been erected by St Patrick for a library, in Irish screne (scrinium), hence the etymon of Ballynascreen "the town of the library." It appears to be the spot named Skrine in Glen-kan-ki, in the map of the Pacata Hibernia. St Columb afterwards converted it into a church or more probably into a monastic institution, as it stands in the midst of the termon or errenach lands, most of which are known to have been procured by his means as endowments to monasteries. His temporary residence (Bolea na Columbkille) during the alteration of the building is still pointed out on a neighbouring height.

Whether as a monastery or place of study, nothing could have been chosen with a better taste. The building, from its sequestered site on the bank of a bright stream, with lofty mountains and narrow dark glens behind, the sleepy bank in front, broken with ravines or swelling into hills, the vale below stretching away in lovely expansion, was admirably suited to the solitude of study or the seclusion of the monastic life; but as a church it must always have been at an inconvenient distance from the great body of the worshippers. It is sometimes designated in Irish by a name which implies "that it was 9 miles distant from 9 other churches."

The erection of this building was, as is fabled of most ancient churches, obstructed by some supernatural agency, so that what had been erected by day was demolished by night. At length the astonished workmen heard the sound of a bell, which continued tolling in the air many days and, becoming visible, each man spread his mantle and the bell dropped on that of McGillian. The church was raised on the spot and the bell remained till lately in possession of McGillian's reputed descendants. In time the rude people, impressed with an idea of its peculiar sacredness, used to swear by it on occasions of extraordinary solemnity; and an oath taken on the heaven-descended instrument could not be violated but with infamy eternal.

Its more special use is in expurgatory oaths, and perjury in such case is always followed by alienation of mind in which some overt act proves the falsity of the deponent. Hence the bell is called Dia Dheultagh or "the vengeance of God." It is long, narrow, of a square form, very curiously embossed, and fame, who loves the marvellous, tells that each of its sides once held a diamond of great value. It is certain that sockets still remain in its sides, in which some rare stones may have been set by way of ornament. The bell is now removed to Tyrone.

Desertmartin Church

The old church of Desertmartin presents nothing worthy of notice. It stands near the village of that name and, unlike most ancient churches, in a low, dull and damp situation, roofed with shingles. This church is said to be of great antiquity and to have been dedicated to St Martin, uncle of St Patrick. It was occupied by the Catholics till the revolution and was used for the service of the Establishment till the building of the present new church.

Calmore Castle

Westward of the village of Tobermore are some vestiges of the ancient castle of Calmore, once a place of very considerable strength, which commanded the mountain passes and the fords of the Moyola. From the almost complete removal of the materials the extent of the works cannot now be traced. It was burned by the Irish on the retreat of their army from Derry in 1689 and not afterwards repaired.

Ancient Coins

Many ancient coins have been found in the district, particularly about Desertmartin. The late Revd N. Bryan had an extensive collection of these coins, which it is believed are now in the museum of the Royal Dublin Society. The most curious of these which have met the eye of the writer is a small coin lately found in Longfield by Hagan. It appears to have been a silver penny, the obverse surmounted by a cross, the inscription "Edw Rx Angldns HvB," "Edward, King of England, Lord of Ireland." The reverse is a cross, whose point of intersection forms the centre of 2 circles. At each angle of the cross are 3 points placed triangularly. The outer circle forms the raised border of the coin; between it and the inner one are the words "civitas London," "city of London." The whole is very coarsely executed. It is probably a coin of the first Edward: at least the regal style assumed in the inscription proves that it had been struck before Edward III asserted his claim to the crown of France.

Another silver coin of superior workmanship is in possession of Dr McKenna, Moyheelan. The one side is nearly defaced, but appears to have been a crowned head round which was the legend "rosa sine spina," "the rose without a thorn." The reverse is a shield parted quarterly with the arms of England and France in the alternate compartments. Nothing remains of the legend but the word "civitas." This was probably a groat, or a 3d piece, coined before the union of the crowns in the person of James I.

Shillings of Elizabeth, with her usual inscription "posui deum adjutorem meum," "I have taken God for my helper," have been often found, as also half-crown pieces of Charles II and 3d pieces of William and Mary, with well-executed heads of both. Many of the latter were found in digging up the garden at Fort William.

A very small brass coin, now in possession of the writer, was found in the same place. On one side is a cross and an inscription apparently running "ste vicar." The reverse has the usual papal insignia, the keys with the title "pont m." If the obverse have been rightly deciphered, this coin must be of the 11th century.

Arrowheads

Arrowheads of flint are often dug up; these are the elf-bolts. A drawing of one of them is annexed. [There] is a drawing of a brazen instrument dug up in Moneyninea. It is 6 inches long and weighs 18 oz. Each side contains a groove in which a handle was probably inserted. Another of these was found in Longfield, together with a brazen skean or knife, the blade of which was 14 inches long.

Urns

Earthen urns have been dug up in Longfield, Dromore and Turmagh. Their outside was rudely carved; they contained only a blackish earth. Those found at Turmagh had been placed in an inverted position.

Ancient Fence

In Coolsara moss a subterraneous paling was discovered some years since at the depth of 5 or 6 feet. The stakes of this paling had been pointed by some tool of the most exquisite sharpness.

Cromlech

At Strawmore, on the north side of the road leading from Dungiven to Cookstown, is a cromlech or slaught named Slaght Illeran "the death place of Illeran." It is composed of several large stones of coarse imperfect granite placed endwise in a line curving from east to north west and forming an arc whose chord is about 50 feet. The superincumbent sloping stone or altar, which once blazed with the beal fire or streamed perhaps with human gore, is now partly demolished. That and others of the huge stones composing this rude relic of druidical superstition were bored, split and carried off a few years since by one Devlin, a neighbouring farmer, who has since restored them as nearly as possible to their former position; from what motive he cannot be induced to explain.

Contiguous to the cromlech stands a chapel, proclaiming, as it were, the triumph of the blessed gospel over the barbarous and bloody rites of heathenism.

Giant's Grave

On Kill-na-hough "the cemetery among the caves," a hill in Drumderg, is a spot pointed out as the grave of a giant. 4 immense stones forming a parallelogram are set up on a raised tumulus in a line of about 10 feet from south to north. At the southern extremity are placed 2 immense barrows or headstones overtopping the others. Old men remember these to have been covered by another vast stone, which in that position must have formed a complete cromlech. This upper stone was removed to be converted into a millstone and, according to the report of the inhabitants, had nearly burned the mill to the ground when applied to so profane a purpose.

A large cave is said to have opened here but it cannot now be traced.

Burial Places

There are 2 rude monuments reported to be burial places on the top of Sliabh Gallion. They are called the Tummocks. One of these is a mere cairn or lofty conical heap of small stones thrown together confusedly. The other, called the Tyrone Tummock, is a verdant tumulus apparently of earth; but on being lately explored, proved to be also a cairn on which immense stones had been reared edgewise, forming a tomb as in that of Killnahough but not more than 6 feet long. The standing stones had been buttressed by others driven deep and firmly wedged so as to support the weight of the enormous covering stone.

Danish Forts

The Danish forts are too numerous for particular notice. The most remarkable is that of Drumbally hill in Coolsara. It is on the top of a beautiful conical hill, of easy ascent on all sides and commanding a very extensive prospect. There are 2 ramparts, an outer and inner. The dry ditch between is about 10 feet deep and nearly width. The inner part is about 50 feet in diameter. The entrance was on the east side.

SOCIAL ECONOMY

State of the Population

Previously to the colonization of this district by the Scotch in 1609, much of it was waste or overrun with wood, forming part of the domain lands of Shane O'Neill. The inhabitants, his immediate and willing lieges, shared in all the glories and in the numerous disasters of that brave unfortunate prince and his successor, in their unsuccessful struggle for liberty and independence. Hence, when despotism at length accomplished its purpose, the settlers found the low fertile land utterly dispeopled and deluged with the blood of its bravest defenders. A feeble, spiritless remnant had escaped to the woods and the hills where, under tenure from the colonists, they finally settled, the former retaining the fat of the land; but civil bloodshed, barbarous laws and odious jealousies, that for more than a century subsequently desolated the land and divided its people, rendering property and life insecure, prevented the natural increase of the population.

Progress of Improvement

There are no data by which to investigate the ancient state of the population of this obscure district; yet its rapid increase surprises and startles the most incurious observer. There are several townlands, the houses of which have been trebled in the memory of men not very old; and all agree that no such increase had been remarked in the days of their fathers. The last decade of George II may be assumed as the point whence it began to start towards its present density. Since that it has increased in a greater ratio than for a century and a half previous.

We owe this to domestic peace, to the limitation of pasturage, above all to the increased facility of subsistence from the extended cultivation of the potato. At the period above mentioned none but the most fertile and accessible grounds were cultivated: the life of the people was quite pastoral. In May every family removed with its flocks and herds to the woody glens and upland heights, then rich with the most luxuriant herbage, now tamed by the plough. There they lived during the summer on a scanty supply of oatmeal but abundance of butter, curds, cream; in short, a milk diet in all its various preparations. It is not quite 60 years since this custom of boalying ceased.

The actual state of the population may be seen in the appendix, but the enumeration by classes, so desirable in a statistical work, is in this instance quite impracticable. The division of labour is so little practised that a single family can hardly be named which subsists solely by agriculture; nor again any manufacturer who does not consider himself a farmer.

Substantial Farmers

The number of substantial farmers in this district is inconsiderable: 30 would perhaps go beyond the mark; at least no more can be said to have sufficient command of capital. These are men of fine appearance, "bacon-fed knaves," well clothed, wanting few of the real luxuries and none of the comforts of life. Tea is used by their families and their tables are well supplied with butcher's meat and poultry of their own feeding. Their snug, thatched, stone and lime houses are quite comfortable and clean, whitewashed, kept in good repair, the apartments generally floored and carpeted with suitable furniture in very good style, indicating the possession of hereditary wealth. But there is one all-pervading defect which is so general as to leave the impress of negligence and inefficiency on their whole economy, namely the construction of their office houses and yards, which are in every instance ill situated and utterly inadequate to any useful purposes.

However, as this important class of men have caught the spirit of improvement, and as the Drapers' Company have lately erected at Gortnaskeay a very neat farmhouse, with suitable buildings in the English style, all slated, and have given encouragement to a respectable tenant to erect another on the same model, but on a larger scale, at Iniscarn, it is to be hoped that miniature copies, at least, of these useful buildings may soon arise over all their property and at length through the whole surrounding country.

Poor Farmers

The lower and more numerous class of farmers

present a sad contrast to the men above mentioned. Their very appearance bespeaks them victims of rapacity and rack-rent. They are indeed ground down by an insupportable burden, and all labour under a deficiency of capital. Their numerous families are quite adequate to the consumption of the farm's produce, yet the crops must be hurried to market to meet the November rent and the summer's provisions purchased at an advanced rate.

In short, their lives are a continued struggle for existence, and they live, as one of themselves emphatically observed, "merely by pinching the back and pinching the belly." The rent, the tithes, the leases, the necessaries, the very few luxuries of the family are in a great measure derived from female industry. The yarn spun by the wives and daughters, and woven perhaps by the sons, forms the principal fund which supports the family expenses. It is occasionally augmented by annual sales of butter and pigs. In the mountainous townlands the little money in circulation is derived from the sales of young cattle and sheep, from illicit distillation and from smuggling. In the southern part of the district they make money by burning and selling lime in the summer season.

The clothing of such men is in most instances of the coarse home manufacture, in a few of old second-hand purchase. During the greater part of the year all the family, especially the females, are forced to go barefooted.

Their food differs from that of the cottier in this, that they can mostly command a scanty supply of winter's milk and occasionally a side of beef or bacon.

Their dwelling consists of 2 divisions, the kitchen with its outshot, a projection in the wall beside the fire, in which outshot the parents sleep, and an inner apartment seldom having a fire, though the floor is earthen. As to the interior, the mean shabby furniture is huddled together in disorder and too often does little credit to the cleanliness of the housewife. The exterior is unsightly. It is generally in bad repair and, particularly in Ballynascreen where lime is dear, wants the cleanly, cheerful air that whitewashing alone can bestow; and as the cowhouse and barn are mostly under the same roof with the dwelling house, there is generally an accumulation of filth in front.

Cottiers

Let us now take a view of one yet lower in the scale of personal and domestic comfort: the cottier, whose claims are strong to our sympathy and admiration too, if, with the stoic moralist, we admit suffering and forbearance to be characteristics of the perfect man. Before he has attained to reason and reflection, ere he has provided a second coat, he hastens to become a father and takes as the partner of his future fate some creature as young, as ill appointed, as unprovident as her mate. He then receives a subdivision of his father's plot (for in this class should be placed the cultivator of a 2 or 3 acre farm) or else he rents, and dearly rents, a patch with a cabin, mud-walled or built of stones uncemented, often without a window or but dimly lighted by a window of the smallest dimensions, firmly nailed, never to open, and which, were it to open, could admit little else than the putrid effluvia of the dunghill.

Such is the house. The furniture, not unmatched to it, comprises only articles of prime necessity: the loom, the spinning wheel, the pot and pitcher, a few stools or rude chairs, a chest, a frail table, a thin deal dresser with its wooden array of dishes, noggins and spoons, all, as are the dress and complexion of the squalid inmates, tinged with a smoky hue; the bedding the most indifferent of its kind, and spread not seldom on the bare damp floor, beside the goat or the cow.

The food too of such persons is of the humblest sort. They can sometimes procure a mess of stirabout but the perennial fare is potatoes and buttermilk. The supply of the latter fails in the spring months. Then the potato is seasoned with salt, an egg, or perhaps in favourable times with a salted herring or an eel from the Toome fishery. Towards August even the potato fails. They are then constrained to make a meal of cabbage leaves, their only garden vegetable, with a morsel of butter. From butcher's meat their abstinence is more rigid than that of the most austere eastern ascetic. Their voluntary Lent is perennial, excepting the festivals of Christmas, Shrovetide and Easter. This is miserable enough, but some are doomed, alas, to fare still more disgusting. In the memorable summer of 1817 many lowland farmers were obliged to bring home their cattle from the mountain pastures, lest they should be bled to death by the herds, who boiled and ate the blood!

Thus fed, thus lodged, the easy prey of oppression, of fever, of famine, this unhappy being passes his toilsome years, rising, however, with gaiety and elasticity of spirit, above the gloomy despondency which, in such a state, impels the impious, pampered kind of another land to self-destruction or aims his hand against the life of his wealthier neighbour.

Employment

It has been already observed that the division of labour is unknown and unpractised. There is therefore, strictly speaking, one separate class, quite detached from agriculture and diverting its whole substance and attention to manufactures. Of course the population, wholly agricultural, is more numerous than the present state of agriculture requires. This applies more particularly to Ballynascreen, in which the linen manufacture has been but partially introduced. In the other 2 parishes weaving is carried on in almost every farmhouse. Hence from the former parish there is a constant flow of emigration to America and of periodical trips across the Channel to the labours of the British harvest.

Thus employment, independently of its public advantages, has the effect of retaining the people in their native land. It has also the important moral effect of keeping the young men under their parents' eyes, of debarring them from improper nightly meetings and practices injurious to individual happiness and social order. It may be mentioned here, even at the risk of prolixity, that a remedy for this evil want of employment enters into the plans of the Drapers' Company. That body has resolved to offer inducements to the superfluous population to devote itself to handicraft trades and manufactures. It appropriates certain annual sums for the purchase of decent clothing for young men and binding them apprentices to persons wholly engaged in handicraft trades and manufactures.

Physical Appearance

Generally speaking, the men are of good stature, active and athletic. They excel in the gymnastic exercises, such as running, leaping, throwing the sledgehammer, lifting and throwing the stone, playing football and bullets. Little can be said in praise of their personal cleanliness: in fact they are rather slovenly in their persons.

The females are seldom put to field labours, except in the flax and oat harvests, yet they are not remarkable for gracefulness of shape. The girls dress neatly, considering their situation; indeed, fame and fashion soon waft the modes of the city even to this remote spot; but these nymphs of the hills and glens have a freshness of colour, a richness of complexion which the city belle would sigh for and sigh in vain.

Fuel

Turf is the only article of fuel. In the long winter nights are added chips of bog fir which, besides heat, furnish a bright cheerful light, superseding the necessity for candles; or where candles would be used for ordinary purpose, the fir is divided into thin reeds called splits. The supply of turf is plentiful and cheap in Kilcronaghan; in ordinary seasons a load may be bought in Tobermore and Desertmartin at 8d to 1s. However, the increase of population and extension of agriculture have in many townlands of the other parishes so exhausted the bog that turf is now becoming scarce and valuable. In some places the farmer has to draw his turf a distance of several miles; some cannot bring more than 4 loads a day from the [?] drag.

In other places the bog mud is baked into turf, and again in one part of the churchlands of Ballynascreen, where an individual possesses a large tract of bog, it is let in half-acre lots at a guinea a year; the lot includes the space on which the turf is cut and dried. Some landlords charge the bog 8s an acre; others 5s a fire yearly. In Luney turf bog is charged 3 pounds an acre; about Desertmartin 2 guineas. On Mr Ogilby's and some other properties the tenants have bog free of any expense.

It has, however, been the general policy of landlords to reserve the bog as a check on the tenant, who thus takes his turf merely by sufferance; and on the least abatement of servility or the slightest show of independence, he is by the deprivation of fuel made to feel most sensibly the heavy hand of power. This is no longer practised on the Drapers' property: to every tenant is assigned a proportionate share of turf bog, for domestic use only. This he holds by the same tenure as his land and therefore he may be expected to use it more economically.

Health

Generally speaking, the state of health is good all over the district. The diseases of most frequent occurrence are inflammatory sore throat, pleurisy and low fever, arising most probably from the uncomfortable damp and imperfect ventilation of the poorer dwellings, from severe labour without adequate nourishment, and lastly from want of cleanliness. Catarrhal afflictions principally confined to children are prevalent, induced by the damp atmosphere.

Dispensary

The Drapers' Company have established a dispensary in Ballynascreen, subsidiary to the general dispensary at Moneymore. This is the only establishment of the kind in the district and its advantages are confined to the sick poor of the Drapers' estate. The surgeon Dr Savage has a yearly salary of 80 guineas, besides fuel and lodgings. His duties are to attend 2 days in the week at the dispensary, to see patients and deliver medicines, and also to visit at their own dwelling such patients as are disabled from coming to the dispensary.

Longevity

There have been several instances of remarkable longevity; a few are subjoined: the Revd Francis McNamee attained the age of 90; his successor, the Revd Roger Gormly, died at 100; Patrick Walls lived to 101, John Hutchinson to 105. The latter often mentioned that he remembered to see almost the whole country from Tobermore to Lissan covered with wood.

Local Government

The peace of the district is protected by a few sub-constables, under the direction of the 3 rectors, who are the only magistrates. To each of the great proportions is attached a manorial court exercising a jurisdiction over the tenantry in matters of small debts.

A military detachment with a gauger has been stationed, for some months past, in Ballynascreen, for the protection of the revenue.

Inhabitants

The district, as before observed, is inhabited by 2 distinct races of men, the aboriginal Irish and the descendants of the Scotch colonists who settled here on the planting of the country by the London companies. Few, if any, English appear to have fixed their residence here. The native race have nearly exclusive possession of Ballynascreen. Of the other parishes they mostly occupy the portion adjacent to the base of Sliabh Gallion and are also less thickly diffused over the other parts.

Principal Families

The principal septs are those of McKenna, O'Hagan, McRory (Anglice Rogers), Henry and O'Neill. Being the most numerous class, they claim the first place in this delineation.

Character of the Irish

The most striking features in the character of the natives are a social disposition, generous affections, a natural vivacity, an open-hearted frank deportment, an affability of manner, and the warm welcome of hospitality freely given by the rich farmer in his opulence and by the cottager amid his penury.

Their communicative disposition prompts them to give, even to the veriest stranger whose appearance bespeaks sympathy, the whole tale of their joys and their sorrows. From their gay humour and flow of spirits they excel in conversation; whether in narrative or in sketches of character, nothing can be more admirable than the dramatic keeping and animation of their style.

Taken as a body, if not better educated than the race of settlers, their exertions to attain education are greater. They are unquestionably more active, more enterprising, more intelligent and, when placed in situations favourable to the development of their faculties mental and physical, their superiority is quite manifest.

They have been often taunted, and by professed friends too, with their clannish propensities and servile submission to leaders. Formerly, perhaps, they have been too lightly caught by the magic of a name and have leaned too oft on broken reeds. This confiding temper is now nearly effaced: it can scarcely be reckoned among their present foibles. And yet, in the ordeal of persecution and bondage which they had to undergo, a recourse to patronage might have been pardonable.

There are shades yet darker in the portrait. Their thoughtlessness, their irritability, their improvidence, their stoical indifference to personal and domestic convenience, and the apathetic acquiescence of the poor under the privations of their abject state are the greatest obstacles to their improvement.

Character of the Scotch

The disposition of the Scotch is cold but not unsocial; their manners reserved but not impulsive; their affections mostly bounded by the family circle but not irresponsive to the call of benevolence; their habits frugal, yet capable of softening occasionally into generous relaxation; and in cool perseverance, calculating prudence and command of temper they deserve to be taken as models by the Irish. As on the other hand, their intermixture with the native race, while it has not effaced their more amiable qualities, has removed the preciseness and smoothed the asperity which still adhere to their isolated fellow settlers in other parts of the country.

Contrast between Irish and Scotch

In no trait of character, however, is the contrast between them more striking than in their ideas of country and the effects of those ideas on their conduct. The Irishman is distinguished by his fixed attachment to the soil of his native land. Though ever so poor and abject, he takes a deep interest in the tales of her ancient greatness and feels himself ennobled in her bygone glories. Hence, if necessity forces him to emigrate, it is with violence to the best feelings of his nature.

> And even those ills which round his mansion rise
> Enhance the bliss his scanty fund supplies
> Dear is that shed to which his soul conforms
> And dear that hill which lifts him to the storms.

But the heart of the settler is not bound by ties so endearing: he more prudently makes country to consist in comfort and independence; for these he forgets all abstract romantic ideas. Indeed to him Erin's ancient story possesses little interest: nay his most triumphant historical recollections are connected with her degradation and her downfall. To Scotland he yet looks as his mother country, and with her name associates everything distinguished in intellect, valuable in science and venerable in religion.

Character of the People

Among the better portion of these rival tribes ancient prejudices are fast sinking into oblivion or subsiding into a generous emulation. They rarely intermarry, but in other respects the difference of creeds, by which they are as strongly marked as by national descent, seldom breaks the harmony or intrudes on the charities and civilities of social life. Some inconsiderable party riots, excited by a few malignant spirits, the partisans of the Orange and the Green factions, outcasts of society and detested by all, do not invalidate this assertion; the great mass of the people is peaceful and tranquil.

Industry of the People

They are laborious and industrious in the extreme. The weaver who had plied his shuttle from the morning's light, the day labourer who had drudged from dawn for his scanty hire, are seen working by the twilight in their own little plot till the night dew chills the sweat of the day. In Ballynascreen there is the appearance of idleness, especially in the winter season: this, however, has its source not in indolence but in want of employment. In winter the nature of their soil precludes all farm labours but the brief business of the barn.

They are naturally of a commercial turn, and in the intervals of labour many engage in little trading projects and speculations of industry to improve their capital. Their native shrewdness and acumen in this line bespeak them born for trade, insomuch that their less sagacious neighbours of Keenaught <Kenaught> scruple not to brand them with the name of sharpers. This imputation has even passed into a tramontane proverb which, like most general censures, has been preserved for its point long after it should have been discarded for its injustice.

Temperance

Notwithstanding the late surprising increase of illicit distillation, the prodigious number of shebeen houses, the facility of procuring spirits and the general use of them, habitual intemperance is very rare and without intentional offence.

Morality

One instance of their moral purity shall here be adduced by way of contrast. Mr [?] Curwen, whose residence is in Cumberland, the pride of England for education and morals, informs us that in his parish the annual number of destitute bastards is to that of children born in wedlock in the ratio of 1 to under 20; whereas in the populous parish of Ballynascreen 1 child only has been thrown upon the parish during the last 10 years!! A proud reflection for our country! Well indeed may Erin boast not only the superior loveliness but the brighter virtue of her daughters.

Language

The English language has come into very general use, except among the most infrequented recesses of the mountains where it has not yet supplanted the native tongue. The latter is understood probably by all: it is certainly spoken by most of the people, and there may be seen not only Catholic manuals but also the Book of Common Prayer in the Irish language.

The Scottish dialect is become obsolete.

Customs: Pilgrimage

Few particular customs remain among these people. Such as have been noticed shall be here subjoined. Lough Patrick, a small lake in the mountains in the north west of Ballynascreen, seems to have been anciently a station or pilgrimage. Its waters are said to have been hallowed by St Columbkille. There is a yearly assemblage on its banks indicative of an ancient patron. It is held on the eve of St John, with which throughout all northern Europe are associated so many legendary tales and so many freaks of superstition. On that thrice hallowed Eve

    When goblins haunt from fire and fen
    And wood, and lake, the steps of men

numerous crowds of both sexes assemble and, while the neighbouring hills and the plain below are blazing with the Midsummer bonfires, indulge themselves in rustic amusements, dances and thus pass the evening in harmless pleasures. But the priests seem to think it has ceased to be harmless: they now exert themselves to prohibit such meetings.

Superstitions and Fairies

In a mountainous region, such as that under review, superstition holds longest her old domain. Witchcraft is now forgotten, or perhaps never had footing here, though fascination or the effects of an evil eye both on man and beast are commonly believed. There are still some ghosts seen.

The popular creed, both of natives and settlers equally, admits the existence of fairies. In Irish they are called shigeogh, and similarly in the vernacular tongue, by way of propitiation, the gentry or gentle people. They are supposed to reside in the old thorns of the Danish forts, which thorns are often seen to blaze with their unreal fires. They are the same diminutive, playful, capricious, malevolent beings that we find depicted in ancient northern poetry. They have the same propensity to the abstraction of unchristened children and of women at the period of *accouchement*. The lot of such changelings is a severe one: to bolt the suspected imp in a riddle over a strong fire; if a fairy, it will ascend in the smoke.

It has not been ascertained whether the order of fairies called luchre in the native dialect be composed of mortal children or of enchanted Danes (for with the name of Dane is associated, in the minds of the old Irish, everything malignant). These luchre are they that give the fairy gold to those whom they lure into intimacy with them. A tale of immense treasure got from one of these is told by Patrick Devlin of Owenreagh. Poor Patrick's bushels of gold, however, faded away when he related his good fortune to his family.

An abstracted woman must be gained by force: a man is known to have actually watched a whole night for the fairy procession to get an opportunity of recovering his wife, who had died in child bed but whom he supposed to have been carried off by the gentry. They are believed to shoot at cattle and the bolts thus launched are, when found, religiously preserved, for, happily, a drink of water in which the elf-bolt, with 3 pieces of silver, has been immersed, is an effectual cure for the elfic wound. They are never named by the believers in them but with a superstitious dread; even an incidental illusion to them often calls forth the deprecatory ejaculation of:

    "Fair may they come
    Fair may they go
    But their heels aye to us."

The sticklers for their existence maintain that they are a remnant of the fallen angels who had swerved indeed from their allegiance but, not having proceeded to actual warfare against Heaven, were not reserved in chains under darkness. Strange as it may seem, a person whose veracity in ordinary matters is unimpeachable insists most seriously that he saw 2 of these green-clad gentles issue from the wall of his cowhouse and pass close by him at noon day.

Banshee

The superstition of the banshee arose probably from the belief of women having been carried off by fairies. The banshee is a native modification of the genius or demon in classic mythology and is peculiarly attached to certain septs or families, to whom she announces by loud lamentations any coming calamity. She always appears dressed in the old Irish mantle.

Belief in Prophecy

The vulgar everywhere are deeply imbued with the belief of prophecy. This remark applies equally to both tribes in this district: the prophecies falsely applied to Columbkille and the reveries of James a-Hood, a native seer, are not more eagerly listened to by one class than are by another those of Thomas the Rhymer and the godly Mr Peden. One charm has already been mentioned, but many are practised. There is one for taking a mote out of the eye which deserves notice, as several persons of education and sound judgement declare that they have been relieved by it.

Other Superstitions

Many minor observances might be adduced to show the state of the vulgar mind. Among others: if a cock crow after roosting, it is the omen of hasty news from the quarter to which he looks.

They firmly believe in the existence of magic as a systematic science. The settlers have brought with them, and increased the fame of, Michael (uniformly pronounced Mitchell) Scott.

The name of Cornelius Agrippa is even now pronounced by all with horror and detestation, as one adept in that black art. They relate many wonders effected by his book *De occulta philosophia* which gave such umbrage to the clergy, his contemporaries. Many an over-curious scholar, opening the forbidden volume, has unconsciously called around him legions of malevolent spirits, who caused no small perplexity, and often death, to their summoner, if unable to lay them or give them suitable employment. The usual expedient was to suggest some work surpassing human skill. The Giant's Causeway formed from an adventure of this kind: a shorter method of accounting for that stupendous work than by dull geological theories; but the usual device was to employ the demons in twisting ropes of sand.

Their faith in glamour or glamoury is no less fixed. This is a species of magical imposition on the eyes of the spectator by which the sorcerer makes every object appear magnified beyond reality. The counter charm is to look at such an object through a piece of wood having a natural hole, or to have on the person a shamrock leaf. At a late fair a man was seen to view through such an aperture the feats of a tumbler and rope dancer.

Employment of Children

The children of the poorer classes are trained up to the hardy habits of their fathers. They run about at all seasons without shoes, hat or cap till earned by their own labour. It is rarely but in winter that the poorer children can be spared to school. In the spring they are employed to drive the plough, and in summer to weed the crops and tend the cattle of the better farmers. The wages of such herdboys vary from 7s to 15s with board, according to the difficulty of the charge or the pressure of the times. In the seasons of planting and raising the potatoes children get from 3d to 4d a day. Those of the weavers are also very usefully employed in preparing and winding the yarn for the shuttle. Such children continue at school perhaps 3 or 4 winters, and often much longer, from mere want of employment; and their years pass on thus diversified with the winter's study and the summer's labour, till they acquire vigour enough to engage as apprentices to some trade or as labouring servants.

The children of the better farmers are put to school at 6 years old, or earlier, according to the vicinity of the school or the ability of the parent. This is their employment till 14 or 15, except at intervals of the busy seasons when all ages are summoned to the labours of the field. The education of the girls has hitherto, from various causes, been much neglected: being much less actively employed, education has not been thought so necessary to them as to the boys. Besides, necessity puts them early to the spinning wheel, and the rapid increase of the family makes their assistance indispensable to their mothers, or to women similarly situated; and for such purposes they are often hired.

Such girls as are put to school go at the same age and to the same schools as the boys.

Schools

The parish of Desertmartin has 4 day schools containing 249 male and female children. In Kilcronaghan are 5 schools attended by 258 scholars. One of these schools is patronised by and conducted on the plan of the Society for Promoting the Education of the Poor of Ireland. The cleanliness, discipline, good order and proficiency of the children are truly creditable to themselves and their teachers.

In Ballynascreen 603 children are educated in 12 schools. The prices of tuition are: for reading 2s 6d, writing 3s 4d, arithmetic 5s. The plan of education goes no further, except at one of the Kilcronaghan schools, in which, it is said, algebra and geometry are taught. In all these schools the books read are unexceptionable; not a single immoral book has ever been observed among them.

Drapers' Schools

When the Drapers' Company made a census of their estates in 1818, the Ballynascreen division of their property contained 631 poor children under 12 years of age, and that in the other 2 parishes 896. With true feelings of benevolence they seized on the opportunity thus offered of effecting a great moral improvement. They were aware that what is commonly called education was widely diffused over the population, but they wished to superinduce regular habits, the love of comfort and order.

With these philanthrophic views the company have erected 4 schools, included in the above enumeration, viz. one at Iniscarn, another at Cranny, a third at Duntybrian and the fourth at Ballynure. These buildings, besides their mighty moral use, form an ornament in the landscape. The 2 latter stand conspicuously on the opposite banks of the Moyola. The schoolrooms are large, airy and well lighted. Contiguous to each schoolhouse, apartments are in course of erection for the master or mistress, who is paid solely by the company. The annual salary of the former is 50 pounds, that of the latter 35 pounds, besides comfortable dwellings, rent free.

2 of the schools are for boys; these have been in operation since August 1819. The other 2, the girls' schools, were established at November 1820. All the schools have hitherto been carried on in temporary buildings with very considerable success. Against November, it is understood, they are to remove to the new schoolhouses, where the classes are to be augmented so that each school shall contain 100 pupils. The Madras mode of instruction and the British system of needlework have been adopted. Thus all are trained to order and usefulness, but the girls in particular. From this happy improvement in their education must produce manifold advantages to their little circle of society, in their various relations of sisters, wives and mothers.

These schools are confined to the tenantry, but like all others in the district are open to children of parents of any religious tenets; and the judicious selection of the governors and committee precludes any improper interference with the religion of the pupils. Good clothing forms the principal subject of rewards for good conduct and proficiency, from a view of infusing into the poorer classes a taste for comforts and conveniences of a higher order than they have heretofore aspired to.

Loss of Schools

Intentions so benevolent are above all praise; yet even from so much good one evil, a temporary one let us hope, has arisen. The neighbouring small schools, particularly in the parish of Desertmartin, are broken up; and till the aid of other landlords can be obtained or till the legislature thinks proper to intrust the Catholic clergy with adequate funds for the erection and partial endowment of other schools, the poor are likely to remain uninstructed. And partial aid only is wanted: the people are extremely anxious to procure education for their children, and in every instance that has fallen under the writer's observation they would prefer paying for it. Why then should they not be allowed the means? This would be preferable to the gratuitous system of instruction adopted in the Drapers' schools; that system has a manifest tendency to abate the laudable spirit of independence which it is the first duty of a patriot landlord to support and foster.

Provision too might have been made in at least one of those schools for a higher department than is comprised in the present plan. The munificent fund appropriated by the company to the promoting of education would fully admit this encouragement to rustic genius; and such a school would find ample support in the taste and spirit of the better farmers. This opinion is deduced from a fact which, while it is creditable to the taste of the country, is also illustrative of the present state of learning among the people.

Teachers

Of natives of this district, sons of farmers, there are at present engaged as teachers of religion: 24 Catholic priests, 10 ministers of the Establishment, 15 Presbyterian ministers, besides 3 barristers, 12 army and navy surgeons, 8 graduates in surgery and physics, without taking into account the numerous unsuccessful aspirants to professional honours. Such a contribution of learning, sacred and profane, to the general fund of human knowledge cannot probably be matched among the same class of society in any mountainous tract of equal extent in the United Kingdom.

But it would be unfair to note these advantages without gratefully adverting to the source whence most of them have flowed. In the village of Moyheelan there is a school exclusively classical, conducted by Mr Patrick Murphy, a gentleman distinguished for his classical abilities and not less for his modesty, whose little seminary has sent forth most of the above-mentioned gentlemen. This school has sometimes contained 72 scholars; the present number does not exceed 20. The price of tuition is 11s 4d ha'penny per quarter.

Sunday Schools

There is 1 Sunday school at Killytoney containing 40 scholars and another in the village of Desertmartin which contains 30 scholars. The most numerous schools of this kind are those of the Catholic chapels in Ballynascreen. The number attending these schools amounts during the summer months to about 450, but in winter the school is unavoidably suspended. The Lancasterian system is used to a certain extent; placards have been purchased by congregational collections. These schools are all managed by gratuitous teachers.

One important benefit arising from having Sunday schools in the different places of worship is the inducement it holds out to bring children at an earlier age and more regularly to participate in social worship.

The solemnity of the place too accords well with that moral and religious instruction which should make a principal part of Sunday school teaching, and without which, indeed, every other teaching is little better than the tares sown by the enemy.

State of Learning

Such are the opportunities of instruction afforded to the people; and, generally speaking, they have fully availed themselves of these advantages. In Desertmartin and Kilcronaghan the bulk of the population may be called *well educated*.

Ballynascreen has not attained so enviable a distinction, yet the number of persons unable to read is not considerable. Many have an education superior to their place in society; many have given unquestionable proofs of genius and its flame has beamed not seldom from the lowly hut of the cottier; poetic talent is common and some very promising specimens might be selected "sed nunc non erat hic locus."

Manuscripts

Few, if any, Irish manuscripts are now believed to remain in these parishes. Some that could have lately been gleaned up have now perished, or fallen into the oblivious grasp of collectors. Last year 3 were transmitted to Maynooth. These had been in the collection of the late Revd John McLaughlin of Ballynascreen. They consisted of a translation of Kempis' inestimable work *On the imitation of Christ*; a historical poem of about 900 lines; a mutilated fragment of some work, interlarded with ranns, or poems. Being written on paper they have no claim to remote antiquity, though probably they are transcripts of some ancient works.

Poetry

Many fragments of Irish poetry linger yet in the memory of the inhabitants. The sweetest are always ascribed to Ossian and the bards approaching to his time. The greater part are of later date, chiefly songs, in the beautiful plaintive strain of our native music. Of this number, are the laments of the Boyne and of Aughrim, mainly nervous elegies, the writers of which, while they deplored the wounds of their country, could duly appreciate the character of that craven king in whose cause they suffered. Even very lately this district contained some versifiers in the olden tongue, degenerate successors of the ancient bards whose stores of imagery and sentiment the[y] plundered at will. Their compositions are mostly amatory or satirical. To the latter, the genius of the language and the disposition of the people are strongly inclined, but this race too is extinct.

There is now little leisure for tuneful avocations. The landlords have ejected the muses, the children of Mammon have prevailed over the sons of song "and doomed them to oblivion of their art."

Religious Establishment

Each of the 3 parishes is a rectory in the patronage of the Lord Bishop of Derry.

The present incumbent of Desertmartin is the Revd Charles Colthurst. The value of this living is estimated at 700 pounds, derived from the tithes and from the rents of the glebe lands, which lie partly in Desertmartin, partly in Tamlaght O'Crilly.

MODERN TOPOGRAPHY

Glebe House

Mr Colthurst's residence, the Glebe House of Dromore, is beautifully situated and surrounded by a grove which contains some very fine old oaks and chestnut trees. The house is an old one, but its well-chosen situation, the ancient planting, the recent tasteful improvements of the glebe grounds and the singular neatness of the new church rank the parsonage of Desertmartin among the prettiest spots in the county.

Desertmartin Church

Contiguous to the Glebe House, on the brow of a hill, stands the church, a beautiful building though small; it has no steeple but a small square turret with pinnacles. It is visible from all parts of the neighbouring country and has given additional ornament to the scenery. This church was built in 1820 by a loan of 800 pounds from the Board of First Fruits, to be repaid by instalments. It is to be lamented that differences have arisen between Mr Colthurst and his parishioners on the propriety of erecting this new church. In consequence, the latter persist in refusing to pay any part of the loan and still keep the old church in repair.

Lecumpher Meeting House

There is a meeting house at Lecumpher belonging to a congregation in communion with the Associate Synod of Ireland. It was erected in 1795 by Seceders from the Magherafelt and Moneymore congregations. The place of minister is now vacant: the people, out of gratitude to the memory of their late pastor, are reserving it for his son. The minister's emoluments are regium donum 50 pounds, stipend 40 pounds, to which the Drapers' Company annually add 10 guineas.

Roman Catholic Chapels

There are 2 Roman Catholic chapels in the parish, one at Anagh, another at Cullion. The latter is thatched, and both are in bad repair and too small to contain the congregation attached to them.

The Revd James McCabe is priest of Desertmartin and Kilcronaghan. His stipend may be estimated at 75 pounds, besides an annual subscription of 10 guineas by the Drapers' Company.

Kilcronaghan Glebe House

The Revd James Spencer Knox, eldest son of the Lord Bishop of Derry, is rector of Kilcronaghan, which he holds united to Maghera. He is supposed to derive 550 pounds per annum from Kilcronaghan, viz. 400 pounds of tithes and 150 pounds from the rents of his glebe, which contains about 107 Irish arable acres.

The parsonage of Kilcronaghan is a neat comfortable house situated about half a mile from Moyheelan, on the east side of the road leading to Desertmartin. It is built on the gort or tithe field anciently allotted to the parson for collecting his tithe corn and which, in this instance, is far distant from the glebe lands. The natural dreariness of the place is further heightened by a grove of gloomy Scotch firs; and Mr Knox's contemplated removal to his living of Maghera precludes the hope of any immediate amelioration, a hope which might well be indulged from his known taste and the zeal with which he had commenced some improvements. The parochial duties are performed by his curate, the Revd R. McCausland.

Church

The church adjoins the glebe house; it is small, without any ornament and was rebuilt about 10 years ago on the site of the old church which is said to have been of great antiquity, but the era of its erection is unknown.

Meeting Houses in Tobermore

There are 2 meeting houses at Tobermore: the oldest, a branch of the Maghera congregation, was erected in 1728 and is under the jurisdiction of the Synod of Ulster. The minister, Revd William Brown, has a stipend of 60 pounds, besides 75 pounds of regium donum and 10 guineas from the Drapers' Company.

The other belongs to the followers of the Revd Alexander Carson, a gentleman who in 1805 was separated from communion with the Synod of Ulster for the introduction of some theological tenets connected, it is said, with the doctrines and practices of the Anabaptists. Mr Carson, then minister of Tobermore, was, with his adherents, driven by violence from his meeting house, in a manner which does little honour to the presbytery.

The present meeting house adjoins that from which he was thus forcibly ejected. It was reared in 1814 by the zeal of his followers, who form a numerous congregation. As a tribute to his talents, exemplary character and benevolent disposition, the Drapers' Company annually add 10 guineas to his stipend of 100 pounds.

Ballynascreen Glebe House

About a mile south east of the village of Moyheelan, on the road leading to Tobermore, stands the Glebe House of Ballynascreen. It is a commodious building, in a very good style and having quite the air of the residence of a country gentleman of fortune and taste, but it stands in a situation which commands little variety of prospect. There is some good timber in the extensive and thriving adjacent plantation. The grounds are in a very improved state and stocked with the best breeds of cattle. This house is now occupied by the rector, Revd William Knox, second son of the Lord Bishop of Derry. The living is supposed to be worth 1,000 pounds, derived from the tithes and glebe lands, independently of the parsonage and its fine farm of 98 acres which are not connected with the glebe-town.

Moyheelan Church

The church is in the village of Moyheelan; it is about 60 feet by 24. The body of the church was built about the beginning of the last century and enlarged in 1757. The square turret, with its stately octagonal spire, was erected under the administration of the late bishop.

Catholic Chapels in Ballynascreen

There are 2 Catholic chapels in the parish, one at

Straw, the other at Strawmore. The former is a large slated house with the newly erected galleries but the latter strongly bespeaks the poverty of its numerous congregation. The estimated stipend of the parish priest, Revd James Murphy, and his curate, Revd Francis Quin, is 110 pounds, besides 10 guineas yearly from the Drapers' Company.

SOCIAL ECONOMY

Tithe

Tithe is chargeable on all grain crops, on flax, potatoes and meadow. The tithe bill of the last session of parliament is about to be put into operation in this district. No other complaints, however, are made on the subject of tithes than arise from the nature of this ungracious tax on husbandry.

Poor

Poor rates are totally unknown in the district: the charity of the people is ardent enough to relieve extreme cases of suffering. The most abject have a laudable aversion to begging, or at least remove from the scenes of their better days. Their room, is, however, filled by other vagrant beggars to an indefinite and ever varying number.

The collections in the churches, amounting to about 2 pounds in each parish, are distributed annually at Easter among the resident poor, at 1s 3d to 2s each.

Church Records

The writer is unacquainted with any parochial records in the district. The vestry books, indeed, contain the "short and simple annals" of the different parishes, as far as relates to any imposts on the people for the maintenance of the Established worship or other assessments for local purposes.

Methodist Preachers

Some Methodist preachers resort to the district but they have hitherto formed no permanent society. Their hearers are mostly of the Established religion.

PRODUCTIVE ECONOMY

Proprietors

The principal proprietors of these parishes are the Drapers' Company; Robert Ogilby Esquire, lessee of the Skinners' Company; Lord Garvagh, James Stevenson Esquire, Henry Bruce Esquire, lessees of the churchlands; the owners of the Bellaghy estate; representatives of the late Mr Conolly; and Sir George F. Hill.

Farms and Rents

In the Drapers' and the Bellaghy estates, in the churchlands, the glebe-towns and Mr Carey's, land is let by the Irish acre; in the Skinners', Lord Garvagh's, M. Harren's and Judge Torrens's, by the Cunningham acre. The highest rent is 2 guineas per Irish acre. This is for land of the best description in the district; such land is also let at 30s to 26s, the middling at 1 pound, the worst at 16s. In Mr Ogilby's estate the best land is about 1 pound, middling about 15s and inferior arable 11s 4d ha'penny per Cunningham acre; moory pasture is a mere trifle. Tithe may in general be set down about 2s to 2s 6d per arable acre; church rates inconsiderable.

These rents are quite too high. It may be fairly affirmed that, except in some favoured fertile spots such as Fort William, the parsonages of Desertmartin and Ballynascreen, and some others on which capital has been liberally expended, no land in the district is worth more than 1 pound per Irish acre.

Farms vary from 60 acres to 1 acre; one grazing farm in Desertmartin contains 250 acres but the average of arable farms may be put at 10 and a half acres.

Leases

The general run of leases is from 31 years and 3 lives downwards to 21 years, as in the churchlands. In the Drapers' estate there is to be a classification of tenures according to the amount of rent: the lowest class, under 5 pounds rent, are to have leases from year to year; those paying 10 pounds, 15 pounds and 20 pounds are respectively to have leases of 14, 21 and 31 years. It will be optional with tenants of the highest class to have freehold leases, but such freehold interest to be surrendered at the end of 31 years, if the life or lives shall exceed that term.

As a stimulus to industry and a motive to the gradual enlargement of farms, admission to the first class will be reserved as a premium for successful industry and superior exertion in the acquisition and the application of capital. The leases will contain clauses against underletting and to secure a better system of cropping and encouragement for planting; but as the whole scheme seems nothing less than to make poverty penal, it will encounter difficulties in the execution.

Improvements in Farming

The tenantry of the Bellaghy estate form our only body of yeomanry. They hold in perpetuity at an easy rent, so low in many instances as 2s 6d an acre. These persons therefore, with Messrs Glenholme, Porter, Dickson, Sinclair, Hanna, Quin, Patterson, Hass, Getty and few others, form that class of persons who can be said to have such a command of capital as to enable them to introduce and recommend improved methods of husbandry; and yet, heretofore, their capital, care and attention had been diverted into so many channels and distracted by pursuits so various that their whole system was crippled and defective.

Now, however, they have caught the flame of emulation and begin to apply to agriculture the same spirit and intelligence which they evince in other pursuits. Most of them, too, deserve honourable mentions from their zeal in forwarding the interests of the Farming Society. The description of our modes of agriculture is not, therefore, strictly speaking applicable to the system pursued by those persons. Some of them have introduced the improved plough, have sown artificial grasses, reclaimed considerable tracts by the most [useful?] methods of paring and burning, and have successfully tried both under and surface draining; other improvements will soon follow.

The other class, that is the great body of our farmers, is utterly destitute of either skill or means for effecting any improvements. The ploughing matches have indeed given a stimulus to them which, if properly followed up, may lead to happy effects.

Modes of Cultivation

The mode of cultivation practised may be best described by its negative characteristics. There is here, then, no second ploughing, no harrowing before sowing, except, and that rarely, in the case of flax, no green crops, no artificial grasses; an exhausted field is, indeed, said to be laid out in grass, which being interpreted means not that grasses are sown, or that any means are taken to promote their growth, but that the natural grass is permitted to grow if it can conquer the weeds. There is little draining, no irrigation; the steam ripples idly by and the slope vainly invites its fertilizing waters. The meadows here are mostly natural. They are sometimes manured with ashes, but in general their management is quite barbarous: they are grazed down late in summer, the aftermath is cut late and the grounds are thus poached by the cattle.

Recent Improvements

The most remarkable recent improvement is the almost total abolition of the rundale system. Farmers are becoming more sensible of the importance of enclosures, both as fences and drains. Most farms are divided into small fields, rather well fenced. The usual fence is a gripe and bank commonly small and planted with thorn quicks. Hedgerows sometimes meet the eye, of ash, alder, sloe tree and black sallow. In the dry sandy grounds, and on the hillsides, whins (furze) are sown and grow well; they are even said to thrive where thorn quicks fail. And besides, the green succulent tops of the whin form, when pounded, an excellent resource to the half-starved cattle in the spring months.

Recent improvements in the vehicles and the implements of husbandry have scarcely yet been fairly introduced. In Ballynascreen the slide car is the commonest vehicle; very few farm carts are seen in the district. The more improving farmers have cart-cars; these have a spoked wheel of large diameter revolving on the axis, which diminishes the friction and admits of wider body. The iron plough has not yet made its way: some wooden ploughs of the improved make are held with reins and tackling to correspond.

Manures

The manures in use are farmyard dung mixed with bog, also compost of bog or clay and lime in alternate layers. Great exertions are made in liming: the quantity used in husbandry is increased, perhaps, in the ratio of 15 to 1 compared with that of the opening of this century. In Ballynascreen the poor farmer draws the limestone not only from Desertmartin but even from Cookstown and Dungiven. The better cultivators spread it also on lea a year before ploughing, to the amount of 50 barrels to the acre.

Clay is burned in little smothered heaps but on a very limited scale. It is merely a resort of the patch farmer to eke out his scanty portion of manure, so that its merits have never had a fair trial. If the practice were regularly introduced into Ballynascreen, where lime is so expensive and clay so accessible, it would effect a mighty improvement.

The owner of the tuck mill in Ballynascreen has sown a few perches of woad this year, in drills about 27 inches apart. The soil is gravelly but neither rich nor dry enough, yet the crop looked pretty well in the first week of September. Whether, or how often, it had been cut during the season is not yet ascertained.

Crops

The culture of turnips has not been attempted by any of the farmers. The Revd William Knox has about 3 acres of turnips this year; his transplanted swedes have been rather unsuccessful. This gentleman has also introduced the cultivation of rape and mangel wurzel. Wheat is grown on a few farms in Desertmartin and Kilcronaghan but the quantity is inconsiderable. The species is the red or spring wheat, sown in October and November. Rye has latterly been introduced about Tobermore and the cultivation of it is spreading.

Those are the rare crops; the common succession is: 1, potatoes, 2, flax, 3, oats, 4, oats; or 2, barley, 3, flax, 4, oats; or 2, oats, 3, oats; then lea for 2 or 3 years. In the first year of lea there is no grass whatever. The second and third years give a close verdant pile embellished with the daisy and perfumed with the fragrance of the natural white clover. Such a series of crops applied to any soil must exhaust it, but in this very indifferent one is truly pernicious.

Potatoes

Potatoes are planted in ridges over the manure, or kibbed, that is dibbled, after which the manure is spread and covered. The season of planting is from the beginning to the middle of May, but some sluggards prolong it till the middle of June. The seed per acre is 25 bushels, produce 240 to 300 bushels. The favourite seeds are the red and black.

The soil of Ballynascreen is not favourable to potatoes: they are rather viscous. As a remedy most of the farmers store them on rude lofts in contact with the smoke of the chimney. Potatoes raised on the ground which had been planted the year before are found best for the table.

Barley and Oats

Barley is much grown in this district. The only kind sown is the common 4-rowed barley. It is sown from the middle to the end of April and reaped about the end of August. The quantity sown is from 4 to 4 and a half bushels per Irish acre, according to the condition of the soil, the produce from 6 and a half barrels upwards to 10 barrels.

Oats are generally sown in the last fortnight of March and thence till May. After sowing the ridges are usually trenched and shovelled over the seed. The species sown are the lightfoot, Poland, Blantyre, Angus; and in Ballynascreen the black oats. Potter's oats have been introduced: this may prove a favourite kind if its thickness of skin be not found injurious. This year, however, it has failed in the district, even in the richest clover soils. 7 bushels of Potter's and of potato oats, 8 bushels of the other kinds are usually sown on an Irish acre and in Ballynascreen weak land takes 10.

Flax

In Ballynascreen flax always succeeds potatoes. The land is either ploughed once then harrowed before sowing, or more usually dug, and this is the only instance of spade husbandry. Flax has the same place in the rotation of the other parishes but there it sometimes follows barley or the first crop of oats; in this case it is sown on land which had been purposely manured with mere dung. Much of our soil is unfavourable to flax: it grows short. The seeds most in request are the Dutch and New York. The former is almost solely used in the southern part of the district: the plant of that seed strikes a deeper root and is not so subject to the disease called *firing*.

In Ballynascreen both kinds are sown but the New York is preferred to the Dutch. The quantity of seed is about 4 bushels to an Irish acre, produce from 100 to 160 green stooks. In clay grounds, after the removal of the crop, the ridges are now always trenched up: an excellent practice in such soils. It turns up the clods to be pulverised by the frost, it carries off the water by the deep furrows and thus permits an earlier ploughing than could otherwise be attempted. Hitherto little or none of the seed has been saved. The flax is always kiln dried previously to beetling and is mostly prepared for use by hand.

The district does not furnish enough of flax for its internal consumption: the defect is supplied, however, from the more plentiful markets of Moneymore, Cookstown and Magherafelt.

Landlords

Such is our husbandry. Little can be said in its favour and the most powerful argument in extenuation of its defects would probably be deemed idle declamation.

The whole district, with the exception of the Ballynascreen churchlands and the 3 glebe-towns, has the misfortune to be parcelled out among absentees. In many places the sole evil of this system is that the great body of cultivators have no leading person to spread among them the influence of enlightened example, to exhibit for their imitation models of perfection in agriculture and rural economy.

Here the disease sinks deeper. These landlords are absentees, not only in body but in spirit: they take no measures to improve the morals, the comforts or the health of their tenantry. They are known solely through the half-yearly visitation of the agent, the frequent foray of the bailiff, or the meaner mission of the hen-gatherer. Avarice is their ruling passion; their cry, "give, give." Equally backward to promote a good object and to prevent an evil one, their nature yields most pliantly to that competition for farms which unfortunately prevails among the peasantry and the offer of an increased rack-rent puts the high-bidding adventurer over the head of the old deserving tenant.

A different conduct would soon change the face of the country and the habits of its people. Other measures would fix and invest in the soil the small floating capital which is even now in the hands of the farmers, but which, uselessly to themselves and to the community, is employed in precarious speculations, in the petty traffic of some marketable commodity, offering a quick return with trifling profit.

But this improvement no foreign aid can accomplish. The North West Society may do much; the local farming society may have a good effect; the philanthropic zeal of the Drapers' Company (absentees only in their doctrine of rent) must be beneficial; but the main improvement must proceed from the justice and patriotism of the landlords. Let them give the farmer that positive interest in the soil which arises from a good tenure at a reasonable rent. Industry will then take the proper direction, then will follow better husbandry and an improved soil, increase of capital and decrease in the cost of production, comfort to the tenant and rent to the landlord.

Horses and Oxen

About 12 farmers in the district are in the habit of breeding horses. Mr Henry of Ballynagowan has a stallion whose foals promise well, but the horses of the better farmers are reared in the counties of Armagh and Tyrone, they are stout, middle-sized and well suited to agricultural purposes.

The poorest farmers never consider themselves established without a horse. It is a matter of regret they are not aware of the advantages resulting from the use of oxen; these patient, easy-fed animals are infinitely superior to the scrubby half-famished garrans <garrons> now in use, and whose number is becoming really alarming. Among the mountains are to be found some hardy, vigorous, light nags of the Highland and Manx breeds, well adapted to the place as far as feeding is concerned.

Dairies

There are no regular dairies here, no manufacture of cheese; but there is considerable export of butter.

Cattle

The breed of black cattle in this district appears to be the old Irish, or perhaps a cross between that and the Lancashire. It has received some recent improvements. Mr Quin of Coolsara and the other cattle dealers have conferred this benefit on their country by the judicious introduction of good bulls and cows from the south and west of Ireland. Bullocks and heifers are reared here by almost every farmer. They are well suited to the soil and climate, and no cattle find a more ready market in Lancashire and Cheshire.

The Revd Messrs Knox and the other gentlemen have introduced the Ayr, Devon, Leicester and other foreign breeds to their grounds. Crosses of these have, most injudiciously, been procured by some farmers and the experiment has failed, as the best judges had anticipated. The system of farming must be improved before those breeds can succeed, even in the lowlands. And how are they to live on the rough mountain pastures, whither our dry cattle are always sent in the summer months? If change be necessary, and if a foreign breed can be superior to the native, a position which may well be questioned, the Galloway or the Kyloe would perhaps be found to suit this district best. The bullocks of either breed are rather preferable to heifers and both are exportable at a much earlier age than cattle of the short-horned breeds.

The grazing farms and heathy pastures are generally stocked with young bullocks and heifers of the native breed, from 1 to 4 years old, either reared by the owner or bought up in the neighbourhood, or taken to graze for the summer. The poverty of the small mountain graziers has a deteriorating effect on the breed of cattle. It would be a valuable improvement to introduce good bulls to the mountains, instead of the degenerate starveling race that is now kept by those people.

Grazing is let at 7s 6d to 10s a summ, that is a bullock or heifer of 3 years old. Sheep are charged at 1s 8d to 2s 2d a head.

Sheep

The breed of sheep most sought after by the farmers of the lower and more fertile grounds is brought from Fermanagh and the more southern counties. It is always recognised here as the Connaught breed; their size, the quantity and quality of their fleece entitles them to a place in the stock of every farmer. They do well here, even under the very paltry management of the present mode. Indeed, the nature of the soil in most parts of Desertmartin and Kilcronaghan will be found, when grasses shall have been introduced, well suited to an improved breed of sheep. The number of the above breed is, however, very limited; in winter they are housed and fed. There are few individuals of the Cheviot breed, highly prized for the fineness of their wool.

The most numerous flocks are found about the glens and mountain sides, where indeed they form a principal resource to the owners. They are the common native breed with long white faces and thin light fleece. Small, but hardy, without fold or house or fodder, they resist all weather, except when there occurs a winter so lengthened and severe as the last, in which many of them perished. A wether of this breed which had been housed and fed for some months sold for 2 guineas last spring, mutton 6d per lb. There are instances of shearing twice a year, but the practice is not liked: the wool is too short. It is sometimes tried after a wet harvest as a preventive of wool casting.

Many of the Ayrshire or Galloway moorland sheep have been imported into the Banagher and Munterlowney mountains. Some too have found their way into the hills of Ballynascreen. These are mostly horned, with black faces and black legs. Their extreme hardiness and their propensity to fatten in the roughest and scantiest, in the barest and bleakest, pasture would render them a valuable acquisition, but their wool is so coarse that they can never be popular in this district. Happily, however, the cross between these and the native breed is equally hardy, of better bone, more delicate mutton, and the wool is so superior, that this bids fair to become a favourite breed with the mountaineers.

Pigs

There is a very good breed of swine in the district. In no animal is such attention paid to selection: every man rears (but seldom alas! fattens) a pig and is anxious to procure the biggest and best breeds. Many Berkshires have also been introduced. The fair of Moyheelan has become quite an emporium of store pigs. From it the whole barony of Keenaught is supplied.

Poultry and Bees

Little attention is paid to the rearing of poultry; the same remark applies to bees, both proofs of diminished care. About 15 years ago the garden of one farmer in Desertmartin parish contained 27 beehives: it has none now.

Price of Goods

The following are the prices of provisions and grain, as nearly as they could be collected: potatoes 3d ha'penny to 4d per stone, oatmeal 2s 6d per score, beef 2d to 3d ha'penny per lb., mutton 2d ha'penny to 4d per lb., lamb 4d ha'penny a lb., pork 2d to 2d ha'penny, barley, new, 1s 3d ha'penny to 1s 5d per stone, old, 1s 7d to 1s 9d, oats 6d ha'penny to 9d per stone, rye 1s 2d per stone.

Employment

There are no public works in the district to give employment to the poor, except roadmaking which is often a monopoly. During the seed time and harvest there is too much employment and at other seasons little or none. Some farmers get their work performed by cottiers who rent a house and garden, sometimes with, sometimes without, a half acre of land and the summer's run of a cow. The cottier works so many days in the week or the year to his landlord; in the interval, if not a weaver, he is often idle. The rent of such cottier is, in Ballynascreen (with half an acre), from 4 guineas to 5 pounds; in Desertmartin, without it, 4 pounds, though in some townlands the half acre and cow's grass are let so low as 2 pounds 10s. The regulations of the Drapers' Company, however, prevent the settlement of cottiers, so that the married labourer can no longer find a resting place on their property.

The present rate of wages is: for male servants 4 guineas to 6 pounds a year, females spinning a hank per day 2 pounds; day labourers in northern part of the district 8d boarded, 10d in busy seasons, the latter rare, in the south 9d to 1s not boarded, except in busy seasons; 2 horses with tackle and man 4s 6d a day, with dinner to man and feed to horse; single horse and man 2s 6d without meat; blacksmiths 1s 1d for making and driving a set of shoes; hacklers with board 6d per stone of dressed flax, without board 8d; shoemaker boarded 1s 8d to 2s 1d per pair; tailor boarded 5s 5d, making suit of clothes.

Weights and Measures

There is no diversity of weights or measures: the long hundred and the score are in general use. The measures used at the lime quarries are a subject of complaint. Some sell by regular barrel of 4 bushels, others by one of 3 bushels, while many use an arbitrary measure to the great detriment of the trade.

Fairs

There are fairs in the villages of Tobermore and Moyheelan, for the sale of cattle, pigs, yarns, coarse linen and woollen cloth for domestic purposes.

The Tobermore fairs are held on the following days: January 17th, February 13th, March 28th, April 28th, May 31st, July 5th, August 12th, October 19th, December 11th.

The fairs of Moyheelan are held on the first Friday of every month and are custom free.

There are also 2 fairs in Desertmartin, one in May and another in December, but they have declined so much that little business is now done in them.

North West Society

The Tobermore branch of the North West Society comprises the parishes of Killelagh, Termoneeny and Maghera, besides the 3 which form the subject of the present essay. The efforts of this society have hitherto been tolerably successful: the ploughing matches and the distribution of the different premiums have excited a spirit of emulation among the farmers which promises the happiest effects, if properly directed. The actual number of subscribers is 22, of whom 19 are in this district; of 6 claimants of the premium for saving flax seed, these parishes contained 4; of 4 premiums given this year for clover, 2 were awarded to farmers of the district; and last year the competitors for clover were all in this district.

Cattle Trade

There is a considerable trade in cattle carried on from this district. A few of the principal farmers purchase cattle in the Connaught fairs and export them to the northern and midland counties of England. Persons of smaller capital pick up suitable beasts at home and sell them to those traders. An accurate view of this trade is given in the appendix.

Tanning

A small tanning establishment is carried on in Ballynascreen with considerable energy, though cramped by some injudicious legislative restrictions.

Wool

The woollen manufacture is of some domestic importance. It consists of druggets, flannels, blanketing and the coarse cloth worn by the men. There is a tuck mill with dye works in Ballynascreen, which finished 5,334 yards from 1st September 1822 till 4th September 1823. The small wheel only is used in spinning the wool. Stockings are knit but not for sale, chiefly by labourers and children in the winter nights, at 1s a pair.

Linen

The linen manufacture is the principal support of the district, its best source of peace and comfort. Yet during the last 10 years it has been rather stationary than progressive. It is indeed slowly advancing in Ballynascreen. Formerly there were 5 bleach greens in the parish of Desertmartin and 1 in Ballynascreen; there are none now in any of the parishes. The water of Ballynascreen is said to have been unfavourable to the bleaching process, but, from whatever cause, the failure of such means of employment is deeply to be lamented.

Weaving

The parish of Desertmartin contains 220 weavers, the other 2 parishes contain perhaps 200. The cloth manufactured here at present is mostly the three-fourths narrows; the set from 6 to 9 hundreds. These are mostly sold in Cookstown, Moneymore and a few in Kilrea, at 9d to 11d per yard. The finest are the seven-eighths wides of 11 and 12 hundreds, sold in Magherafelt and Moneymore at 10d ha'penny farthing to 1s 1d per yard. Yarn is spun in Ballynascreen as fine as 9 hanks to the lb., in the other parishes to 7 hanks, but the ordinary grist is from 2 and a half to 5 hanks.

The present prices are: for 6 hanks yarn and upwards 3s 2d to 3s 6d per spangle, for the coarse kind commonly used in the seven-eighths webs woven here 2s 7d ha'penny, the low yarn 2s 4d. The finer work is sold in Maghera, partly to manufacturers and partly to dealers in yarn, who dispose of it in distant markets. Such persons also attend the fairs of the district and purchase the surplus left unbought by the weavers. In almost every instance flax is grown by the spinners, or else purchased on the foot. None but the most destitute poor spin by the spangle for hire. Those who spin the coarser quality of yarn earn about 3d a day; 5d a hank is generally paid for the finest sorts; but then, such payments are mostly in kind.

The double wheel was introduced by the Drapers' Company and by Mr Ogilby but it has been laid aside. Whether the trial was a fair one is not known to the writer, but that machine is not calculated to produce a fine grist of yarn.

The weaver, in every instance, purchases his yarn in a raw state, trusting to his own skill or the vendor's honesty, for the assortment of the article and its facility in bleaching equally. The expenditure of stuffs in preparing a web is about 4s 6d; but taking into account the serious waste of fuel and time by the present process, the total expense may be taken at double the amount. In this point of view the establishment of yarn greens, furnishing an equally assorted material, would prove a great national benefit. And the modern improvements in machinery and chemistry warrant the belief that the bleached yarn could be afforded so much cheaper as to effect a considerable saving in the weaver's annual expenditure, as well as to benefit the community by improving our staple manufactures.

Flax Mills

There are 2 flax mills in the district, Mr Glenholme's of Anagh and Mr Hanna's of Moyheelan. The scutchers are on the vertical plan, with rollers attached. The mill rates are 1d per lb. of rolled and scutched flax. Mr Glenholme has procured ripples, scrapers and other implements from the Linen Board and has taken a very laudable interest in acquiring and propagating the Dutch method of preparing flax.

Corn Mills

There are 7 corn mills, viz. 3 in Ballynascreen, 2 in Kilcronaghan and 2 in Desertmartin. The machinery of these mills is tolerably good; all have fanners and, excepting 2 of the Ballynascreen mills, tile kilns are attached to each of them.

The Drapers' Company very properly led the way in abandoning that relic of feudalism, suit of mill, in favour of their tenantry, an example which some other landlords have imitated. The toll of mulcture has, in consequence, fallen from a 16th to a 32nd. At Desertmartin mill the toll is a 28th, the miller providing fuel to dry the grain. Such has latterly been the extent of illicit distillation in some parts of the district that during the last year 1,200 sacks of malt were ground in one of the above mills at 1s 3d a sack and 142 distillers kept regular running accounts with the miller.

Shops

Several petty trading shops are dispersed over the district, besides those of the villages. Ballynascreen contains 10 of these and the other 2 parishes together may have an equal number. In these places are sold tea, sugar, tobacco, deals, iron and leather. The owners of such shops often take payment in kind, butter, yarn and raw hides, to vend in distant markets. It may be necessary to remark that the only circulating medium is the paper of the Belfast banks and the silver tokens of the Bank of Ireland.

Lime and Quarrying

The lime trade is too important to be omitted in a report of this district. In the less busy seasons almost every farmer in Kilcronaghan and Desertmartin is engaged either in quarrying or burning. The superior quality of our lime ensures a constant demand but the supply is neither constant nor regular. It would, in this respect, be a very desirable change if 3 or 4 skilful persons with some capital could obtain leases of the quarries and erect suitable kilns.

About 45 to 50 barrels of the raw stone may be bought at the quarry for 15s. In the Drapers' estate the principal quarries are reserved to the company, who have appointed a man to raise and sell the stone to tenants only, at 1s 3d a ton of raw stone. Our limestone is easily burned in most places; turf alone is used. Small pot kilns are adopted in Ballynascreen, pipe kilns in the other parishes. The mode of burning is by filling the kiln with the stones broken into pieces about 2 lbs weight, leaving an arch or pipe through the centre of the kiln from the front to rear, about 2 feet wide and 4 feet high, to contain the fuel which is constantly supplied from without. The common sized kiln takes about 36 hours in burning, contains upwards of 50 barrels of roach lime and consumes about 50 gauges of turf, each a cubic yard.

The appendix shows the ordinary prices of

lime in Desertmartin; in Kilcronaghan it is 2d to 3d ha'penny per bushel, slacked.

SOCIAL ECONOMY

Natural Curiosities and Remarkable Occurrences

Some information on the first of these heads has been already given in the former parts of this essay. To enumerate the different subjects of natural history produced in the district would lead to a detail quite incompatible with the limits of this report.

The sequestered situation of the place, the simple uniform life of its inhabitants and the total want of any existing records of their actions will, it is hoped, account for the absence of information on remarkable occurrences.

Protestant Clergy

The following list of the incumbents is given not as authentic but as the most accurate that could be obtained under the circumstances.

The parishes of Desertmartin and Kilcronaghan appear to have been united until lately; Revd Dr Mushett was the incumbent after the revolution, Dr Strachan about 1730, Revd Walter Mottley, Robert Bryan.

After this gentleman's decease the parishes were disunited. His successors in Desertmartin have been Richard Waddy, James Magee, Gabriel Stokes D.D., F.T.C.D., died in his 73rd year, April 28th 1806, Revd Charles Colthurst A.M.

Since the division of the parishes Kilcronaghan has been held by Revd Clotworthy Soden, James Jones, William Bryan, James Spencer Knox A.M.

The Revd Andrew Henderson was rector of Ballynascreen at the revolution. The tradition of the inhabitants is that he was a most benevolent kind-hearted man, but that during the prevalence of James's party he was obliged to flee the country, and his glebe house was burned.

A chasm occurs in the series of rectors till the days of Dr Blackall about 1755. His successor, Revd Dr John Torrens, died January 1785, having nearly completed his 76th year. This gentleman was grandfather of the Honourable Justice Torrens, of Major-General Sir H. Torrens K.C.B., adjutant general, and of Archdeacon Torrens. After presiding over the diocesan school of Derry for some time with distinguished applause, he was promoted to the living of Ballynascreen, which he held for many years. He was also vicar-general of the diocese. He was succeeded by his relative Dr Thomas Torrens F.T.C.D., father-in-law of Judge Torrens; Revd Gardner Young, Revd William Knox.

Presbyterian Clergy

Succession of Presbyterian ministers: the first minister of Tobermore was in 1728 Revd Mr Reid; Revd Mr Turrettin; 1758, Revd James Whiteside, who discharged the pastoral functions 40 years, and died in March 1798 aged 65; Revd Alexander Carson, ejected in 1805; Revd William Brown.

The only minister of the Lecumpher meeting house was the Revd John Wilson, who died in 1821. Mr Wilson was generally beloved, not more for his talents than for his integrity, uprightness and independence of mind. The circumstance of the congregation's reserving the charge for his son is the highest testimony of his worth and efficiency as a minister; but it may not be useless to add that his memory is not less dear to his neighbours of every religious denomination and that in his limited sphere of action his death was felt as a public calamity.

Catholic Priests

Roman Catholic priests of Desertmartin and Kilcronaghan: the following is the succession of the Roman Catholic priests as communicated by a gentleman of that body. Revd Francis McNamee was priest of Desertmartin and Kilcronaghan at, or shortly after, the revolution of 1688. He died aged 90, on the 2nd June 1715.

Revd Roger Gormly (Rory More), his successor, died November 6th 1759, aged 100. This gentleman met various turns of fortune. He had in his youth received a good education and obtained a commission in Tyrconnell's army. After the revolution he was reduced to great difficulties and at length became a priest. Conway the poet, mentioned hereafter, introduces Roger himself, thus recounting his multifarious occupations to his host, Walter Kirkpatrick.

> Gualteri conjux audit, Gualterus et ipse;
> Rogerius reboans, haec sua gesta refert.
> Seneschallus eram; merui sub rege Jacobo;
> Caupo fui necnon, ludimagister eram,
> Occidi Scotos, Batavos, fortesque Britannos;
> Dersa et Limesicum facta relata sciunt."

Rory More was succeeded by the Revd John O'Regan, who died February 27th 1788 in the 68th year of his age. Revd Mathias McCosker promoted in June 1798; Revd James Murphy promoted March 1792; Revd Francis Havlow died 1802; Revd Patrick McKenna promoted

November 1809; Revd [blank] Higgins, ord. F. praed. was administrator during a year.

Revd Andrew Bradley died April 16th 1823 aged 65. This gentleman was the last priest of the Bradleys (in Irish O'Brullaughan), a name so much distinguished, both at home and on the Continent, in the annals of the Catholic Church. Among his relatives were Dominick Bradley, commonly called the "Brahr Ban" or "white friar," author of the work *De missione et missionario*, and of whom De Burgo (*Hibernia Dominica*) says "Nulli ea in regione concionatori secundus;" Patrick Bradley, Roman Catholic Bishop of Derry and chaplain of the Sardinian ambassador to the Court of St James (*Hib. Dom.*); Dr McDonagh, Roman Catholic Bishop of Kilmore, and who, whilst at Rome, says De Burgo (*Hib. Dom.*), "Serenissimo Carolo Edwardo Stuarto Walliae principi a confessionibus fuit."

But Mr Bradley's merit rested not on the fame of his family. Animated indeed by the example of these worthy men he became an exile from his country, in order to qualify himself for the priestly functions. He studied philosophy in St Patrick's College, Lisbon, and, assisted by the present principal of the Royal College, Maynooth, sustained a philosophical thesis with unbounded applause. Having finished a course of theology in the College of the Oratorians, he declined a most respectable situation in Lisbon and returned to his native land to preach the gospel to the poor. Even about 3 years since, he was invited to accept the rectorship of an Irish seminary on the Continent but declined it from motives of conscience.

As a priest he was deservedly dear to his flock and his well-known love of order and hearty exertions in support of the laws and tranquility of the country gained him the general goodwill of the community. As a general scholar few so long engaged in parochial duties could be called his rivals, none, perhaps, his superior. In the vigour of his intellect he was a perfect master of the Greek and Roman classics, with the Spanish, Portuguese and French languages; and it is probable he left few behind him in Ulster so well skilled in the ancient language of Ireland. His successor is the Revd James McCabe.

Catholic Priests of Ballynascreen

The earliest of the Ballynascreen priests whose name has reached us was Terence Rogers, who died in 1735. His successor Right Revd Dr Conway, Roman Catholic Bishop of Derry, died in 1738. Denis Rodgers, who was commonly called "Sagart Francach" or "the French priest," having been sometime rector of a parish in France. The time of his death is unknown. Bryan Rogers, died 1772; Matthew Rogers, 1776; John Wall, 20th March 1778; John Ward, promoted 1785. John McLaughlin, a native of Inishowen, succeeded Mr Ward. McLaughlin was eminently skilled in the Irish language. He studied at the Irish College, Paris, and during his residence there was many years employed by order of the Dublin Society, or of some other public body, in transcribing a part of the *Book of Leacan*, that inestimable remnant of Irish literature, from a copy in the Royal Library. He was appointed first professor of the Irish language at Maynooth but declined the offer. He died 28th October 1803. Revd James Murphy is the present priest.

O'Neill Family

The family of O'Neill appear to have been distinguished in this district.

The last of that name of whom any authentic notice occurs in history was Brian O'Neill, who was appointed a burgess of the Corporation of Londonderry, when that body was remodelled by authority of James II (vide Archbishop King's *State of the Protestants*). The incident is thus mentioned in a doggerel poem of that period (published in the *Derriana*), which records the principal events of the siege of Derry.

"Brian O'Neill of Ballynascreen is chose,
Whose fathers did the English troops oppose,
In Queen Eliza's reign most barbarously.

Remarkable Men

Bryan O'Donnell, commonly called Bryan McCon, the Ulster antiquarian, resided in Ballynascreen, where he died, it is thought, in the year 1747 at a very advanced age.

Dryden somewhere observes that historians who give immortality to others are often badly requited by posterity: poor McCon met this fate. Even his descendants know little of his history. He was a native of Glenfin in Donegal, married in Ballynascreen and resided long in Banchran. O'Donnell was probably the last of our seanachies or antiquarians. In this capacity he frequently visited the most respectable Irish families of Ulster, and was hospitably received by them. The antiquarian remunerated them by relating the deeds of their illustrious forefathers, or by soothing them with the strains of our once famous bards. In these peregrinations he had collected a great number of ranns and transcribed, or obtained, many curious ancient manuscripts which are now, from the ignorant and shameful indifference of his family, irrecoverably lost.

O'Donnell was constantly employed, whilst at home, in transcribing rare manuscripts and preserving the many fragments of ancient Irish poetry which he had collected. An anecdote of him has been preserved which evinces extraordinary absence of mind. One day while O'Donnell was busied in transcribing, some women came in from the neighbourhood to spin and, of course, talked copiously on several subjects. On collating afterwards his copy with the original, he was mortified to find the tale of the historian sprinkled with the gossip to which he had been an unconscious listener and indignantly vowed that he would never again write within reach of woman's tongue. O'Donnell was thus complimented by the Revd Daniel McLaughlin (Donald Gorm), rector of Culdaff.

Failte dhuit MacConn
Agus do labhart ghrinn gan aon gron
Le shealgaraght chlann na milidh,
Agus gach gaisgedheach a sil na Righ reamh.
Da mbeadh an choill so fa na blaith
Agus gan Gaeil a bheidh faoidh mhistah
Gheofadh ar an chrain abhain
Do chruasach alig go umlan.
Achd, nir fhagadar clan na Gall,
Mur fhag siad feolan a frail.
Ach faseadh slat as bun an chroin
A mbeis go so na mor choill.

Henry McConn O'Donnell came with Bryan, whose brother he was, from Donegal and settled with him in Ballynascreen. He was considered equal to Bryan as an Irish scholar, but much inferior in his knowledge of the English language. He was therefore a useful copyist but never travelled as a seanachie. He died before Bryan but at what age, or in what year, is not known.

Poets

The Revd Christopher Conway, a Roman Catholic priest, and relative, it is believed, of the above-mentioned Bishop Conway, was celebrated for his wit and poetic talents. He resided long in the parish of Desertmartin, where he was reduced to the necessity of teaching a small classical school. The period of his death is unknown to the writer.

His numerous poetical pieces have never been published; in the present instance a few only of his Latin verses could be collected. Yet he wooed the English muse too, with success. A poem of his on the victory of Culloden attracted considerable attention at that time and introduced him to the notice of Mr Dawson, ancestor of our present county member.

The subjoined verses, being taken down from memory, are necessarily imperfect.

The following is an edict of Apollo and the Muses for the apprehension of one Cassidy who, it appears, was a violator of prosody and taste.

Nos Phoebus vatum rex, et regina Minerva,
Pieridumque chorus et quos colit unda Medusae,
Mandatis nostris vobis praecipimus hisce,
Prendere Cassidium prensumque adducere vinctum
Ad nos, vel alias nostra de classe Camoenas,
Syllaba namque brevis semper producitur illi;
Contrahit et longam, nec servat jura poesis.
Utque luat poemas, nostrum mittatur in antrum
Mensibus et quatuor discat Palemonis artem
Potando, semper sobrius, Piremidas undas."

Satires

One Phelim O'Neill, having become rich, deserted his religion and changed his name to Felix Neele, was thus satirized by Conway.

Omnia mutavit Felix, mutavit et ipsum:
Ipsius inque ipso, non manet esse sui.
Monticolas inter puduit terpere colonos
Erubuitque braccas, erubuitque brogas:
Signa suae gentis, nomenque rejecit O'Neilli:
Nec ratis, aut salmo, aut rubra retenta manus.
Poeniteat liquisse tuas nunc, transfuga, partes;
Infelix Felix, ad tua castra redi.

A certain devotee, on his return from a pilgrimage to Lough Derg, was reported to have pawned his horse to indulge in a drunken frolic. This incident is thus recorded by Conway. Arthur is the landlord of the public house.

Ivit eques, rediitque pedes, Franciscus ab antro
Patritii, tantus religionis amor!
Fertur equum sacris ideo mersisse sub undis
Ut brutum sanctum, sanctus et ipse foret:
Rectius ast alii, gelido non flumine mersum,
Sed calido justius deperuisse ferunt.
Patritii infelix animal non perdidit unda,
Arthuri e medio Bacchica lympha tulit
Arthuri e vita vitae rapuere liquores:
Quod vita est domino, mors fuit illud equo
Sed de Francisco nunc altera fama vagatur,
Quadrupedem Baccho sacrificasse suum:
Hunc etenim quondam inter numina magna colebat.
Patritio solitus proposuisse Deum,
Ne foret iratus, contempto numine, divus
E cymba timidum vix tulit ille pedem
Cum saepe Arthurum inclamet, (fuit ille sacerdos

Miscellaneous Papers

Numinis) Arthurum littus ab omne sonet.
Ecce Arthurus adest Divi semiebrius aede
Quem sic affatur vocibus ille piis.
O vates, cui scire dedit Semeleia proles
Secreta et regni mystica sacra sui
Per triduum omisi divo mea solvere vota
Delusus geniis, O mea culpa malis.
Jam supplex venio, supplex me limine sterno.
Exores numen, propitesque precor.
(Non capere, aut haedus non restat ovicula quidem
Qui solus restat, sacrificabo equum).
Amanit Arthurus, positamque e cespite mensum
Fraxineis onerat fagineisque scyphis;
Accedunt tumidi, solita de more, botelli,
Grataque Francisca pocula larga duo.
Ramsaei dulces modulatur gulture [culture?] versus
Franciscus quavis dulcior ipse lyra.
Et jam littereis vates sua tempora juncis
Franciscique, hedera deficiente tegit.
Ecce furor subito mentes et corpora versat
Et manus atque oruli, cunctaq[ue] membra tremunt.
Perula larga cito, nobis ait, pocula ferto;
Ecce furo, furo, jam pocula ferto cito.
Et jam nox aderat, cerreptus uterque furore
Invadunt vulgus fustibus omne suis;
(Nam Thyrisi deerant) lacerantur vestes et ora.
Et lapidum nimbi, proxima tela, volant.
Confusis resonat turbae clameribus aether;
Undique strata solo corpora caesa jacent.
Bacchatur donec tenebras nex intulit erbi,
Et Martis placido fine diremit opus.

PRODUCTIVE AND SOCIAL ECONOMY

Suggestions for Improvement

Some hints of this nature incidentally occur in the previous sections. A few shall be here proposed with respectful diffidence.

The present state of the cottage houses is really disgraceful to the country. The Tobermore Farming Society have done well in appropriating a part of their funds to reward superior neatness in the dwelling and office houses of the farmer, but they will have effected little if they shall not extend their sympathy to the hovel of the cottier. The farmer is bound to keep his cottier's dwelling in repair, but generally speaking it is very miserable and, in many instances, incapable of withstanding the winter rain. Nothing is more common than complaints of the bad order in which farmers keep the houses of their cottiers, and not only in this district but elsewhere.

It would be extremely desirable that chief landlords would pay some attention to the state in which these middlemen keep the cottages on their farms. Much of the disease and filth of the country arises from these wretched habitations and though there is no direct control over the middlemen, yet any landlord can make it a point with his immediate tenant that the house of the cottier, who too often pays an exorbitant rent, shall at least be watertight.

Agriculture

It would be idle to insist here on the advantages of cultivating green crops, yet the subject cannot be too often mentioned. It is painful to see the farmer obliged to sell or hire out his milch cows, at the approach of winter, to curtail his stock, when it would be most beneficial to increase it. It will be for the parent society to press this matter most earnestly on the different branches.

Nor is the cottier to be overlooked. What would be more desirable than the addition of an occasional feed of turnips or cabbages to the scanty portion of sapless straw on which his cow is half starved. And this object is within his reach: the Swedish turnips or ruta baga, transplanted, would exactly suit his purpose. His plot of flax is pulled and cleared off about the middle of August. The preparatory tilth of the flax ground has fitted it well for the reception of any bulbous rooted plant. A few square yards of the garden sown in June would bring the plants ready by August. The ground ploughed in, or dug fresh, the plants dibbled in drills over a small quantity of dung or scouring would soon push up, even with our August or September sun. The finger weeding or hoeing with small hand hoes might be easily performed by the children.

If the excellent practice of planting potatoes in wider rows on the ridges, so as to admit more frequent shovelling, were introduced, another easy mode of procuring green food would be the setting of curled kale in the furrows after the last shovelling. Mangel wurzel might also be transplanted after early potatoes: the soil of this district would suit that plant, but it would, perhaps, require too much manure for the cottier. The same objection, indeed, may be urged against the turnip project; but the experiment is worth trying.

The society might, by a small premium, originate the measure. There are landlords who would countenance it. The increased comfort from an increase of milk and butter would insure its success, and greater exertion would be made to enlarge the quantity of manure. Besides, the turnip plot would require little or no manure for potatoes and would produce excellent oats or flax.

Education

An epitome of the *Code of Agriculture*, combined with the *Farmer's Calendar*, should be published under the auspices of the society, adapting both to the soil and climate of the north west district. This work, enriched besides with some of the plainest and most pertinent principles of political and rural economy, should be put into the hands of the grown boys in all the schools of the district. Some of the works read in those schools are not calculated for the most important purpose of education: giving that knowledge which may be useful in after life. Would not the future farmer be better employed in learning to conquer his enemies, the weeds, than in poring over the conflicts of the petty states of Greece and in discussing the details of the Punic wars? And, while he wastes his time and his lungs in spouting young Norvals' exploits on the Grampian hills, would it not be as well to turn his attention to the stocking of his native hills with suitable breeds of cattle?

Appendix to Statistical Report by J. McCloskey

Occupations

Distribution of employments in Tobermore: 2 medical men, 1 watchmaker, 4 spirit dealers licensed, 4 grocers licensed, 4 master blacksmiths, 4 master nailers, 5 shoemakers, 4 carpenters, 3 wheelwrights, 6 weavers, 7 tailors, 4 hacklers, 1 mason, 2 butchers.

Employments in Moyheelan: 1 doctor, 1 blue dyer, 3 shoemakers, 1 master wheelwright, 2 master nailers, 2 master blacksmiths, 3 licensed spirit dealers, 1 licensed grocer.

Employments in remaining part of Ballynascreen: 28 masons, 5 stone cutters, 14 carpenters, 5 coopers, 11 blacksmiths, 4 wheelwrights, 15 master tailors, 18 shoemakers.

Journals

Public journals received through Tobermore post office: *Belfast Newsletter*, 7 copies; *Irishman*, 6 copies; *Derry Journal*, 1 copy; *Dublin Evening Post*, 1 copy; *Warder*, 2 copies; *Dublin Evening Mail*, 2 copies; *True Patriot*, 1 copy; *John Bull*, 1 copy; *Times*, 1 copy; *North West Magazine*, 1 copy.

Exports of Cattle

[Table] Number and value of the black cattle exported by inhabitants of the district in the year 1819, 1821, 1822.

Ballynascreen, 1819: Robert Smyth, 308 cattle, value 2,117 pounds; John Dickson, 200 cattle, value 1,000 pounds; Thomas Smyth, 200 cattle, value 1,500 pounds; total: 708 cattle, value 4,617 pounds.

1821: John Dickson, 100 cattle, value 500 pounds; Peter Duffy, 28 cattle, value 147 pounds; John Smith, 90 cattle, value 270 pounds; total: 218 cattle, 917 pounds.

1822: John Dickson, 140 cattle, value 490 pounds; Peter Duffy, 30 cattle, value 98 pounds; John Smith, 80 cattle, value 240 pounds; total: 250 cattle, value 828 pounds.

Desertmartin, 1819: H. McGuckin, 290 cattle, value 1,740 pounds; Robert Burns, 170 cattle, value 1,020 pounds; total: 460 cattle, value 2,760 pounds.

1821: H. McGuckin, 325 cattle, value 1,625 pounds; Robert Burns, 250 cattle, value 1,250 pounds; William Patterson, 60 cattle, value 300 pounds; total: 635 cattle, value 3,175 pounds.

1822: H. McGuckin, 360 cattle, value 1,260 pounds; Robert Burns, 336 cattle, value 1,176 pounds; total: 696 cattle, value 2,436 pounds.

Kilcronaghan, 1819: Robert Bryan Esquire, 154 cattle, value 1,540 pounds; James Quin and Company, 1,700 cattle, value 17,000 pounds; Bernard Quin, 624 cattle, value 3,744 pounds; Quin and Otterson, 560 cattle, value 3,360 pounds; Arthur Otterson, 470 cattle, value 2,820 pounds; A. Hanna, 75 cattle, value 600 pounds; total: 3,583 cattle, value 29,064 pounds.

1821: Robert Bryan Esquire: 340 cattle, value 1,700 pounds; James Quin and Company, 760 cattle, value 6,800 pounds; A. Hanna, 82 cattle, value 410 pounds; total: 1,182 cattle, value 8,910 pounds.

1822: Robert Bryan Esquire, 230 cattle, value 805 pounds; James Quin and Company, 500 cattle, value 3,500 pounds; A. Hanna, 60 cattle, value 359 pounds; total: 790 cattle, value 4,664.

DIVISIONS

Holdings of Drapers' Company

[Table] Census of the Drapers' property as taken in the year 1818.

Desertmartin: Tirgan, 373 acres, rent 176 pounds 10s, 60 families, 8 Churchmen, 40 Presbyterians, 266 Catholics, 314 individuals, 248 supposed incapable of paying for medical aid, 109 poor children under 12 years of age.

Carncose, 295 acres, rent 141 pounds 15s, 39 families, 14 Presbyterians, 178 Catholics, 192 individuals, 163 supposed incapable of paying for medical aid, 86 poor children under 12 years of age.

Gortanury, 195 acres, rent 202 pounds 10s, 40 families, 7 Churchmen, 156 Presbyterians, 36 Catholics, 199 individuals, 87 supposed incapable of paying for medical aid, 28 poor children under 12 years of age.

Cranny, 258 acres, rent 195 pounds 10s, 38 families, 30 Churchmen, 114 Presbyterians, 108 Catholics, 252 individuals, 124 supposed incapable of paying for medical aid, 30 poor children under 12 years of age.

Lecumpher, 191 acres, rent 166 pounds, 37 families, 19 Churchmen, 183 Presbyterians, 8 Catholics, 210 individuals, 89 supposed incapable of paying for medical aid, 35 poor children under 12 years of age.

Brackagh Sliabh Gallion, 433 acres, rent 140 pounds 5s, 34 families, 223 individuals, all Catholics, 199 supposed incapable of paying for medical aid, 101 poor children under 12 years of age.

Dernascallon, 291 acres, rent 209 pounds 15s, 42 families, 35 Churchmen, 135 Presbyterians, 54 Catholics, 224 individuals, 81 supposed incapable of paying for medical aid, 82 poor children under 12 years of age.

Iniscarn, 432 acres, rent 187 pounds 5s, 31 families, 24 Presbyterians, 139 Catholics, 163 individuals, 128 supposed incapable of paying for medical aid, 49 poor children under 12 years of age.

Boveagh, 228 acres, rent 103 pounds 15s, 24 families, 9 Churchmen, 40 Presbyterians, 88 Catholics, 137 individuals, 135 supposed incapable of paying for medical aid, 68 poor children under 12 years of age.

Cullion, 506 acres, rent 128 pounds, 21 families, 133 individuals, all Catholics, 127 supposed incapable of paying for medical aid, 86 poor children under 12 years of age.

Longfield, 260 acres, rent 199 pounds 10s, 28 families, 43 Presbyterians, 154 Catholics, 197 individuals, 125 supposed incapable of paying for medical aid, 55 poor children under 12 years of age.

Kilcronaghan: Keenaugh, 162 acres, rent 70 pounds 10s, 26 families, 151 individuals, all Catholics, 128 supposed incapable of paying for medical aid, 67 poor children under 12 years of age.

Gortahurk, 588 acres, rent 148 pounds 5s, 35 families, 26 Presbyterians, 152 Catholics, 178 individuals, 128 supposed incapable of paying for medical aid, 61 poor children under 12 years of age.

Coolsara, 311 acres, rent 269 pounds 5s, 30 families, 18 Churchmen, 65 Presbyterians, 138 Catholics, 221 individuals, 85 supposed incapable of paying for medical aid, 32 poor children under 12 years of age.

Killytoney, 121 acres, rent 86 pounds, 15 families, 65 Presbyterians, 27 Catholics, 92 individuals, 21 supposed incapable of paying for medical aid, 7 poor children under 12 years of age.

Ballynascreen: Moykeeran, 113 acres, rent 101 pounds 5s, 17 families, 68 Presbyterians, 32 Catholics, 100 individuals, 33 supposed incapable of paying for medical aid, 104 poor children under 12 years of age.

Moyheelan, 310 acres, rent 313 pounds, 50 families, 33 Churchmen, 85 Presbyterians, 149 Catholics, 267 individuals, 149 supposed incapable of paying for medical aid, 156 poor children under 12 years of age.

Gortnaskeay, 252 acres, rent 201 pounds 5s, 33 families, 9 Churchmen, 180 Catholics, 189 individuals, 169 supposed incapable of paying for medical aid, 5 poor children under 12 years of age.

Duntybrian, 126 acres, rent 86 pounds, 25 families, 10 Churchmen, 73 Presbyterians, 43 Catholics, 126 individuals, 66 supposed incapable of paying for medical aid, 23 poor children under 12 years of age.

Moneyguigy, 273 acres, rent 399 pounds 10s, 29 families, 27 Churchmen, 47 Presbyterians, 114 Catholics, 188 individuals, 90 supposed incapable of paying for medical aid, 34 poor children under 12 years of age.

Dunlogan, 1,041 acres, rent 127 pounds, 15 families, 73 individuals, all Catholics, 69 supposed incapable of paying for medical aid, 36 poor children under 12 years of age.

Moydamlaght, 594 acres, rent 115 pounds, 26 families, 125 individuals, all Catholics, 99 supposed incapable of paying for medical aid, 35 poor children under 12 years of age.

Dunmurry, 479 acres, rent 106 pounds 5s, 21 families, 106 individuals, all Catholics, 92 supposed incapable of paying for medical aid, 37 poor children under 12 years of age.

Cloane, 645 acres, rent 199 pounds 10s, 47 families, 260 individuals, all Catholics, 109 supposed incapable of paying for medical aid, 45 poor children under 12 years of age.

Carnamoney, 560 acres, rent 284 pounds 5s, 59

families, 79 Presbyterians, 257 Catholics, 336 individuals, 152 supposed incapable of paying for medical aid, 84 poor children under 12 years of age.

Ballynure, 358 acres, rent 204 pounds 15s, 36 families, 7 Churchmen, 45 Presbyterians, 174 Catholics, 226 individuals, 94 supposed incapable of paying for medical aid, 69 poor children under 12 years of age.

Coolnasillagh, 483 acres, rent 133 pounds 5s, 36 families, 180 individuals, all Catholics, 126 supposed incapable of paying for medical aid, 48 poor children under 12 years of age.

Total: 894 families, 280 Churchmen, 1,234 Presbyterians, 3,548 Catholics, 5,062 individuals, 3,116 supposed incapable of paying for medical aid, 1,572 poor children under 12 years of age.

Townlands in Desertmartin

Area and population of the district, 1821. [Table contains the following headings: name of townland, signification, size, number of houses, number of individuals].

1, Killboggan: Coill Bog "the wet wood;" 177 acres, 21 houses, 131 inhabitants.

2, Cranny: Crannidh "the trees;" 258 acres, 46 houses, 267 inhabitants.

3, Knocknagin: Cnoc-na-gin "wedge-shaped hill;" 72 acres, 27 houses, 154 inhabitants.

4, Stranagard: Sraith-na-gairbhe "the rough marsh;" 104 acres, 37 houses, 171 inhabitants.

5, Curr: Curr "the corner or the pool;" 128 acres, 30 houses, 152 inhabitants.

6, Bally McPherson: Baile Magh Fearshoin "the plain for meadows;" 98 acres, 24 houses, 148 inhabitants.

7, Lecumpher: Leac Omure "the stone;" 191 acres, 35 houses, 189 inhabitants.

8, Dernascallon: Doir-na-sgalain "the huts in the waters;" 291 acres, 40 houses, 235 inhabitants.

9, Anagh: Aonach "the public meeting;" 279 acres, 47 houses, 259 inhabitants.

10, Dromore: Drom Mor "the great back;" 250 acres, 33 houses, 187 inhabitants.

11, Ballynagowan: Baile-na-gobhan "town of the pointed stone;" 108 acres, 9 houses, 49 inhabitants.

12, Roshure: Ruis Ur "beautiful valley," (cur vallis hebraire, or "wood of yew"); 119 acres, 19 houses, 109 inhabitants.

13, Gortanury: Gort-an-ur "field of heath or yews;" 195 acres, 32 houses, 181 inhabitants.

14, Tirgan: Tir Gain "the sandy land;" 373 acres, 54 houses, 303 inhabitants.

15, Carncose: Carn Cois "the mound at the foot of the hill;" 295 acres, 36 houses, 193 inhabitants.

16, Brackagh Sliabh Gallion: Bracagh "spotted land;" 433 acres, 41 houses, 214 inhabitants.

17, Iniscarn: Inniscarn "the insulated mound;" 432 acres, 31 houses, 155 inhabitants.

18, Boveagh: Bev Beog "the young cattle;" 228 acres, 23 houses, 136 inhabitants.

19, Longfield: 260 acres, 33 houses, 193 inhabitants.

20, Cullion: Cuilean "the holly trees;" 506 acres, 24 houses, 129 inhabitants.

21, Motalee: Mota Lia "the stone mount or grey mount;" 198 acres, 65 houses, 344 inhabitants.

22, Rosgarron: Rosgaran "beautiful underwood;" 126 acres, 28 houses, 175 inhabitants.

23, Grange: Grainge "corn land," from grainseach "a barn;" 390 acres, 42 houses, 217 inhabitants.

24, Luney: Luaneach "marshy," from lua "water;" 207 acres, 46 houses, 242 inhabitants.

Total: 5,718 acres, 823 houses, 4,533 inhabitants.

Townlands in Kilcronaghan

1, Killytoney: Coille Tonidh "the woody bottom;" 121 acres.

2, Coolsara: Coile Scarra; corna "for mowing," scarra "scythe;" 311 acres.

3, Gortahurk: Gorta Coirce "the field for oats;" 588 acres.

4, Keenaugh: Canaigh "the pool of water," or caonach "mossy;" 162 acres.

5, Killynummer: Coille Nuimhir "the great wood;" 131 acres.

6, Ballinderry: Bal-an-doire "place of oaks;" 290 acres.

7, Gortanury: Gortamonadh "the field of division;" 296 acres.

8, Moyasset: Magh Assadh "the plain of the weasel;" 125 acres.

9, Calmore: Coll Mer "the great head;" 198 acres.

10, Cloane: Cluain "a level recess between woods;" 279 acres.

11, Monishinare: Moin-a-sinner "mountain of yew trees;" 300 acres.

12, Brackaghrowley: Braccagh "a spotted land;" 748 acres.

13, Drumsamney: Druim Samhna "the pleasant back of the hill;" 190 acres.

14, Moybeg: Magh Beg "little plain;" 95 acres.

15, Drumballyhagan: Druim Baile "place on the back;" 240 acres.

16, Drumcrow: Druim Cro "back of the hill with nuts;" 60 acres.
17, Mormeal: "the bog of hares;" 395 acres.
18, Granny: see Cranny; 123 acres.
19, Tamnyasker: Tamnaidh, [Greek letters] temenos, Scarrina "a separate field;" 185 acres.
20, Tullyroan: Tully Rathan "the place of ferns;" 247 acres.
21, Cloughfin: Clochfinn "the white stone;" 151 acres.
Total: 5,235 acres.

The first 4 towns and no.14 belong to the Drapers' Company; no.5 to the Revd Lucius Cary; nos 6 and 15 to the Bellaghy estate; from 7 to 10 inclusive to the Right Hon. Sir George F. Hill Bart; no.11 is the property of [blank] McCausland Esquire, as also no.20; 12 that of Colonel Howard; 13 is the glebe-town; 16, 17, 18, 19 belong to the heirs of the late Sir H. Bruce, held under the see of Derry.

Townlands in Ballynascreen

1, Dunlogan: Doonlogan "the brown district;" 1,041 acres.
2, Moydamlaght: Magh-dam-lachd "the milk house on the plain;" 594 acres.
3, Dunmurry: Dun Muraim (marus) "the fenced hill;" 479 acres.
4, Cloane: Cluain "a level recess between woods;" 645 acres.
5, Carnamoney: Carn-a-moiniadh "the mound of stones in the bog" or Cuir-na-moinead "the pits in the bog;" 560 acres.
6, Ballynure: Baile Nur "the heath town or yew trees;" 358 acres.
7, Coolnasillagh: Cuil-na-sailleach "the corner of willows," or Sailseach "of druidical fires;" 483 acres.
8, Moneyguigy: Moin-a-giagiu "the shaking bog;" 273 acres.
9, Duntybrian: Dunlig Breon "the spotted hill;" 126 acres.
10, Moyheelan: Magh Callean "the beautiful plain;" 408 acres.
11, Moykeeran: Magh Caeran "the marshy plain;" 113 acres.
12, Gortnaskeay: Gort-na-sciog "field of thorns;" 252 acres.
13, Glengavna: Glean Gabhanagh "the close glen;" 1,279 acres.
14, Doon: Dun "the hill;" 466 acres.
15, Strawmore: Straith Mor "the great marsh;" 395 acres.
16, Straw: Straith "the marsh;" 666 acres.
17, Leabby: Leaba "a bed, a druidical altar;" 452 acres.
18, Deesart: Desart "stony land;" 312 acres.
19, Brackagh: see above, 355 acres.
20, Cloughfin: Cloch Finn "the white stone;" 264 acres.
21, Tonnagh: Tonnach "wavy ground;" 245 acres.
22, Drumard: Druim Ard "the lofty back;" 663 acres.
23, Mulnavoo and Drumdoo: Mual-na-bea "hill of cattle;" Druim Dhu "black ridge;" 204 acres.
24, Drumderg: Druim Dearg "the red back;" 745 acres.
25, Moneyninea: Moin-a-monach "the spotted mountain;" 910 acres.
26, Derrynoid: Doire Nodh "the noble oaks;" 760 acres.
27, Banchran: Ban Crann "the woody bottom;" 320 acres.
28, Cahore: Ca Or "place for sheep or for berries;" 320 acres.
29, Corick: Comherac "meeting of the waters;" 751 acres.
30, Glensiggan: Glean Beagan "the little glen."
31, Stranahinch: Straith-na-innis "the insulated marsh."
32, Altaeasga: Alt (altus) Easge "the narrow glen with waters."
33, Cavanreagh: Cabhan Reagh "the rugged plain."
34, Owenreagh: Abhuin Reagh "the rugged water."
35, [?] Moranstown and Tullybrick: Tulla Breac "the speckled field;" [total of last 6 townlands:] 7,900 acres.
Total 22,339 acres.

From nos 1 to 13 inclusive belong to the Drapers' Company; from no.13 to 24 inclusive to Robert Ogilby Esquire, from 30 to 35 inclusive to James Stevenson Esquire, lessee of the see of Derry; 27 is the glebe-town; 25 the property of Revd Lucius Carey; 26 that of the Honourable Justice Torrens; 28 of Messrs Gregg and Campbell; and 29 that of Mr Wright, held under the primacy.

SOCIAL AND PRODUCTIVE ECONOMY

Population

[Table] Population of Ballynascreen and Kilcronaghan in 1821.
Ballynascreen: 1,263 inhabited houses, occupied by 1,308 families, 20 houses building, 33 other houses uninhabited, 1,114 families em-

ployed in agriculture, 141 families chiefly employed in trade and manufacture, 53 families not comprised in 2 foregoing classes, 3,224 males, 3,470 females, total of persons 6,694; towns, cities and villages: Cross, 131 inhabitants.

Kilcronaghan: 605 inhabited houses, occupied by 625 families, 8 houses building, 17 other houses uninhabited, 385 families employed in agriculture, 142 families chiefly employed in trade and manufacture, 102 families not comprised in 2 foregoing classes, 1,700 males, 1,781 females, total of persons 3,481; towns, cities and villages: Tobermore, 507 inhabitants.

No particular abstract designating the population of each townland in the above parishes was taken. The above is the return forwarded to government.

Barony of Loughinsholin

[Table] General summary of the district and comparative view of it with respect to the barony of Loughinsholin, in area, population and public expenditure.

Desertmartin: 5,718 acres, 823 houses, 4,533 inhabitants; quota of county assessments: Lent assizes 1820, 162 pounds 19s 6d; Lent assizes 1821, 344 pounds 2s 4d; Lent assizes 1822, 206 pounds 19s 1d.

Kilcronaghan: 5,235 acres, 605 houses, 3,481 inhabitants; quota of county assessments: Lent assizes 1820, 113 pounds 3s 7d; Lent assizes 1821, 239 pounds 3s 2d; Lent assizes 1822, 149 pounds 19s 4d.

Ballynascreen: 22,339 acres, 1,263 houses, 6,694 inhabitants; quota of county assessments: Lent assizes 1820, 229 pounds 1s 2d; Lent assizes 1821, 482 pounds 18s 4d; Lent assizes 1822, 315 pounds 1s 9d.

Grand total of district: 33,292 acres, 2,691 houses, 14,708 inhabitants; quota of county assessments: Lent assizes 1820, 505 pounds 4s 3d; Lent assizes 1821, 1,066 pounds 3s 10d; Lent assizes 1822, 672 pounds 2d.

Barony of Loughinsholin: 100,000 acres, 13,805 houses, 75,933 inhabitants; quota of county assessments: Lent assizes 1820, 2,250 pounds 16s 2d; Lent assizes 1821, 4,741 pounds 19s 7d; Lent assizes 1822, 3,038 pounds 4s 1d ha'penny.

Thus it appears that the district is to the barony, taking the latter at 100,000 acres in area, as 1 to 3 very nearly; in houses as 1 to 5, more nearly as 7 to 36; in population as 1 to 5, more nearly 6 to 31; for public assessments 2 to 9.

Value of Land

[Table] An attempt to exhibit the progressive increase in the value of land in this district.

Rosgarron townland: 26 acres 26 perches arable and pasture land, 3 acres 3 roods bog and mountain, let at 6 pounds 3s in 1734.

19 acres 3 roods 39 perches arable and pasture land, let at 16 pounds 16s in 1788.

11 acres 2 roods 30 perches arable and pasture land, 20 acres bog and mountain, let at 8 pounds 3d in 1788.

7 acres 1 rood 21 perches arable and pasture land, let at 4 pounds 14s 6d in 1788.

2 acres 18 perches arable and pasture land, let at 1 pound 11s 6d in 1788.

9 acres 2 roods 9 perches arable and pasture land, let at 7 pounds 10s 6d in 1788.

Motalee townland: 63 acres 1 rood 16 perches arable and pasture land, 28 acres 1 rood bog and mountain, let at 13 pounds 6s 6d in 1734.

34 acres 3 roods arable and pasture land, 18 acres 2 roods 20 perches bog and mountain, let at 15 pounds 10s 3d in 1764.

Luney townland: 24 acres 2 roods arable and pasture land, 52 acres 2 roods 20 perches bog and mountain, let at 6 pounds 3s in 1734.

19 acres 3 roods arable pasture land, 4 acres 1 rood bog and mountain, let at 4 pounds 12s in 1734.

30 acres 2 roods arable and pasture land, 17 acres 2 roods bog and mountain, let at 9 pounds 4s 6d in 1734.

15 acres 14 perches arable and pasture land, 7 acres 24 perches bog and mountain, let at [blank].

21 acres 3 roods 12 perches arable and pasture land, 2 acres 3 roods 29 perches bog and mountain, let at 13 pounds 15s in 1788.

Grange townland: 163 acres 3 roods arable and pasture land, 226 acres bog and mountain, let at 36 pounds 7s 9d in 1734.

www.ingramcontent.com/pod-product-compliance
Lightning Source LLC
Chambersburg PA
CBHW051211290426
44109CB00021B/2415